Nuggets of Gold

POLITICS AND CULTURE IN THE
TWENTIETH-CENTURY SOUTH

SERIES EDITORS

Bryant Simon, *Temple University*
Jane Dailey, *University of Chicago*

ADVISORY BOARD

Rebecca Brückmann, *Carleton College*
Erik Gellman, *University of North Carolina, Chapel Hill*
Charles McKinney, *Rhodes College*
Sarah J. McNamara, *Texas A&M University*
Elizabeth McRae, *Western Carolina University*
La Shonda Mims, *Middle Tennessee State University*
Robert Norrell, *University of Tennessee, Knoxville*
Anke Ortlepp, *Universität zu Köln*
Vanessa Ribas, *University of California, San Diego*
J. Mills Thornton, *University of Michigan*
Allen Tullos, *Emory University*
Brian Ward, *Northumbria University*

Nuggets of Gold

FURTHER PROCESSED CHICKEN
AND THE MAKING OF THE
AMERICAN DIET

Patrick Dixon

The University of Georgia Press

ATHENS

Published by the University of Georgia Press
Athens, Georgia 30602
www.ugapress.org
© 2024 by Patrick Dixon
All rights reserved
Set in 10.25/13.5 Minion Pro Regular by Kaelin Chappell Broaddus

Most University of Georgia Press titles are
available from popular e-book vendors.

Printed digitally

Library of Congress Cataloging-in-Publication Data
Names: Dixon, Patrick, 1984– author.
Title: Nuggets of gold : further processed chicken and the making of the American diet / Patrick Dixon.
Description: Athens, Georgia : The University of Georgia Press, [2024] | Series: Politics and culture in the twentieth-century south | Includes bibliographical references and index.
Identifiers: LCCN 2024003487 | ISBN 9780820366357 (hardback) | ISBN 9780820367132 (paperback) | ISBN 9780820367149 (epub) | ISBN 9780820367156 (pdf)
Subjects: LCSH: Food industry and trade—United States. | Processed foods—United States. | Diet—United States.
Classification: LCC HD9005 .D58 2024 | DDC 338.4/7664930973—dc23/eng/20240514
LC record available at https://lccn.loc.gov/2024003487

CONTENTS

List of Illustrations   vii

Acknowledgments   ix

INTRODUCTION   "Ready-to-Use 'Fresh-Like' Products"   1

CHAPTER 1   Dr. Baker and Mr. Nugget   16

CHAPTER 2   "The Poor Hen, She Has Become a Machine!"   34

CHAPTER 3   Broken Bones, Broken Laws, and the Rise of AMC Local 525   63

CHAPTER 4   The Business of Feeding People   92

EPILOGUE   The New Century   127

Notes   137

Bibliography   159

Index   169

ILLUSTRATIONS

IMAGE 1. Robert C. Baker   17
IMAGE 2. The food pipeline   21
IMAGE 3. The repaired food pipeline   21
IMAGE 4. Haggart Manufacturing Company's Luxor battery house   39
IMAGE 5. Holly Farms' Wilkesboro plant workers on production line   53
IMAGE 6. Holly Farms' Wilkesboro plant workers on production line   53
IMAGE 7. Holly Farms' workers sliding trays into heat-sealed plastic bags   53
IMAGE 8. Jennie Joines   91
IMAGE 9. Early McDonald's advertisement for the Chicken McNugget   110
IMAGE 10. McCarty Foods advertisement for processed chicken products   114

TABLE 1. Poultry industry concentration, 1980, 1984, and 1989   59

ACKNOWLEDGMENTS

Telling the story of the Chicken McNugget and the American diet has been both a joy and a weighty responsibility, and I would have been unable to scale these fearsome intellectual heights without the support of many archivists, colleagues, friends, and family members. Returning to Washington, D.C., from one of my first research trips to North Carolina, I pushed hard on the gas on I-95 in an attempt to stay ahead of an oncoming snowstorm. Hitting a patch of black ice and spinning backward down a grassy verge felt like an ominous portent for this project at the time. A stranger with a pickup truck helped me to get back on the road, and the journey continued. This ultimately proved to be a greater symbol of what was to follow than the accident itself.

I've been fortunate to receive assistance from many very smart and generous people as I have built this project over the past twelve years. Joe McCartin has supported my ambitions as a historian for the duration of this time. Besides his extensive guidance in navigating this difficult profession, Joe's careful and thoughtful use of empirical evidence and his respectful and empathetic treatment of historical subjects presented me with a strong methodological example that I have, over time, sought to emulate. Early on I also benefited greatly from the mentorship of Susan Pinkard, who introduced me to histories of food and generously shared her time and expertise, presenting an approach to social history that I found to be instructive and that I was motivated to pursue further. As I was thinking about how to turn a dissertation into a book in 2015, it was Susan who first suggested that I put the McNugget front and center. I was reluctant to do so at that time because I was concerned that such a study would not be taken seriously, having recently been labeled as "eccentric" after I floated the idea of a history of Americans' belief in extraterrestrial life. I am glad that I have ultimately followed that advice, even if *Unidentified Frying Objects* was ultimately dropped as a potential title.

Many people helped me in the various research stages of this book in Washington, D.C., North Carolina, Georgia, and New York. Jackie Nowell and Paul Lechtenberg allowed me to access a unique collection of materials at the United Food and Commercial Workers International Union in D.C. At the University of North Carolina in Chapel Hill, Lawrence Naumoff kindly met with me and shared some of his insights on writing about southern poultry workers. Matt Turi provided excellent guidance in helping me to navigate a large and unwieldy archival collection. The Amalgamated Meat Cutters Local 525 Collection at the Southern Labor Archives at Georgia State University in Atlanta was invaluable to me, a true one-of-a-kind trove of information on the history of poultry work in the United States. Archivists Traci Drummond and Hal Hansen patiently and knowledgably assisted me as I worked through this collection over the course of several weeks on two separate visits. It was in the Local 525 Collection that I learned the dramatic history of Gold Kist in Durham, North Carolina, which appears in the third chapter of this book. Lane Windham kindly allowed me to use the resources that she had gathered when writing about poultry in Durham many years earlier, including her 1989 interview with Laura Green. Mike Golash from Local 689 of the Amalgamated Transit Union helped me to locate Karen Walker in 2013. Meeting and interviewing Karen was one of the highlights of my time as a doctoral student. I am truly very grateful that she was willing to share her memories, and I hope that I have done justice to her brave and tireless work at Gold Kist.

As I developed this manuscript toward its final incarnation I benefited from insightful feedback from a range of great writers. Katie Wells presented me with difficult but absolutely necessary questions that encouraged me to rethink the entire structure of the project in a way that was ultimately highly productive. I was glad to have the opportunity to share a chapter of this book in 2020 with colleagues at the D.C. Area Labor History Seminar, where I benefited from the expertise of Roger Horowitz and seminar regulars Leon Fink, Eric Arnesen, and Nick Unger. It was really a great privilege to work closely with Leon and Eric for six years on the journal *LABOR: Studies in Working-Class History*, and I have relied upon their astute understanding of publishing and the historical profession on innumerable occasions. I have also been lucky to work with James Benton and Debbie Berkowitz as colleagues at the Kalmanovitz Initiative for Labor and the Working Poor in recent years. James has been invariably generous in sharing his vast knowledge of North Carolina, and Debbie's experience with and understanding of issues of workplace safety in the U.S. meat and poultry industries is truly second to none. More recently, I am thankful for the confidence and patience of Bryant Simon, Nathaniel Holly, and everyone at the University of Georgia Press who invested both their time and their trust in bringing this book into production.

In spite of my hermit-like tendencies, I haven't taken this journey alone. I have benefited from the counsel and support of a small but strong group of friends, some of whom are historians and some of whom are not. A significant number of them lived on Varnum Street in D.C. at one point in time. Javier Puente and Alan Roe both provided ever intelligent guidance and bolstered my confidence at times when I think few people were taking my work very seriously. Chris England kindly welcomed me to his home in Georgia and helped me to complete a crucial phase of my research. In the early days, Old Chub offered wise guidelines on negotiating some of the hazards of urban living and sometimes beer. Lawrence and Allison McMahon and Zainab Amin improved my time in this country immeasurably.

Finally, the love and support of family have meant that I have been able to set out on an odd path in an odd place nearly four thousand miles from home with the confidence that I would never be stranded. Andy, Vi, Marie, Geoff, Alex, and Ellen have all been remarkably encouraging and generous at many different steps along the way. As have, most of all, my parents, Michael and Jackie. This book is dedicated to them.

Nuggets of Gold

INTRODUCTION

"Ready-to-Use 'Fresh-Like' Products"

Writing in *Broiler Industry* magazine in March 1986, Wendy's vice president Robert Bauer explained the company's recent change in direction. After a decade of explosive growth that was unrivaled in the chain restaurant industry and characterized by its hearty, plus-sized beef burgers and its direct assault on the market dominance of McDonald's, company executives had been reluctantly forced to reexamine basic articles of faith bestowed on them by founder Dave Thomas. "As more women entered the work force, our customers started to demand lighter fare," Bauer wrote, adding that "many consumers became concerned about health considerations associated with beef." Consumer tastes were not the only change in the market; Wendy's was facing labor shortages "due to the decline in the availability and numbers of teenagers." This could represent a long-term problem. "In the year 2000, if all the fast food feeders meet their strategic growth plan, every person between the ages of 15 and 20 will be employed by a fast food company," he explained. The answer: "Ready-to-use fresh-like products." Among the most successful new offerings at Wendy's was a boneless chicken sandwich. "Further processing—to relieve pressure in the preparation area—is of great importance in the future," he continued. Bauer proffered his vision of the restaurant industry. "Those who are able to innovate and adapt will have the opportunity to grow. Wendy's is challenging you to adapt further to the continued growth and dominance of the food service business. You must create new ideas in products and services to push your business forward," he stressed.[1]

Customers of the 1980s were indeed less taken by the sentimentality of old-fashioned hamburgers than they were by novelty and reinvention, new styles and new tastes. More Americans went out to work than ever before, frequently in sedentary office environments, and many had embraced popular new trends in physical fitness and enrolled in a burgeoning national network of health clubs with the goal of emulating the trim and finely toned bodies that saturated nearly every form of American media from the silver screen to the newsstand.[2] Vigorous physical activity and a carefully selected diet were the yin and yang of a healthy lifestyle for a new generation of upwardly mobile professionals. Even for many who did not abide by this mantra, lighter fare that was quick to prepare and had multigenerational appeal took on a new popularity in the age of drive-throughs and microwave ovens.

Within this context, "further processed chicken" found what seemed to some an unlikely place at the center of the American diet. An industry term that understandably never appeared in the advertising of chicken products, further processing referred to the reclamation of meat that took place once the most popular cuts—breasts, wings, and legs—had been removed from the carcasses. Rescuing edible matter that would otherwise have been designated as waste or, at best, pet food, further processed chicken products represented cleverly redesigned meals using animal components that had been consumed for centuries, and often still were in many countries, but had fallen into disuse in the United States. The approach was both old and new. While reliant on a modern scientific methodology, the resourceful, patched-together approach of processed chicken harked back to a tradition of reuse and recycling that had only in recent decades been displaced by the rise of popular disposable goods.[3] The skill involved in further processing was to transform blood, viscera, skin, feet, meat from the neck and back, and sometimes organ meats into appetizing dinners that would elide consumers' postwar predispositions about better and worse cuts. The project was pioneered by Cornell University food scientist Robert C. Baker (image 1), and the designers of further processed meals pursued an ecological and humane mission; their goals were to reduce food waste and pollution, turning by-products into new sources of protein that could help to alleviate world famine and what many believed to be a growing global crisis of overpopulation. To make this endeavor commercially viable they sought to present consumers with a new menu of exciting, convenient, and light fare, healthy meals in which they could take some delight. These were intended to be everyman meals—affordable to lower-income families, but respectable and free from condescension.

Yet within a few years, further processed chicken, created by food scientists and redesigned by chain restaurants and large poultry-processing companies, had acquired a reputation as a mysterious antifood, refuse disguised as chicken snacks and chicken dinners. As the popularity of further processed chicken's marquee product, the McNugget, soared in the mid-1980s and rivals sought to emulate its success, critics ridiculed it as an approximation of food.

The censure of the nugget was unyielding. As the popularity of organic and locally sourced foods would soar in the 2000s, the nugget achieved the status of a culinary bête noir, a symbol of all that was wrong with fast-food dining and school lunches. For many critics, the kitschness of a breaded chicken snack with a name that invoked gold rush–era discoveries of hidden treasure was just too much. In what became a frequently visited Internet clip, British celebrity chef Jamie Oliver sought to explain to schoolchildren the differences between good foods and bad foods in both the United Kingdom and Huntington, West Virginia. His intention was to show "the most disgusting ingredients in some of the worst processed food." Oliver removes the breast, legs, and thighs from a raw chicken and then violently hacks the remainder of the carcass to pieces with a large knife before placing them, along with some chicken skins, into a blender until they resemble a pink purée. His assertion is that this is how nuggets are made, and his intent is to horrify the children. A year or so later, in another show with a similar theme, he taught schoolchildren how to cook superior homemade nuggets from chicken breasts.[4] Oliver's charges were afforded further credibility by a 2013 study by doctors in Mississippi that asserted that "chicken nuggets have become a staple of the American diet" while adding that "the composition of the present day chicken nugget is not well understood." The report, published in the *American Journal of Medicine*, found that "chicken is not necessarily a major component" of the nugget; rather, "fat was present in equal or greater quantities along with epithelium, bone, nerve, and connective tissue." To even call them chicken nuggets was "a misnomer."[5]

Popular depictions of further processed chicken like Oliver's largely mirror the narrative of culinary decline that has been pervasive in intellectual renderings of the modern history of food in the United States.[6] Often penned by scholars with some affinity for the local and organic food movements, many accounts gaze back in time to an earlier age when the preponderance of agricultural output was the product of family farms and the absence of modern technologies and an advanced international logistics network meant that most people ate foods that were both seasonal and local. It is argued that this system of provision gave way to the twentieth-century technological revolution in food design, processing, and preservation as over time many Americans exchanged this more wholesome diet for one that was centered around foods that were both endlessly durable and convenient, mass-produced agricultural products whose natural tastes, or lack thereof, were obscured by salts, sugar, and artificially created flavors. These new products were crude imitations of actual foods and a catastrophe for public health. Though a great many people did maintain an impressive measure of personal health while including processed and fast-food products in their diet, and wealthier diners continued to indulge in unhealthy and ecologically detrimental delicacies of their own, the choice of many economically stretched consumers to opt for more heavily processed products, including meat and poultry, became the subject of considerable concern, criticism, and even distaste. While most recognized that many working-class families didn't always have the time or the bandwidth to prepare fresh food on a daily basis, the regular patrons of the United States' legion of fast-food enterprises have nonetheless been cast at best as the victims of the capitalism of the American food system and at worst as ignorant and self-destructive. Historian Ann Vileisis would explain eating habits in the United States as the product of a "mental framework" that has been "stretched and fudged" by a "relentless legion of admen and home economists" who created "an unspoken covenant of ignorance between shoppers and an increasingly powerful food industry."[7] Critical analysis of working-class methods of spending and consumption has an extended historical lineage; in his recent study of beef in the nineteenth- and early twentieth-century United States, Joshua Specht highlighted the omnipresent tension between "the simultaneous aestheticization of elite food and obsession with reforming the eating habits of the poor."[8]

This book seeks to offer a new perspective on processed foods, how they came to occupy a central role in the American diet, and how this was reflective of changes in both industrial production and consumer attitudes and aspirations. I do so through a focus on the rise of further processed chicken and the monumental poultry business that supported the country's culinary expectations and became a defining feature of hundreds of small southern towns. I don't disagree with my predecessors that the U.S. food system was at least in part the product of the country's particular brand of capitalism, but it was also one that was steered in certain directions by a heavily state-sponsored set of agricultural policies. The development of the poultry business was an extension of the greater project of industrial agriculture: to make farms more rational and businesslike in their approach and to impose scientific planning and methodologies on nature.[9] It has been commonly contended that many of the products of industrialized agriculture, in particular those served as fast-food meals, have played a significant contributing role to a crisis of obesity in the United States that has resulted in staggeringly burdensome health-care costs to both the state and private individuals. This crisis is often explained in part as the consequence of a constriction upon the options available to consumers whereby successful chain restaurants and their familiar bargain meals strangled out the competition and high-volume grocery retailers abandoned costly inner-city operations, creating what came to be referred to as food deserts.[10]

At the same time, I draw attention to the experiences of many poultry plant workers that exceeded the normal economic and physical hardships of Fordist production practices. Some of these workers walked the difficult path of seeking union representation in North Carolina, an important center of production and a state known for its hostility to such entreaties. Yet I also present a restaurant sector in which both vendors and diners recognized the opening of a whole new range of culinary possibilities. Though nutritional details may have eluded some consumers, and the ambiguous content of further processed chicken items allowed for the addition of even cheaper filler ingredients, an understanding that heavier and heartier meals contributed to personal weight gain did not require any meaningful measure of scientific expertise. Americans knew that foods prepared in vegetable fats contributed to bodily fat and yet nonetheless embraced fried foods as a dietary staple with great enthusiasm, frequently rejecting more traditional forms of home cookery in favor of eating out or on the go. Consumers regarded McNuggets as chicken in the same way that they considered hot dogs to be a pork-based product.

While wealthy families had enjoyed transferring the labor of food preparation to domestic cooks for centuries, when rising levels of postwar income and affordable restaurant dining became available to working-class Americans, they too enjoyed dispensing with these labors and regarded chains like McDonald's, Wendy's, and Kentucky Fried Chicken, among others, as modern, efficient, consistent, and unpretentious. For many, Taco Bell, Pizza Hut, and Domino's offered variety in the form of what were for a time referred to as "ethnic foods," meaning they didn't resemble Northern European fare. Before they accrued a growing middle-class cultural stigma in the 1990s and 2000s, popular chain restaurants were considered by most Americans and indeed many consumers worldwide to be perfectly respectable places to eat and for many families a modern American tradition.[11] Over time, fast-food giants developed great built-in advantages, including considerable leverage over the agricultural sector, access to credit from private financial institutions as well as federal loans, prime real estate, almost unrivalled global brand recognition, and the cultural influence that could be afforded by nationwide marketing campaigns. Later in the twentieth century, chain restaurants would, in some low-income neighborhoods, become seemingly the only viable food businesses alongside convenience stores and gas stations, curtailing the range of available dietary options. Yet in the era of their ascent, these popular brands were the winners of the market contest, offering a new dining experience that many Americans enjoyed. Wendy's gained an impressive market share in the 1970s by offering a variation on this formula: all of the convenience of the new style of dining but with a throwback aesthetic and food that was freshly prepared every morning.¹² But by the 1980s, menus of burgers, fries, and milkshakes were considered tired.

Through innovations that addressed a demand for novelty (in a later decade, Taco Bell would encourage diners to "think outside the bun"), chain restaurants embraced further processed poultry and revived both their menus and the notion that they were offering a contemporary dining experience. While salad bars and non-meat-based options achieved limited market success, chicken products that appeared lighter and were marginally healthier than beef became popular favorites that spawned new lines in frozen food products for home preparation. The evolution of fast food in the late twentieth-century United States was the outcome not merely of the designs of food scientists but also in many cases of the clearly indicated preferences of consumers. As the price of food became more affordable both through the subsidization of large-scale arable crops and through the freedom granted to agribusiness from the negative social and environmental costs created by industrial production methods, cheerful convenience foods became a feature of what for many was the very lifestyle that they desired. Many wealthy consumers continued to patronize fast-food joints even when they could afford what were considered to be better quality options. Bargain meals, service in minutes, and extended opening hours were a double-edged sword, though. As the same few brands proliferated far and wide, in some locales and for some consumers they became less of a preferred choice and instead the only choice in town, a diet that grew increasingly repetitive and detrimental when consumed in excess. Having once represented a new range of eating options in the postwar years, the predictably successful formula of franchise restaurant operations meant that over time chain restaurants represented an increasingly dominant share of new entrants into the market. For workers in multiple jobs and with unconventional hours, people with limited transportation, the unhoused, and people who lived without cooking facilities, the McDonald's Dollar Menu and similar value offers at times represented the food option of last resort. Some independents competed for the same client base by offering menus that closely resembled those of the chains. In neighborhoods flooded by low-cost franchise restaurants, the lack of access to a diverse array of dining options was often correlated to existing racial, geographical, and socioeconomic disadvantages, compounding structural socioeconomic inequities. As the 1990s transitioned to the 2000s, the bloom was off the rose for these iconic brands; their reputation for cleanliness had diminished, and they were treated by some as public restrooms, their menus were pilloried, and they were associated with minimum-wage jobs that were occupied not by high schoolers but rather by adults, often immigrants and people of color, who needed a lot more than they were earning.[13]

Still, further processed chicken remained an established feature within the American diet. Even as the glory days of fast-food adulation were seemingly ending, the poultry business continued to occupy a commanding presence in the U.S. political landscape, adapting marketing messages in response to popular critiques and steadily growing in size and scale while investing in ever more capacious facilities across the South. Wielding influence at both national and local levels as an essential economic and industrial actor, the poultry business attained an optimum regulatory environment with the U.S. Departments of Agriculture and Labor, both of which were amenable to changing production practices and only occasionally imposed what were generally quite affordable penalties for malpractice and negligence. Companies learned to navigate the country's New Deal labor laws with aplomb, especially in a state like North Carolina, where companies were aided by "right-to-work" laws and state and local officials offered generous incentives to promote economic development.[14] Considering low-cost foods to be a boon for many lower-income Americans and a more desirable means of raising living standards than the alternative of elevated income levels, politicians from both parties largely acquiesced when confronted with the darker sides of agribusiness. Poultry companies had become institutionalized as an essential component within the food chain, and they were seldom held accountable for the human and ecological costs that resulted from the relentless methods by which they supplied the centerpiece of many Americans' favorite meals.

Within the past few decades, there has been a trove of innovative and valuable academic literature that has interrogated the past and present peculiarities and eccentricities as well as the power and exploitation that reside within the U.S. food system. As a leading export commodity, as a touchstone of American soft power, as a signal of class, taste, and aspiration, and as an area of persistent rural industrial growth in an era of widespread deindustrialization, food studies has been legitimized by multidisciplinary scholars as an area of important intellectual enquiry, an essential element in understanding a culture, a politics, and an economy across time and space. Some explorations of the U.S. meat-processing sector predated the most recent generation of food studies scholarship and asked many questions of great pertinence to students of the poultry sector. As one of the more powerful trusts of the Gilded Age and as a locus of working-class immigrant community identity and strength, a strength that was translated into political and union power in the New Deal era on a racially fraught battlefield, meatpacking workers, especially in Chicago, have long captured the imagination of historians. In the 1980s, when the beef and pork industries remade themselves anew and deunionized, this dramatic shift was scrutinized by a number of distinguished scholars as a measure of the development of Reagan-era capitalism, as a portent of greater union decline, and as a lens through which to understand working life in rural America.[15]

Until the early 2000s, there were few published studies accounting for the rise of the modern industrial poultry business, which was often considered a lesser power in the shadow of the beef and pork industries, leaving only the pious and self-reverential autobiographies of major protagonists such as Lonnie Pilgrim of Pilgrim's Pride and D. W. Brooks of Gold Kist.[16] The interconnected and more publicly facing chain restaurant industry produced a similar genre of memoir as empire builders from Ray Kroc of McDonald's and Dave Thomas of Wendy's to Chick-fil-A's S. Truett Cathy and Taco Bell's Glen Bell eagerly explained to readers how hard work and honest graft were their secret ingredients for personal success.[17]

While journalists had periodically offered alarming exposés of working conditions in the 1990s through the lens of high-profile incidents such as the Hamlet fire, in which twenty-five workers died, and ex-employee Donna Bazemore's workers' compensation claim against Perdue Farms, Steve Striffler's 2005 anthropological study represented an important early take on both the industry's development and ascendance, as well as a detailed accounting of the problematic conditions faced by many workers at the time of writing.[18] This came shortly on the back of Leon Fink's *The Maya of Morganton*, a fine-grained case study that revealed the transnational migratory flow of workers who represented a mainstay of the modern poultry workforce, seen through the eyes of Guatemalan workers at Case Farms in North Carolina.[19] Kathleen Schwartzman picked up on the threads of Fink and Striffler in taking an expansive view, considering NAFTA and the push-and-pull factors of globalization that transformed work in the rural areas of Mexico and the United States. Rejecting the common refrain that immigrants were only taking jobs that Americans didn't want, Schwartzman described the significant incorporation of Hispanic workers into the poultry workforce not as a natural outcome of market forces but rather as a more deliberate approach to meet the needs of large processors for a cheap and stable labor force, a process that often displaced African American workers.[20]

After these initial accounts, a cluster of valuable case studies added further detail and character to our understanding of southern poultry work. LaGuana Gray's history of El Dorado, Arkansas, centered the experiences of Black women at work, arguing that the central position that they took within the poultry industry was derived from earlier stereotypes attributed to them by the broader white political infrastructure within the state.[21] Gray touches on the tensions between native-born Black workers and migrant workers, a theme explored in great detail by anthropologist Angela Stuesse, who described the challenges faced by workers and activists to forge interracial working-class unity in Mississippi in the 2000s.[22] Returning to the 1980s and 1990s, Bryant Simon similarly located Black women within the engine room of American food production, depicting workers who were both bold and resilient in the face of dangerous and austere conditions at Imperial Foods in Hamlet, North Carolina, and the victims of a process of rural ghettoization, overlooked but nonetheless necessary actors in the national drive to produce cheap foods for everyone.[23] Most recently, historian of science Paul Josephson has contributed a much-needed examination of the ecological implications of mass-scale poultry production, an essential but overlooked element of the livestock sector's damaging footprint upon rural communities.[24] Both Solomon Iyobosa Omo-Osagie and coauthors Michael J. Broadway and Donald Stull consider the local environmental impacts of concentrated animal feeding operations, lagoons of hog waste, and the runoff from industrial poultry farming, topics that remain somewhat joyless and unfashionable but nonetheless are important and underexplored.[25]

For all of the depth and detail the past twenty years of scholarship has provided on the politics, working conditions, and dynamics of workplace struggle in the transnational poultry business since the 1990s, this project was in part born out of a desire to understand the industry's longer history. Did the largely disenfranchised workforces of the 1990s reflect the shop floor dynamics of poultry processing since the industry's inception? The contemporary poultry sector remains majority nonunion, but it is not union free, and there were major facilities, such as Tyson's Glen Allen plant in the suburbs of Richmond, Virginia, which had, until its recent closure, been collectively bargaining for a half century, first under the Amalgamated Meat Cutters and Butcher Workmen (AMC) and later as the United Food and Commercial Workers (UFCW). By the 1990s and 2000s, union-organizing campaigns in poultry plants were a rarity; the UFCW's twenty-year campaign with workers at the Smithfield Foods pork facility in Tar Heel, North Carolina, was a lesson in both persistence and the inordinate levels of chicanery involved in organizing in the rural meat sector.[26] If a leading concern after a growing stretch of falling union numbers was to reverse that decline, there were simply lower-hanging fruit. Yet old union shops in towns such as Glen Allen were clues of past struggles and untold stories. In the Southern Labor Archives at Georgia State University, I found an astonishing wealth of evidence revealing the untold histories of AMC Local 525 in North Carolina and Local 272 in Virginia and their thirty years of work in the southern poultry sector.

As I was considering the nature of southern poultry work, browsing decade upon decade of trade magazines such as *Broiler Industry* and *Restaurant Business*, I concluded that while there was a significant labor history that had yet to be revealed, I would find a narrative that failed to account for broader changes in thought and practice at different points within the food chain to be ultimately unsatisfactory. The growth of the poultry business and of further processed chicken within the American diet may well have been guided by the profits to be accrued by manufacturers, restaurants, and grocery stores, but that growth cannot be explained by profit motives alone. While this corporate triumvirate may have engaged in persistent and invasive advertising and marketing, successful products were invariably a calculated response to stated consumer desires and aspirations, intrinsically tied to changing ideas concerning health, lifestyle, home economics, and taste.

Considering the evolution of poultry's role in the twentieth-century United States, this book aims to make four distinct contributions through thematic chapters that consider Robert Baker and the influence of food science, the industrial development of poultry processors, the contested labor of poultry work, and chicken's place within the American diet. While Robert Baker has started to appear in recent years as a figure within the historical record, chapter 1 examines his work and his goals in closer detail than any previous accounts. Situating his work within global debates about population growth, famine, and the scarcity of protein sources, Baker identified what he considered to be leaks within the food pipeline wherein rich sources of edible matter were lost, phased out of the Western diet in an era of growing affluence. If the rescue and repurposing of animal proteins was the goal, it hardly made sense to create highly perishable products rather than focusing on durable frozen goods. Baker considered the poultry and restaurant industries as necessary partners in the enterprise of transforming food waste into edible meals on a meaningful scale; however, while those industries soon saw incredible economic potential in the production of popular and low-cost further processed chicken products, their near-term commercial priorities did not align with Baker's long-term global goals. For all of the numerous poultry products that Baker had created, by the turn of the 1980s only his chicken franks had made an impact upon the market. Yet various shifts were in motion within both the fast-food industry and among Americans' dining habits and attitudes, and the use of the Cornell scientist's techniques would quickly proliferate.

The second chapter considers the long-term evolution of American poultry production from the origins of battery farming to a full-blown industrial operation. While preindustrial farming is at times characterized as a more humane form of animal raising, my research complicates that picture, demonstrating that commercial imperatives frequently overcame general concerns for animal welfare. The introduction of "apartments" for chickens, later known as batteries, was considered both a progressive solution to common concerns and, for some, an unnatural form of regimentation. Poultry production both adapted and expanded in response to the wartime and postwar economies. While others have tried to tell the story of modern chicken through the lens of one company, the reality is that the poultry industry was never led by one company alone. In the postwar years, it consisted of hundreds of competing companies concentrated in a small number of southern and mid-Atlantic states. In some cases individual companies innovated and in others they emulated the most successful industry leaders. In other circumstances they shared many of the same suppliers of shop floor equipment. That's not to say that certain companies didn't exert greater influence, though. Holly Farms, based in Wilkesboro, North Carolina, was the largest poultry company in the world by the 1970s. It was a significant trendsetter in shaping the relationships between processors and contract farmers, between consumers and supermarkets, and within its own rural workforce, interventions that would survive its ultimate takeover by Tyson Foods in 1989 as investors and financial institutions took on a leading role in reorganizing agribusiness and the food industry.

Holly Farms features again in chapter 3 as I consider the fate of poultry workers in North Carolina between the 1950s and the 1990s. While scholars such as Fink and Simon have offered detailed accounts of poultry work in Morganton and Hamlet in the 1990s, and the latter in particular looms large in the history of the industry, the chapter's primary goal is to uncover an earlier era of workplace conflict within the chicken business. North Carolina represented a leading state in terms of total production; it was also the location of some of the sector's most fiercely contested workplaces. By examining union-organizing campaigns led by AMC Local 525 in the small towns of Wilkesboro and Monroe, we see how a company, forward looking in its approach to marketing and product development, created a violent playbook of union resistance, taking advantage of the limitations of U.S. labor laws and the home-field advantage of remote rural confines. For all of the difficulties involved in southern union efforts, Local 525 wasn't without its victories, though. When it was located in a small city with a history of union activity and political activism, its circumstances changed. In a second case study, we visit Gold Kist in 1970s Durham, where Local 525 had an established presence but where the old guard of union leadership faced an increasingly discontented young workforce in an era of rising inflation and growing expectations of economic freedom. Though collective bargaining from the 1960s through the mid-1970s had delivered job security and steadily improving benefits to poultry workers, when faced with an urban workforce in a post–civil rights environment, union members reneged against the recommendation of local president John Russell in 1978 and embarked upon an improbable two-week strike against Gold Kist. As the 1980s turned to the 1990s and union power declined, processing facilities accelerated their production, and the adverse physical effects of poultry work became increasingly acute. While large and powerful producers maintained political influence and wealth that meant they could afford to absorb the occasional financial penalties imposed by regulatory agencies, smaller companies sought to operate at a breakneck speed as they endeavored to compete with industry leaders and their greater economies of scale.

The fourth chapter considers the infrastructure of fast-food dining, the thousands of chain restaurants that, like McDonald's and Wendy's, established a foothold in the American dining experience during the 1970s. These restaurants were designed primarily as purveyors of beef, fried potatoes, and sodas, but when cattle prices climbed in the 1970s, poultry represented an ever more affordable alternative. As a legion of body-conscious Americans turned to a new trend for personal fitness, joining health clubs and investing in home workout equipment, attentions turned to leaner and less calorific diets as well as meals that were quicker to prepare. Within the context of these evolving attitudes and lifestyles, further processed chicken meals, based upon Robert Baker's designs, entered the mainstream of restaurant dining and occupied a position as a leading source of protein. Led by the Chicken McNugget at McDonald's and followed by countless replicas, further processed chicken products in the form of both nuggets and patties soon occupied frozen food aisles in supermarkets nationwide, representing a wildly successful economic story for poultry-processing companies.

The Chicken McNugget and its imitators entered a highly competitive restaurant sector in which sales models were rapidly evolving. Rather than presenting fresh ingredients and unique methods of preparation, chain restaurants sought to offer greater "value" than their rivals, meaning larger servings at a lower price per pound. By the 1990s, contradictory ideas operated within the same space. Even as McDonald's lent its sponsorship to national and international sporting events and Americans reiterated their commitment to healthy and athletic lifestyles, many customers continued to opt for the most outlandish and oversized innovations on offer.[27] Further processed chicken, relatively tasteless when unadorned, existed within this sphere, but not as the lean cuisine that some had envisioned; instead, it was wrapped in batter and doused with sugary sauces. While the media initially treated extralarge burgers and sandwiches and bucket-sized sodas as a novel and inventive form of Americana, detractors assembled growing evidence of an obesity crisis that threatened both adults and children and recast what they referred to as "junk food" in a more critical and even moral light.

Why should we take the Chicken McNugget seriously? Does further processed chicken really warrant an entire book? In the chapters that follow I argue that it does. The McNugget was the world's most successful restaurant's most influential product innovation, and critics weren't wrong to locate it as an exemplar of late twentieth-century processed foods. Though many sweet and salted processed snacks have contributed to the American obesity crisis, unlike further processed chicken, few of those snacks have occupied a role as a central source of daily protein. According to the definition used on the menu at McDonald's, when McNuggets were accompanied with a side of french fries, a portion represented not a snack but rather a "meal." An economic triumph, further processed chicken was a clever response to changes in consumer demands for new ideas and lighter fare. By the 1990s, the popularity of fast-food diets had reached a critical mass, and while consumers were subject to the coercive influence of the advertising industry, depictions of extralarge meals often stood alongside idealized images of toned and athletic physiques, not of obese bodies. Unsustainable diets were not simply the product of Svengalis on Madison Avenue; the truth was more complicated, an outcome driven by changes in lifestyle, taste, shareholder imperatives, and even good intentions gone awry. What may have been intended as respectable meals for middle-class families when issued at a bargain price point would not retain that social standing.

Exploring the development of further processed chicken sheds new light on the attitudes toward food and consumption that created what Eric Schlosser would famously describe in 2001 as a "fast food nation." For Schlosser, casual dining had assumed a central role in American life by the 1990s. I concur with this underlying premise, but our analyses differ. While I emphasize that violence and coercion were significant features in the development of industrial production and that North Carolina presented a geographical space that was supportive of these workplace dynamics, I don't believe that the U.S. food economy can be explained as purely the outcome of rapacious or exploitative instincts driven by one-dimensional characters. Many of the designers that we encounter in this study very much exist as actors within a highly competitive market economy, but they are also driven by a technocratic motivation to build an optimized food system, characteristics that were not unique to American capitalism. In a recent study of pig farming in the German Democratic Republic, Thomas Fleischman found that, by the 1970s, "agriculture under communism came to be indistinguishable from capitalist agriculture."²⁸ While Americans were central agents in the design of further processed chicken, poultry producers relied on specialized machinery designed and manufactured in a range of different countries and were part of a broader international effort to develop a planned and rationalized global food system.

Neither mainstream poultry processors nor fast-food restaurants were purveyors of boutique products. Like many industries that thrived in the postwar United States, from automobility to home construction to domestic appliances to entertainment, they operated on the central assumption that the key to achieving maximum success was by aiming for a mass consumer base by controlling operating costs and creating products that were able to maintain long-term popular appeal. When affordability could be combined with the sense that products were somehow essential to everyday life, company executives and lobbyists were able to convert this economic heft into political influence and bend governmental agencies in their favor.

Yet I am not presenting a "great company" theory of history. Neither poultry nor chain restaurants can be explained by the success of one market leader alone; Tyson Foods and McDonald's were important companies that made crucial interventions, but even these latter-day giants lacked the power and ingenuity to shape an entire industrial sector alone, more often responding to the maneuvers of aggressive and competitive upstarts that were directly targeting their market share. The trajectories of Tyson and McDonald's cannot be understood in isolation from the decisive interventions of Holly Farms, Wendy's, and PepsiCo, influential actors that this account adds to the historical narrative.

This is a story of a gaudy frozen food product and its success, but it is also a story about the transformation of American society in the postwar decades. And it is about the human costs that those changes incurred. Long before the public exposés of the 1980s and 1990s, long before the COVID-19 pandemic threw the meat and poultry industries into the foreground of public attention, the power dynamics and the routines of poultry plant work were being contested across the U.S. South. The contemporary poultry plant is not a recent invention but the result of decades of shop floor agitation on the part of both managers and workers, sometimes collectively and on other occasions acting in isolation. Many workers accepted the challenging realities of the poultry plant, in some cases accepting managerial paternalism, in others deeply cognizant of the outsized influence that large industrial employers exercised in small towns. Some workers openly contested managerial authority, though. The accounts contained here add to existing case studies by examining febrile workspaces in North Carolina in an earlier era when violent disputes among the mostly female workforce were not uncommon. While this book doesn't claim to be a comprehensive farm-to-table examination of the food chain in its entirety, by exploring the relationships between producers, restaurants, workers, and consumers, it seeks to offer a new appraisal of the rise of poultry to a central place both in the American diet and within the greater sphere of the national political economy.

CHAPTER 1

Dr. Baker and Mr. Nugget

"Shit, he's richer than a motherfucker," observes Wallace, a Baltimore drug pusher in a noteworthy scene from the first season of the HBO series *The Wire*. In conversation with colleagues Poot and D'Angelo, he is referencing the unknown inventor of the chicken nugget. Wallace, played by Michael B. Jordan, reflects on the technical acuity that must have been applied in its design, as well as the nugget's practical benefits as a snack that is easy to consume. "He must have got the bone all the way out the damn chicken," he says. Prior to this, they would have been "chewing on chumpsticks and shit and getting their fingers all greasy." Poot questions whether "Mr. Nugget" was handsomely compensated for his invention, and this is when Wallace responds in the affirmative that he must be very wealthy.

At this point the conversation becomes more interesting because D'Angelo, who is working in a supervisory capacity in the crack-dealing operation, disputes the assertion that the nugget's inventor would have been rightfully rewarded, observing that he is "just some sad-ass down in the basement of McDonald's, thinking up some shit to make some money for the real players." Poot reacts despondently to the injustice of this scenario wherein Mr. Nugget did not receive a percentage cut of future profits. But it is not a matter of right or wrong, D'Angelo states. "Now you think Ronald McDonald is gonna go down in that basement and say, 'Hey, Mr. Nugget, you the bomb! We selling chicken faster than you can tear the bone out, so I'm gonna write my clowny-ass name on this fat-ass check for you.'" Far from it. Rather, whoever "invented them things, he's still working in the basement for regular wage thinking up some shit to make fries taste better or some shit like that."[1]

Robert C. Baker, professor of food science and the chairman of the Department of Poultry and Avian Sciences at Cornell University, did not make a for-

IMAGE 1. Robert C. Baker. Courtesy of the Division of Rare and Manuscript Collections, Cornell University Library

tune from the numerous poultry products that he developed between 1957 and 1989. Though his department received support from the poultry industry, their discoveries were freely published and shared with anyone who wished to utilize them. "They were mailed to about 500 companies," said Baker's former student Robert Gravani in 2012. "He literally gave ideas away, and other people patented them," he added.[2]

The item that came to be known as the chicken nugget was the most popular product to emerge from Baker's three decades of experimentation in the food sciences, closely resembling a dish that he presented as "chicken cubes." It was a wildly successful product enjoyed by millions but quickly reviled and the subject of mockery on the part of critics.

Less than three years after the national launch of the Chicken McNugget, in January 1986 the *Wall Street Journal*'s Martha Bayles invoked the popular dish in a lament about the sorry state of political debate. Writing as Halley's Comet was passing the sun, Bayles singled out television as the subject of her ire, charging that news shows were "bite sized at best" before proclaiming that "television is to reality what the McNugget is to a whole, living chicken." Bayles would not relent in her damning analogy. Whose fault was it? The journalists blamed the campaign managers, and the campaign managers blamed the journalists, "as if chicken farmers and franchise operators were blaming each other for McNuggets, when clearly they create a product together, to their mutual benefit." Was it new? "Many Mondale supporters, both within and without the ranks of the media, feel compelled to declare 1984 the Year of the McNugget," she continued, "the flash-point election where issues and substance finally succumbed to the artificial processing, packaging and pitching of sleazoid media types."[3] What did this situation say about the American people? There were two theories: "Some media critics seem to believe the country is full of cretins who would blindly swallow a McNugget without asking what the devil it is, simply because they have been instructed to do so by a slickly designed ad." Bayles preferred the second hypothesis: "Others say that the cretins are few, that the average consumer has a pretty good idea of how a McNugget is made, and whether or not he should swallow it. After all, he lives in the real world, where he experiences things other than television."[4]

Two years later, the cult British science fiction comedy *Red Dwarf* invoked Baker's morsels in another unfortunate and even more bizarre analogy. Traveling three million years in the future, the show's spacefaring crew encounter an abandoned vessel, and anticipation builds as they wait to meet the ship's attractive female officers. These hopes are dashed when all that they find are the officers' skeletal remains. "They've been dead for centuries," exclaims Arnold Rimmer, one of the crew members. "You've only got to look at them. They've got less meat on them than a chicken nugget," he quips.[5] The nugget was proliferating across the planet as the breakthrough savory snack of the 1980s, but just a few short years after its liftoff it was already gaining a certain unwanted cultural standing as a jocular culinary anomaly, neither natural nor nutritious and perhaps, worst of all, not even chicken.

Yet neither the nugget nor the various forms of further processed chicken to emerge from Cornell University were ever designed to function as what was often being referred to by the 1970s as "junk food," a label Baker would consistently reject. Over time, further processed chicken products were increasingly a reflection of consumers' casual dining habits, but for Baker and his colleagues the emerging discipline of food sciences represented a noble calling, a mission to reconfigure the food supply to match underutilized resources with evolving tastes as a means of alleviating global hunger, a pervasive concern throughout the twentieth century.

Preserving Food

Robert C. Baker did not set out to devise a product with the notoriety of the Chicken McNugget. He did not even envision working with poultry, as he was raised on a fruit farm in the 1920s and 1930s in Sodus, New York, on the southern edge of Lake Ontario. Though his family kept a flock of Rhode Island Reds, he majored in pomology as an undergraduate at Cornell, where he received his BS in 1943, only taking some classes in poultry to satisfy his father. "I guess I fell in love with chickens," he would tell the *Rochester Democrat and Chronicle* many years later. Though he had started studying botany, "I changed later on because I thought the future was brighter in chicken than it was in fruit."[6] Baker worked as an assistant county agent in Orange County, New York, for a couple of years before completing an MS in agricultural economics from Pennsylvania State University in 1949 while serving as an assistant professor of poultry husbandry. He then returned to upstate New York, where he committed to working in the Poultry Extension Service at Cornell while working on a doctorate that he would receive from Purdue in 1956.[7] "The C. doesn't stand for 'chicken,' but maybe it should," cracked local journalist Carol Ritter, referring to Baker's middle initial in a 1982 Sunday profile. "Baker, perhaps more than anyone else in America, can be called the 'Chicken Man,'" she opined.[8]

As a professor of food science, Baker was working in a relatively new area of academic research. "Food science can be defined as the application of the principles of science, engineering, and economics to the processing, formulation, synthesis, distribution and marketing of food," he explained. Baker and his colleagues sought to serve a growing industry, one that "employs 1/7 of the population of the United States." He added, "This is greater than the combined work force in the steel, automobile, chemical, communications, public utilities, and mining industries." While he worked with the assumption that women within families were primarily responsible for preparing food, Baker indicated that this was an evolving situation. If food science was once about cookery and recipes, "times have changed with the rapidly growing popularity of convenience foods for the consumer and the emphasis today is on trained, technically-oriented food scientists."[9]

The discipline of food science operated within the same philosophical assumptions as many of the applied sciences in the postwar United States. In a national economy built upon a foundation of widespread consumer spending power, designers understood that successful products were those that were purchased or adopted by large manufacturers and retailers with a continental reach. The most successful products frequently provided affordability, comfort, and convenience. As spacious and luxuriant automobiles proliferated and became a part of American youth culture in the 1950s, so did drive-in and then drive-through restaurants.[10] Affordable refrigerators and later microwave ovens allowed for a rapid expansion in the range of durable and reheatable products. In the public realm, nationally recognizable burger chains along with restaurants such as Domino's and Pizza Hut acted as lodestars of Americans' tastes.

Yet while Baker employed a systematic methodology of product development oriented toward commercial success, the particular focus of his work was motivated by a broader economic and environmental analysis. Beginning in the late 1960s in speeches and published commentaries, Baker began to frame his work as a response to his persistent and enduring concerns about food waste in the United States. This was not an entirely newfangled concern. Baker had lived through the Great Depression and the many laments directed toward the Agricultural Adjustment Administration's destruction of usable food materials in order to protect commodity prices from a market with a glut of products and an undercapitalized consumer base. Forty years later, mountains of rotting fruit and vegetables were no longer a concern. In the Cold War era, agricultural policy had become an essential component of foreign policy in the form of direct aid and in the provision of new scientific methods and technologies. Trade agreements created by the United States Department of Agriculture (USDA) encouraged farmers to maximize production while actively promoting access to export markets. Instead, concerns lay elsewhere.

Baker consistently employed the analogy of a pipeline between producers and consumers, a pipeline that was leaking because popular foodstuffs were allowed to expire and other less popular resources were underutilized and discarded or wasted through inefficient production processes (see images 2 and 3). He estimated in 1979 that if the leaks in the pipeline could be effectively plugged, then overall losses could be reduced by between 30 and 50 percent, increasing the food supply by 10 to 15 percent without having to cultivate new lands. Fixing the pipeline needed to be a component of long-term planning "if we as Americans are going to have a plentiful supply of food," Baker explained. "Although current projections indicate that this nation will not face a nutrient shortage even in times of crop failures, present diets, particularly high protein foods, will become increasingly costly in relation to income," he said. "As our nation looks for ways to increase food production, a growing awareness of what is happening to the food once it is harvested will become mandatory." Leakages in the pipeline also incurred great ecological costs: "Vast amounts become waste[,] compounding pollution and waste disposal problems. This all includes the enormous amounts of energy used to produce food no one consumes."[11]

When presented with a public platform Baker would repeatedly assert that food waste was a critical national problem, describing a series of examples that included all major food groups. "At least 8 percent of all commercial

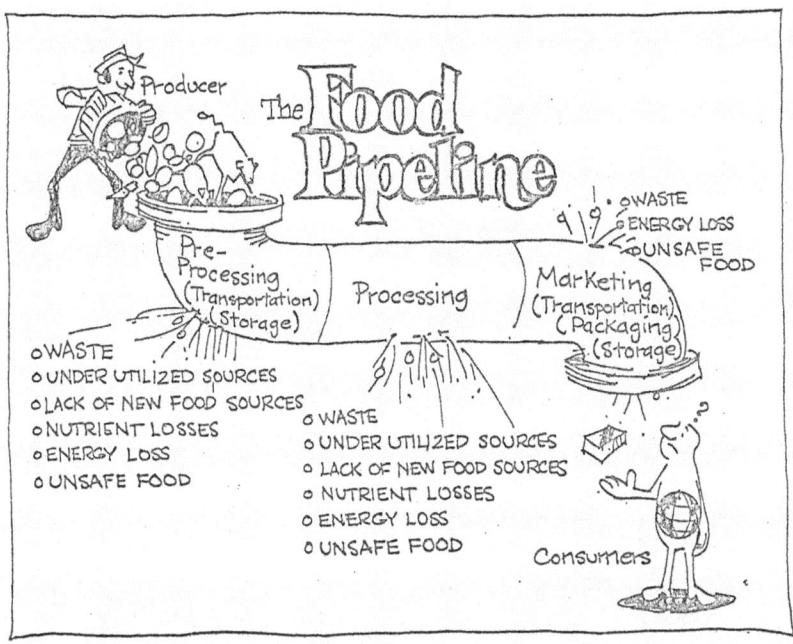
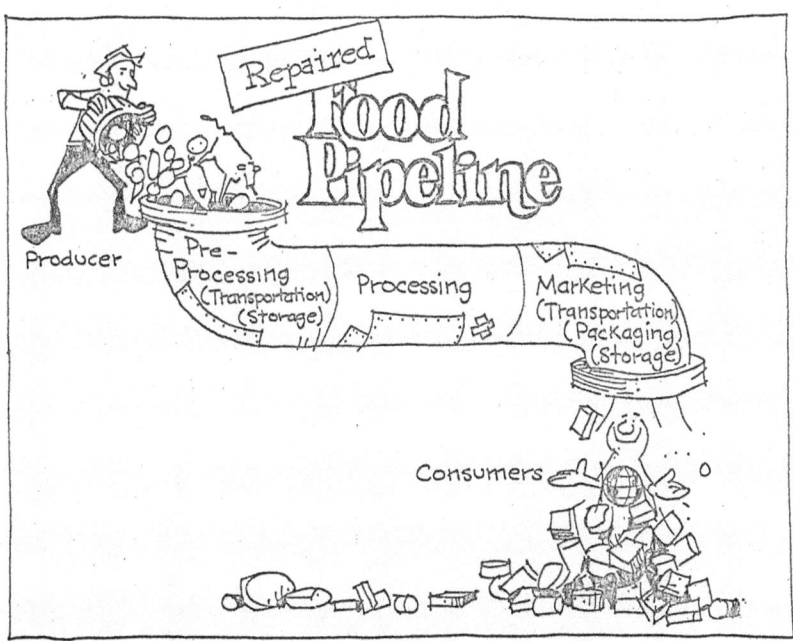

IMAGES 2 AND 3. For Robert Baker, the application of new methods in the processing, preparation, and transportation of poultry products represented an important remedy to the environmental and economic ills that resulted from what he depicted as a leaking food pipeline. Courtesy of the Division of Rare and Manuscript Collections, Cornell University Library

bread stales and is thrown away, never reaching the consumer," Baker wrote. "If one assumes that this loss is somewhat representative worldwide and that one pound of bread is made from one pound of wheat, then the world wheat loss from staling approaches one billion bushels per year," he claimed.[12]

He estimated that 800,000 tons of protein from corn milling were wasted or fed to animals in the extraction of starch and oil, and 1.7 billion pounds of milk were wasted in processing or on the farm, including one-third of the protein involved in cheese production.[13] "A fourth of all fruits and vegetables harvested are lost through spoilage between harvest and time of purchase," Baker charged.[14] This did not include misshapen fruit that were not deemed saleable by supermarkets or even nature's own wasteful ways: fruit that fell from trees and crops that were destroyed by weather or insects.

Then there was the fishing industry, a particular cause of concern. "Did you know that each year we waste or 'underutilize' millions of tons of fish?" he asked the League for International Food Education in its 1978 newsletter. "It is estimated that as much as 70% of the fish in the oceans are underutilized." The same could be said for lake-dwelling fish too. Why were fish underutilized? "Some have tiny, needle-like bones which make them difficult to eat," he explained. "Others have unfortunate names, like sucker, crappie, or cancer fish. Still others are considered too small to be worth the effort to prepare them." When these "trash" fish were returned to the water dead they served as a pollutant.[15] Besides fish, animal blood was commonly washed away from abattoir floors. "This blood, an excellent source of high-quality protein, could be used to feed humans," Baker wrote. "From the red meat industry alone, over 300 million pounds of blood protein could be added to our diet."[16]

Food that had been purchased was often wasted too. Baker cited a two-year study in Tucson where intrepid researchers inspected the contents of garbage cans and estimated that around 10 percent of a family's total food resources were discarded. If this estimate was accurate, then Tucson's 450,000 residents wasted around 9,500 tons of edible food annually, worth a market rate of about $10 million.[17]

And then there were poultry meat losses, the problem to which Baker would commit the greatest share of his time and creativity. In poultry processing, the yield of a chicken is the difference between a bird's live weight and the amount that is salvaged as saleable product. The higher the yield, the more effective use the processor or butcher is said to have made of the chicken. A 1973 report by poultry scientists P. L. Hayse and W. W. Marion asserted that the average total yield in the United States from broilers was 70 percent for females and 72 percent for males. In their experiment, the average weight of the females was 1,494 grams, while the males weighed 1,841 grams. Of the eviscerated meat, the most popular cuts—breast, thighs, drumsticks, and wings—constituted 72–73 percent of the meat. The remaining 27–28 percent consisted of the neck, tail rack, rib rack, heart, liver, and gizzard. For females, this amounted to 282 grams and for males 364 grams per bird.[18] By the 1970s, these components, historically deemed highly edible, were in most places unpopular. "The necks and giblets of broilers are placed in the body cavities of the carcasses and sold to consumers, who often throw them away," Baker wrote. "If both necks (deboned) and giblets were further processed, a potential 300 million pounds of neck meat and 487 million pounds of giblets, or a total of 787 million pounds of edible meat would be available."[19]

Then there were the Leghorns, an active and energetic breed by nature, the most popular and prolific egg-layers in the United States, only sold as a cheaper meat when their productivity waned. "Leghorns have not the eating quality of the heavier breeds," explained Milwaukee merchant John Grajek in 1943. "The meat in Leghorn fowl," he added, "is more stringy, tough skinned and dry." Subsequently, their resale value had invariably been several cents per pound less than other more popular breeds.[20]

Where many saw beleaguered battery hens, Baker saw great potential. Like later critics of processed foods, he identified attributes associated with older foodways in need of recovery. "Back a few years, Leghorn fowl were very popular for meat and I can remember their selling for as much as forty-five cents a pound on the farm," he reminisced in a speech in Bogotá in 1978. Tastes had changed, though: "Today in the United States we are raising broilers[,] and consumers much prefer the tender broiler to the Leghorn fowl. At present Leghorn fowl are bringing about seven cents a pound on the farm and they have been as low as two cents."[21] As of 1978 there were an estimated 292 million pullets and hens of egg-laying age in the United States.[22] Once these birds had passed the point of optimum productivity they were generally sold to pet food manufacturers, but the market for human consumption was limited. For Baker, a change in the American agricultural paradigm was called for. "In the past we have used most of our research dollars to increase production. We have carried out all kinds of studies on improving grain yields, increasing pounds of milk per cow and eggs per hen. This has been excellent research and the results have really paid off." Baker predicted that "in the future, however, scientists are not going to be able to continue to make large gains in food supply by breeding, feeding, pest control, etc. We must obtain our large increases elsewhere and a logical place is the food pipeline." This was a frugal as well as an environmentally sensitive approach. "The cost of preventing waste and making use of underutilized sources is less in dollars and energy than [the] cost of increasing primary production," Baker concluded.[23]

A Hungry World

So was Baker a fantasist, or was he responding to serious, widespread concerns? A range of different indicators, including the persistence of crop failures in developing countries, galloping population growth, and the continued suburban capture of American farmlands, lent credibility to anxious forecasts concerning the world's future food supply.

Economist Stephen Devereux has estimated that around seventy million people died of famine in the twentieth century and that almost half of these deaths occurred in China between 1958 and 1962. While most famines did not reach the extraordinary levels of those in China, in the Soviet Union in 1921–22 (approximately nine million deaths), 1932–34 (approximately seven to eight million), and 1946–47 (approximately two million), as well as during the Bengali famine of 1943 (approximately two to three million), the persistence and catastrophic impact of crop failures continued to cast a pall over many populous countries in the 1960s and 1970s.[24] The Rockefeller Foundation first entered into the area of agricultural development in Mexico in the 1930s, but by the postwar years, the specter of red revolution in China and white revolution in Iran had convinced U.S. policy makers of the need for a strong American presence in what would be termed "international development" beyond the Western Hemisphere.[25] While the Soviet Union offered a successful theory of industrial planning, U.S. officials believed that their model of agricultural technology offered an alternative pathway to modernization that would strengthen democratic political development, Nick Cullather has argued.[26] Poor crops and drought in India in 1966 and 1967 accelerated the country's implementation of the "Green Revolution" in farming, producing bumper harvests and long-term social and environmental repercussions. Yet the most scarring example of the potentially explosive consequences of famine occurred in Ethiopia, where droughts in the northern Amhara region in 1973 led to the starvation of as many as two hundred thousand people and contributed to the usurpation of the imperial government of Haile Selassie by the Marxist Derg in 1974.[27]

Famine was not limited to East Africa. "In West Africa and Bangladesh, people are starving by the millions, and in Washington, officials are scratching to find quite small amounts of spare food—food not committed to be sold—for relief," read an editorial in the *Washington Post* in 1973. The editorial went on to assert that this crisis was "a condition very much aggravated in the last year by Soviet grain purchases on a scale which all but erased the United States' (and other exporters') 'surpluses,'" adding that "it was on these 'surpluses' that humanitarian food programs had been built."[28] The grain deal "sharply altered the global supply picture" and "permanently modified America's complacence with respect to food abundance," wrote J. Don Looper of the Foreign Agricultural Service in the 1981 annual USDA yearbook of agriculture, which was titled *Will There Be Enough Food?*[29]

Signifying the importance of food in global policy discussions, in 1978 U.S. president Jimmy Carter appointed the Presidential Commission on World Hunger, which was chaired by respected career diplomat Sol Linowitz and included famed agricultural scientist Norman Borlaug, nutritionist Jean Mayer, poultry executive D. W. Brooks, and John Denver and Harry Chapin, both popular musicians and high-profile public advocates. Reporting that as many as eight hundred million of the world's population did not get enough to eat each day, Linowitz recommended that "the U.S. makes the elimination of hunger the primary focus of its relations with the developing world."[30] The commission warned that "when people consume fewer calories and less protein than their bodies need . . . it diminishes physical and mental capacities and thus makes people less energetic and able to learn," while it "also increases susceptibility to disease." Whereas daily protein consumption in "developed countries" averaged ninety-seven grams, the commission noted that in "less developed countries" it was as little as fifty-four grams; accordingly, life expectancy rates were seventy-one years and fifty-two years, respectively.[31]

Fears of famine were often coupled with anxieties about the implications of uncontrolled population growth. Biologist Paul R. Ehrlich's best-selling 1968 book *The Population Bomb* introduced the concerns of scientists to a broad audience as his projections of social upheaval entered the public consciousness. "The battle to feed all of humanity is over," the book began. "In the 1970s and 1980s hundreds of millions of people will starve to death in spite of any crash programs embarked upon now." The duration of time required for the earth's population to double had shrunk exponentially, Ehrlich explained. Whereas it had taken around one thousand years for the earth's population to double to a total of five hundred million from 650 to 1650 CE, there were as many as a billion people just one hundred years later. By 1930 there were two billion, meaning a 100 percent increase in just eighty years. The global population would reach four billion by 1974. Even if one was to set aside the logistical difficulties of moving billions of people off the planet, "it would take only about 50 years to populate Venus, Mercury, Mars, the moon, and the moons of Jupiter and Saturn to the same population density as Earth," Ehrlich observed. Never mind Venus's eight-hundred-degree temperatures. Crisis was inevitable. "It is difficult to guess what the exact scale and consequences of the famines will be. But there *will be* famines," Ehrlich projected.[32]

In 1957 in *The Fight for Food*, J. Gordon Cook observed that the "lack of animal protein and vitamins in the diet of the under-developed nations has been the cause of deficiency diseases, such as pellagra and beri-beri, which are endemic in many countries."[33] Ehrlich, like Cook and Linowitz a decade later, identified protein as the crucial dietary component that would be most difficult to provide in sufficient quantities if the health of humankind were to be preserved. "Without enough high-quality protein in a mother's diet during pregnancy and in a child's diet during the first few years, the child may suffer permanent brain impairment and be mentally retarded," he wrote. Other consequences included "dwarfing, crippling, and blindness." Ehrlich thus concluded that "protein is the key to the world food problem—it is high-quality protein which is most expensive to obtain, both in economic terms and in terms of the ecological cost of getting it."[34]

In light of these concerns, some invoked the nineteenth-century English cleric Thomas Malthus and his forecasts that world population would outstrip the capacity to produce food, leading to a "Malthusian disaster" where famine and pestilence would reduce the number of people to a manageable level. Malthus contended that, whereas population increased geometrically (1 + 2 + 4 + 8 + 16, etc.), the productive capacity of land only increased arithmetically (1 + 2 + 3 + 4 + 5, etc.). Perhaps the most strident work claiming vindication of these theories was *Homage to Malthus*, published in 1975 and written by English American historian Jane Soames Nickerson. In her bold effort to revive Malthus's reputation, Nickerson went so far as to state that "Malthus was a prophet, and prophets are notoriously unpopular." Prophets, she explained, "possess a gift which they have to share, however beclouded by uncertainties, however unwelcome to their audience." Up until that point, improved technologies had meant that the world food supply had been able to keep pace with increases in population. That said, "the time of crisis is getting very near," Nickerson warned. "It seems certain, according to the competent authorities in many related fields, that in the not distant future the question of who shall have enough to eat will become a political question: to which of the hungry will the societies that possess a surplus allocate that surplus?"[35]

Leon Bates, a former air force electrician and the founder of the Texas-based Bible Believers Evangelical Association, remarked in his 1977 book *Projection for Survival*, "It is still hard for most people to believe that our civilization is on the brink of DISASTER." Bates's studies led him to assert that "evidence continues to increase that Universal Famine may be our next MAJOR CRISIS." He also contended that UFOs were probably the result of demonic activities rather than the more common assumption that they were aliens visiting the planet Earth, so his view may well have been somewhat astray from the mainstream of American thought.[36]

Changes in land use represented another significant area of concern for many agriculturalists. By the 1980s, around one million acres of cropland were taken out of service every year. While poor land management and soil conversation continued to create severe erosion in some places and food-generating acres were converted to biofuel production elsewhere, real estate developers were the greatest aggressors.[37] Growing waves of suburban expansion beyond urban areas had transformed many former rural enclaves as farmers sold off croplands to developers. "Mowers Replace Feed Grain in New Suburb," read a *New York Times* headline in a 1988 article detailing the cosmopolitan tastes of recent homebuyers in Raritan Township in New Jersey.[38] A 1987 USDA report warned that urban sprawl, highway construction, salt pollution, and soil erosion could eliminate from production farm acres equal to the size of the state of Missouri in the coming decades. "Assuming the current rate of conversion continued, the cropland rate would be reduced nearly 48 million acres, or 12 percent, between 1982 and 2030," the report read.[39]

Ehrlich's forecasts of a population disaster were far from unanimously accepted. Conservative economist Julian Simon became an increasingly outspoken critic, arguing that rather than presenting a problem, population growth created greater productive capacity and that unshackled human ingenuity could meet the challenges of drought and starvation while providing ever greater living standards.[40] For the purposes of the USDA, both analyses led to the same outcome; whether growing populations posed an existential threat or not, the inexorable mission of the department to expand the output of U.S. livestock and crops would continue into the distant future, a mantle the department increasingly carried alongside private sector actors such as Archer-Daniels-Midland and Monsanto, companies that invoked the problems of the global poor to validate their aggressive international strategies. Under these circumstances, Robert Baker's broader objectives were clear. "Waste and starvation should not go together," he wrote in 1978. "Hunger in the world is on the increase—a fact that is complicated by the projection that there will be 80 percent more people in the world by the year 2000," Baker stated before adding that "food to supplement scarcity in industrial and developing nations" had become a critical issue in the United States.[41]

Baker's Kitchen

Baker realized that he faced a significant obstacle. Most of the forms of wasted animal protein that he identified were considered unappetizing. In earlier ages, Americans had been willing to eat older hens as well as the less prized cuts such as hearts and necks, and home cooks employed their skills to improve the appeal of this meat. Early nutritionists Elmer V. McCollum and Nina Simmonds, both at the School of Hygiene and Public Health at Johns Hopkins University, charged in 1920 that, even when consuming meat, Americans were failing to take advantage of the nutritional variety that was available to them. "When a rat or a weasel makes a raid on a chicken coop . . . it cuts the throats of the birds and sucks blood as its first choice," they observed. "Later it opens the body cavity and eats of the internal organs, or the brain cavity and eats the nervous tissue. It is remarkable that civilized man should from choice limit himself largely to the cuts of meat which are derived from muscles. It has not been found possible by the meat packers to educate the public to eat the glandular organs to any great extent when they can afford muscle cuts of meat," McCollum and Simmonds concluded.[42]

Secondary cuts of beef were minced into burgers and pork scraps used for sausages, and cookery books of a previous generation made similar recommendations pertaining to poultry, often stressing economy as a central component of home management. In the case of small animals like fowl, it was most common to cook the body in its entirety as a single dish and then to make use of leftovers in the subsequent days. *The Perry Home Cook Book*, a collection of typical American fare, also published in 1920, presents a clear representation of this. Accompanying instructions on how to bake, roast, fry, or press a chicken, Mrs. E. G. Jenkins of Oskaloosa, Kansas, details her chicken croquettes. "After slicing all that can be sliced from a baked chicken, pick the remainder from the bones and mince fine," she says. Then add salt and pepper, one egg, a tablespoon of mashed potatoes, and a half-cup of sweet milk. Molded in cracker crumbs and rolled in a little flour, the least relished parts of the bird are thus reconfigured into a tasty snack that saves on waste.[43]

Recipes of this type may have retained value for the prudent domestic cook, but they did not represent products that could be prepared at an industrial facility for the frozen food market in an era of culinary abundance. By the 1970s, there was a readier supply of broiler meat available than ever before. In 1932 there had been a total of 450 million chickens in the United States, about three and a half times the number of people.[44] By 1978 there were 3.6 billion broilers, about sixteen per person.[45] For underutilized sources of animal protein to be marketed to the American palate, they had to be reconstituted into something more appetizing. It might even help if the original form was obscured entirely.

For new products to be successful, their utility needed to be married to changes in consumer tastes. Baker recalled that when he conducted a survey in Syracuse in the 1960s, he found that "we just weren't giving the consumers what they wanted. Mrs. Consumer wanted convenience items and we as an industry just weren't obeying her wishes," he told *Broiler Industry*.[46] By 1968 he had developed thirty-eight new poultry and egg products. By 1985 he was able to list fifty-two, as well as "easy to use" Frozen Minced Fish and Fish Crispies and a breakfast pizza with a base made from egg whites.[47] Baker's poultry products were often envisioned not as wild new inventions but rather as imitations and substitutes designed to fit within the framework of consumers' existing eating patterns. "Many were copied from the red meat industry," Baker observed. "We have found that we can make any product that has been made from red meat," he added.[48]

Concurrently, one of Baker's first attempts to present further processed poultry to the public was the chicken hot dog, introduced as the "bird dog" in 1962.[49] Mastering the science behind the bird dog would pave the way for further inventions and ultimately lead to the nugget. "There were Germans who knew the art of making beef or pork franks, but they didn't know how to make chicken or turkey franks," Baker recalled years later.[50] He initially experienced difficulties in achieving a sausage with the right texture and consistency. "They were somewhat mushy due to a fat content of 28%, and chicken meat didn't fit the consumer image," Baker said in 1985. "There's no question we were going at it more or less blindly in the early years, simply because no technology existed for making products out of poultry meat."[51]

Mirroring the fat content and the method used in making red meat sausages did not work. "One of the principal ways in which chicken meat differs from beef, pork and lamb is that the skin is generally considered an integral part of the meat, while with red meats this is not the case." Different quantities of ground skin were added to samples of chicken meat with varying ratios of protein, water, and fat. The resulting sausages were then tested for tenderness, taste, and deformation at both hot and cold temperatures. Achieving the correct balance of skin was crucial. Tests showed that as the proportion of skin increased, tenderness and chewiness did likewise, but in the process, juiciness was incrementally reduced. Baker reported that a threshold of 20 percent skin had to be reached before there was any noticeable difference. "This would indicate that the amount of skin normally present in boned-out chicken (about 15 percent added skin) makes little difference to the texture," he wrote.[52] In utilizing skin, as opposed to any other ingredient, he attempted to keep the proportion of meat as high as possible. When the content of chicken links received some scrutiny in the 1980s, Baker wrote in defense of one of his proudest inventions. "I am very familiar with the production of chicken and turkey hot dogs and can assure anyone that everything that goes into chicken or turkey hot dogs is wholesome," he commented in 1989. "Approximately 98 percent of chicken or turkey franks is meat," he stated. Baker went on to defend the use of additives such as sodium nitrite and sodium erythorbate. The former protected the hot dog from pathogenic bacteria, while the latter prevented color changes.[53]

Chicken frankfurters, like all sausages, maintained their shape through their containment within a skin of their own. However, reclaimed and deboned poultry meat would not hold together and maintain a shape through cooking merely as the result of its initial compression. If this problem could be effectively resolved, then poultry products of any shape and size could be constructed. Finding the correct binding agents had to accompany an emulsifier that would suspend water and fat particles. "When chicken is cooked twice, extra water is lost and this gives a mouth feel which is described as 'warmed up' flavor," Baker wrote.[54] To counter this, he built off the work of previous studies on both red and white meats that had attempted to bind meats together using different ingredients, such as salt-soluble proteins, food-grade phosphates, egg albumen, and gluten. His tests in 1970 found that a considerable level of binding was achieved when sodium chloride (salt) was combined with Kena blend FP-28—a sodium phosphate mixture—and beaten for three minutes. "Beating enhanced binding in all cases," he found.[55]

After three minutes of beating, the texture of the broiler muscles the researchers were testing was affected. "The tensile strength values for this treatment combination were almost 5 times the control (no treatment)," Baker and his team reported.[56] Sodium phosphates were soluble, meaning that they did not alter the appearance of the meat in a way that would disturb the consumer. Beyond just helping in the binding process, sodium phosphates also had the effect of stabilizing meat through the cooking, freezing, thawing, and recooking processes. This meant that the meat would not suffer from oxidation, and it would retain nutrients, taste, and color. As stabilizing agents, sodium phosphates would ensure that the chicken did not become too acidic or too alkaline. Baker asserted that the binding of proteins was most successful at a mildly alkaline pH of 8.0. When the pH dropped down toward acidic 5.0, proteins would carry no electric charge, and they would become inactive and insoluble.[57]

Baker was open and declarative in his defense of phosphates in poultry hot dogs, in contrast to the later image of the mysterious McNugget. "Just compare phosphated versus non-phosphated chicken, cooked or warmed up a second time," he instructed. "If you haven't done so, you will have a pleasant surprise. You will become a believer. The phosphated will have a pleasant fresh flavor while the non-phosphated will taste 'warmed up' or stale."[58]

Baker and his colleagues at Cornell were not the first to experiment with the use of Kena FP-28, also known as sodium tripolyphosphate. They were building on the recent work of other scientists working with meat products, and they devised a formula of protein, fat, water, and additives whereby mechanically deboned chicken could be pulled apart and put together again in a shape that would survive the experience of cooking, freezing, and reheating. These robust products maintained the form that the processor had selected and retained the essential characteristics that were expected of meats: tenderness, juiciness, texture, and color. Whatever flavor they possessed in the first instance was not lost either. With this formula chicken could be shaped in any manner of different ways.

Equipped with these essential findings, Baker and his team designed numerous original poultry products. Many were fairly limited in their levels of success, falling into one of two opposite but connected traps. Some were direct imitations of red meat dishes, and while beef and pork remained inexpensive, these poultry products were surplus to requirements to consumers who may have been averse to experimentation. While new products such as Chick-A-Links and Chicken Hash held some appeal, other designs, including "Bake and Serve" Chicken Loaf, Chicken Ham, Chicken Bologna, and Chicken Chili Con Carne, remained strange curiosities that left potential venders unconvinced of their mass appeal. Catchy names like Chicken Crispies, Chickalona, Chicken Chunkalona, Chicken Chunk Roll, and Poulet Supreme failed to persuade purchasers.[59] Though items like Spam, thought of by many as an austerity dish, represented a precedent for successful densely processed meat products, by the 1970s many of Baker's proposals fell short of capturing the imagination of poultry company or retail executives and their marketing teams.

By the 1980s over one hundred companies made some variation of chicken franks after their sales grew from 3 percent of the frankfurter market in 1977 to 13 percent three years later, but in a nation where burgers were very popular, Baker continued to promote the potential of his patties as he searched for a second major success.[60] Through the early 1980s, he would repeatedly make the case that twenty-one-month-old Leghorns, sometimes referred to as "mechanically deboned spent layers" and commonly used in canned soups, presented an undervalued resource. In 1983 the College of Agriculture and Life Sciences at Cornell issued a press release to this effect. "Chicken burgers made from dark meat are just as tasty as or better than those made from all white breast meat or even ground beef for hamburgers," it proclaimed. Researchers had tested a variety of different recipes but found that 50 percent Leghorn thigh, 40 percent broiler necks and backs, and 10 percent ground skin to be among the most appetizing, as good as if not better than the more expensive broiler breast burgers that were making their way into restaurants. Breast meat was considered "the Cadillac of the product," Baker said. Nonetheless, "many panelists felt that dark meat was tastier and juicier than breast meat," he explained. This was good news for everyone. "Poultry producers would be able to receive a more realistic market value for their producers"; meanwhile, "consumers would pay a fair price for chicken burgers without sacrificing quality," he added.[61]

Describing the product to journalist Mark Frank, Baker acknowledged that Americans were "big hamburger eaters regardless of the price and always will be" and noted that "when people look at it, they're a little surprised. But it looks like a hamburg grind, except it's ground finer. The color is like hamburg." Tradition remained an obstacle: "It always takes a while to break down psychological barriers and to get people used to a new food product. The one that had the worst barrier was chicken hot dogs. But now the younger generation doesn't have any hangups about them."[62]

By the mid-1970s Baker's chicken franks had achieved a respectable level of success, and poultry companies were maintaining an interest in the latest innovations and recommendations emerging from Ithaca. Chicken production and consumption were increasing nationwide, but there was little question that beef remained Americans' favorite source of protein, reaching a historic record of 93.4 pounds per person in 1976.[63] The 1970s represented a decade of hectic expansion for fast-food burger chains as consumers continued to dine out with greater and greater frequency. Whereas around 20 percent of meals were eaten outside the home in 1960, this figure had increased to more than 30 percent by the 1980s and would later reach 40 percent by 2000.[64] McDonald's expanded from fifteen hundred restaurants in 1970 to six thousand by 1980.[65] Meanwhile, Wendy's was the breakout franchise of the 1970s. The company's primary pitch was that it sold larger and fresher burgers than McDonald's did, and it expanded from one store in Columbus, Ohio, in 1969 to around eighteen hundred by 1979.[66] In light of the success of these chains and the rapid growth of Taco Bell to nine hundred stores (another restaurant whose primary ingredient was beef), many concluded that there were certain elements of the American diet that remained perpetually unalterable.

However, changes were indeed afoot. In certain regards, the seemingly unstoppable march of the burger chains up the highways and byways of American towns and cities had started to take a toll on consumers. Growing concerns about obesity in an increasingly sedentary and office-bound population were causing greater numbers to question the nutritious value of the burger, fries, and milkshake or Coca-Cola combination. What if this wasn't an entirely timeless meal after all? Before the leaders in the restaurant industry could fully grapple with the possibility of burger fatigue, they faced a severe spike in the price of beef in early 1979, up by a third in April over the previous year's average and a threat to their bottom-line profitability. In response to this challenge, they would revisit their menus, and further processed poultry products would receive greater consideration than ever before. Yet as they approached these problems, restaurateurs would not share Baker's concerns about plugging holes in the food pipeline, reducing the costs of waste and pollution, and alleviating global hunger. For poultry production companies, providing for America's fast-food restaurants and their millions of daily consumers was no small feat. Meeting the demands of the restaurant industry's largest contractors required an equally vast industry a half century in the making.

CHAPTER 2

"The Poor Hen, She Has Become a Machine!"

Meat is never harmful to the normal person.
—Robert B. Hinman, professor of animal husbandry at Cornell University

"The place of poultry on the general farm must be definitely understood," wrote Rob R. Slocum, from the USDA's Animal Husbandry Division in 1919. "It must be remembered that the poultry flock is merely one of the activities with which the farmer is engaged and that he will be unable to devote to his flock a great amount of his time." He concluded that "the part poultry should play, therefore, is to fit into the general farm management in such a way as to help maintain a proper balance in farm operations and to utilize materials which are suitable for feeding the hens but otherwise would be wasted."[1] A "poultry farm" was still a rarity even through the 1930s, when 85 percent of American farms raised chickens and few flocks were larger than two hundred head.[2] Normally a reliable source of income, cash receipts on poultry sales dropped substantially during the Great Depression from a national high of $333 million in 1930 to just $235 million in 1935.[3] Receipts would never fall this low again.

Children may have lavished tender affection upon hens and enjoyed their eccentric personalities. Commercially oriented farmers, who embraced technological innovation and the scientific husbandry of a narrow range of the most profitable breeds, did not. An emerging class of specialized poultry farmers, raising birds that had been identified and promoted by USDA experiment stations, built a powerful industry capable of transforming the American diet. The relationship between industry and consumer was symbiotic. Executives would often adapt to changes in taste and lifestyle, but as innovators they too would take the lead, guiding consumers toward new products and forms of preparation that conformed to the latest methods of food storage and cookery.

A streak of stiff indifference to both human and avian austerity was characteristic of unsentimental poultrymen, forged by the struggles of Depression-era inequities and memories of youthful hardships. "I have often said that our industry is an industry of 'pennies and grams,'" wrote Lonnie Pilgrim, born in 1928 and raised on a barely profitable cotton and cattle farm in East Texas. "If we can reduce our costs by just one penny per dollar and increase our sales by just one penny per dollar, we improve our bottom line 2 percent," explained the pious founder of Pilgrim's Pride in 2005.[4] Bill Rusch of North Carolina's Holly Farms echoed Pilgrim's view. "This business is made up of thousands of hundredths-of-a-cent per pound, and if you can gain a couple hundredths of a cent by improving one step of the operation, you have an advantage," he told *Forbes* in 1982.[5] "We produce something like 6.5 million chickens a week, and a hundredth of a cent means a lot," Rusch reiterated in the *New York Times* two years later. "People will kill around here for a hundredth of a cent."[6]

Geographically dispersed across the hinterlands of southern states, the poultry industry would enlist the aid of underemployed rural workers, often female and Black and then later of Latin American heritage. The business's leaders were not nearly so diverse. Emerging from regions that had once been successful producers of cash crops and educated on a legacy of mythical southern glories of days past, poultrymen engaged in a hard-fought competition against one another through grit and hard work for market share at the expense of contract farmers and their own production-line employees.

By selling a vision of a new industrial South, poultrymen gained access to capital and accumulated liquid assets, which they poured into gleaming new facilities of concrete and steel, monuments to humankind's mastery of nature and the envy of visitors from overseas. The industry's winners, Fred Lovette, Lonnie Pilgrim, Don Tyson, and Frank Perdue, to name the most noteworthy, retained the modest garb of small-town businessmen but attained an aptitude within the capital markets and learned the lessons of magnates past, absorbing smaller competitors in waves of consolidation and forming powerful alliances with grocery stores, restaurant chains, and food service management companies. In the process, they were able to obtain immense political influence and protection at both local and national levels, often rendering federal agencies such as the Occupational Safety and Health Administration (OSHA) and the Environmental Protection Agency (EPA) effectively inert while benefiting from a close relationship with the much larger USDA.

Building a Commercial Poultry Farm

In the decades before World War II, the farming of poultry retained a secondary role in the preponderance of American farms. Eggs were a profitable sideline, and while some farmers made their own deliveries to country stores, others sold directly to traveling "hucksters," drivers of small trucks who traveled from farm to farm purchasing goods for the market. Even so, these were years of experimentation, as the proponents of a more commercially oriented approach honed their methods in the pursuit of a more profitable hen, laying the groundwork for a dramatic wartime and postwar expansion. In matters of breeding, feed, and housing, scientists and entrepreneurial farmers experimented with methods that would become hallmarks of poultry as an industrial endeavor.

In rural America, farmers' finances were ravaged by the long agricultural depression of the 1920s and 1930s. During World War I, U.S. agricultural output expanded immensely in the service of war-torn European allies, but as the affected nations recovered their own domestic capacity, international markets weakened, precipitating a crisis of overproduction and falling prices for U.S. crops. Even before U.S. consumer spending power began to collapse in 1929, many of the staples of American farming output were unable to turn a good profit. Yet critics charged that outdated methods on American farms, some of which hadn't changed substantially since the nineteenth century, were an essential element within the crisis and that any meaningful recovery must involve a reimagined approach to agriculture that applied the same scientific management and planning that was central to the development of industrial production.[7] With many farms failing, some producers of traditional crops in the southeast and mid-Atlantic regions turned to new models in commercial poultry farming as an alternative with the hopes of seizing upon and expanding a promising but so far underdeveloped line into the retail sector.[8]

In 1923 Cecile Steele of Ocean View, Delaware, is reported to have been delivered five hundred chicks from the local hatchery by accident, ten times more than her original order. Rather than returning them, Steele decided to increase the number of sheds on her property and raise the birds purely for meat. Turning a good profit, she continued to expand both the size of her orders and her capacity until she could house ten thousand birds by 1926.[9] Benefiting from a suitable climate, appropriate soil conditions, sufficient cheap labor, and close access to the lucrative urban markets of New York, Philadelphia, Washington, D.C., and Baltimore, commercial poultry operations on the Eastern Shore had increased exponentially as the 1920s came to a close. By 1928 there were around five hundred broiler growers in Steele's corner of southeastern Sussex County, Delaware, alone.[10] Monica Gisolfi has illustrated how in upcountry Georgia, farmers plowed under their cotton rows, replacing a labor-intensive cash crop with capital-intensive poultry operations. Adapting the credit system that had provided farmers with the pesticides and seed used in arable farming, merchants now advanced the credit required to obtain the chicks, feed, and equipment needed to launch a new model of southern business.[11] If poultry farming could be scaled up to a sufficient level, then this new production line stood to open a new niche in an American meat market presently dominated by beef and pork, transforming an expensive occasional product into a daily alternative for consumers of modest means.

Broiler farming, that is, birds raised to be sold for meat, did not provide the steady source of income offered by a flock of egg-laying Leghorns, but by the 1920s the characteristics required of a successful commercial operation were an area of growing scientific enquiry. A good broiler was less active and energetic than an egg-layer and could gain in size quickly by turning food into meat at an efficient rate, with that added weight then spread evenly across the body so that the bird could maintain a sufficient measure of mobility. Poultry experts, heavily influenced by the eugenic sciences and notions of biological progress, stressed the need to cull the abnormal and the weak.

Willard C. Thompson, writing for the USDA's New Jersey Experiment Station in 1920, insisted that poultry keepers must "separate out the drones from the workers." Thompson continued: "Do not let pity tempt you to give a weakling a chance. . . . It will not be a paying investment." Farmers had to have a long-term perspective. "The chick is the individual that becomes the layer or breeder of tomorrow," he emphasized.[12]

Others stressed the noble purpose of animal improvement. "The wild fowl of the jungle was a small bird, probably laying only one or two settings of eggs a year at best," wrote J. Milton Hover and Marvin S. Pittman, professors at Michigan State Normal College in Ypsilanti, in 1932. Yet animal husbandry had attracted "the best genius of the race," who "for centuries . . . has struggled with the problem of increasing the efficiency and usefulness of livestock through better breeding animals."[13]

Even before the development of high-intensity methods that critics would later label as "factory farming," the final month of a bird's life, during which farmers sought to maximize weight gain and limit activity in preparation for market, was regarded as traumatic. Live poultry were liable to lose considerable weight under the stress of any extended period of travel, a problem that was particularly acute in vehicles navigating the bumpy roads of the early twentieth century. After substantial periods of rain, many roads leading out of rural areas were completely impassable.[14] Farmers commonly shared and discussed their methods and feed recipes with each other. Crate fattening, where as many as six birds were confined to an eighteen-by-twenty-four-inch wooden box for up to three weeks, was a popular solution to travel-related weight loss. Birds were fed broiler mash, a wet mixture that normally contained a combination of cornmeal, oats, wheat, milk, beef scrap, and granulated bone. Whereas yellow corn affected the bird's skin color, wheat was known to produce more abdominal fat.[15] Chickens would consume more mash when simultaneously denied access to water, their only means of avoiding dehydration.[16]

By the 1910s the more labor-intensive method of "cramming" was increasingly in use, something of a risk, given the ease with which birds could be injured in the process. "Chicken will continue to be stringy and tough until the cramming machine is universally adopted," a farmer told the *Los Angeles Herald* in 1906. Questions of animal welfare were present decades before industrialization, but catering to the market was of greater concern. "There is one way—and it's a cruel way—to have perfectly tender and delicious chicken," the same farmer maintained. "That is to pen up the birds a month before killing time, give them no exercise and feed them with a cramming machine," he said. Cramming chicken involved mounting a tube on the front of a wheelbarrow that was attached to a hopper filled with mash. The rubber tube was then inserted in the bird's mouth and the contents of the hopper were expelled with a hand pump. "The chickens squawk and struggle. They don't like to eat that way. In fact they loathe the very sight of the cramming machine," he continued. "But the main thing," the farmer concluded, was that "the birds eat the greatest possible amount of food and take the least possible amount of exercise, putting on healthy fat and developing a tender, fine grained flesh in a manner impossible to the ordinary barnyard, hustling, strenuous chicken."[17] James A. Rodgers noted in the *Los Angeles Times* in 1920 that "one of the greatest feeding crimes is to let them get real hungry."[18]

By the 1930s, farmers increasingly sought modernized forms of housing. Traditional henhouses and their constantly replenished food supplies were of enduring interest to a range of different vermin. Rats presented a particular danger in spring and summer. Harry Lewis, a professor of agriculture, warned that "if a rat once gets into a brooder full of chicks he kills them all on the spot before he attempts to carry them away."[19] Crows would similarly kill chicks, whereas patient hawks could seize full-grown birds. Weasels and minks attacked adult hens, and skunks came in search of eggs. In more built-up areas, stray dogs and cats could terrorize a flock. "In the town where I live a bunch of mischievous dogs ran amuck for a distance of more than a mile early one morning, and created havoc in poultry-yards all along the way," observed C. S. Valentine in 1910.[20] Thieves could also present a problem. "There are always plenty of unscrupulous persons who do not hesitate to steal poultry," Lewis wrote.[21]

A seemingly progressive alternative was on the horizon, though. In 1933

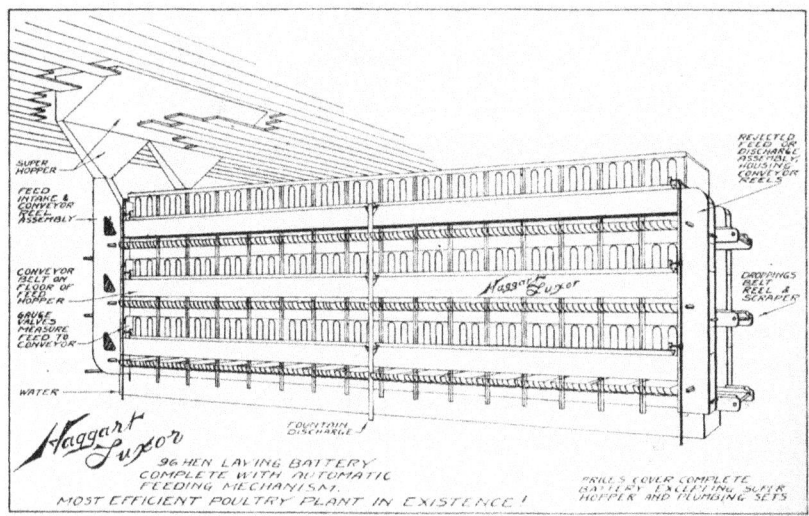

IMAGE 4. The confident high modernism of the Haggart Manufacturing Company's Luxor battery house evinces a model of clean and automated avian living where laying hens drink from a fountain and feed from a super hopper. From Charles and Stuart, *Commercial Poultry Farming*

R. P. Hart of the *Los Angeles Times* visited citrus farmer Peter Wink in rural Fontana, about fifty miles east of the city. "When I came upon a three-story apartment house in the country, I was a bit surprised," Hart wrote. "Upon finding that the tenants were chickens, I became downright inquisitive," he went on. The edifice contained around a thousand birds. "I wondered how the hens were herded up and downstairs until Mr. Wink showed me that there were no outdoor yards or runs, the hens being kept entirely indoors," Hart recalled.[22]

These "apartments," which before long would be more commonly referred to as batteries, were considered an airy and efficient way of housing poultry. They were free from dampness and other animals, and their warmth allowed production to continue uninterrupted by the changing of the seasons. Both manufacturers and observers noted the lack of odor normally associated with henhouses. Running water was piped through, and food was delivered to birds on a conveyor belt that carried away waste in the process (image 4).

"Although 'battery' birds never see the blue sky or the green grass," the *National Grocers' Bulletin* stated, "they get the sun's rays in their diet through the cod liver oil included in their feed" and could "eat whenever the spirit moves them." The article even added, "A little music is thrown in just to keep them contented."[23] In spite of the general sense of marvel at the soaring capacities of these cacophonous warehouses and the lack of bloodshed between fighting hens, some were more ambiguous in their assessments of the severance between chickens and a more natural outdoor environment. "In this day of regimentation, mass production and economy of effort and space, modern science has taken many liberties with Mother Nature," wrote Avery McBee in the *Baltimore Sun* after observing what he described as "mechanized hens." Referring to the hens as "cellmates," McBee was impressed by the ruthless efficiency of an operation that he visited in Cockeysville, Maryland, in 1935 and noted that since the Leghorns involved were unable to scratch for food or run around, "their muscles are underdeveloped and yield nicely to the knives of the ultimate consumer." Through battery farming, "a 5-year old hen would be as tender as a broiler," the manager told McBee. "Outside of each layer's cage is a little card, resembling a hospital chart, which gives the entire record of the hen and her production," he observed. "Woe to her if the curve should take a nosedive, for she shortly will end her days in a pot." It was with a note of sympathy that McBee concluded: "Lo, the poor hen, she has become a machine!"[24]

Farmers' livestock found their way to market via a range of different means that varied from region to region. Some farmers delivered directly to meat markets, wholesalers, country stores, and even the few limited dedicated production facilities. In the late 1910s, farmers started replacing carts and horses with trucks and gained quicker access to more distant markets until motor power became a ubiquitous feature of rural life. "Farmers were the largest users of motor trucks," reported the *Washington Post* in March 1920, "owning 10 per cent more than manufacturers and 15 percent more than retailers."[25] A 1921 survey of over eight hundred farmers estimated that in spite of poor roads, trucks allowed farmers to haul goods to market three times quicker than with horses.[26] Dairy farmers enthusiastically equipped their vehicles with refrigerated tanks to deliver milk. And by the mid-1930s, more than a third of calves and hogs were delivered to Chicago's Union Stock Yards by road. Frank Ridgway, the *Chicago Daily Tribune*'s agricultural editor, wrote in 1935 that "a swift moving fleet of thousands of vans, massive tanks, and 'crates' are kept going night and day, moving live stock, milk, and home grown fruits and vegetables into the city from farms over an area stretching back into the country for a hundred miles or more."[27]

Consumers who did not raise their own hens purchased chicken at specialized butcher's shops, markets, or general stores, often to be cooked on the day of purchase. In *The Story of Meat*, a short volume published in 1939 by Swift and Company, authors Robert B. Hinman and Robert B. Harris emphasized the personal and gendered nature of the retail trade for meat in the era before electric refrigerators. Hinman and Harris stressed that the best customers were those who bought a wide variety of different products and that the clever salesman would broaden his customers' frame of reference while retaining their loyalty. Introducing new items involved certain perils, though, and retailers needed to exercise shrewdness and a measure of caution. "When a customer says in a hesitating fashion 'No-o-o-o,' the man behind the counter had better beware," the authors warn. If he sells her something that her family subsequently dislikes, the customer will think, "Darn that meat man of mine. He's always selling me something I don't really want. I'm going to another market."[28]

Above all, it was important for the retailer to develop a keen sense of the likes and dislikes of a woman and her family and be able to carefully respond to feedback on previous sales. "Most women," Hinman and Harris wrote, "do not consider themselves competent judges of meat quality and often buy where they have confidence in the meat salesman." A good vendor should use appetite appeal so that the purchaser could envision the meal upon completion: "One of those chickens stuffed with dressing—baked to a turn and served with a touch of cranberry sauce—would certainly be good, Mrs. Jones." This might not entice Mrs. Jones. The vendor should "watch her face and if she doesn't show interest," then he should propose a different item. These were characteristics of "the salesman women like." He greets her "in low, cheerful, sincere fashion."[29]

Sinclair Lewis offered a similar appraisal in his best-selling 1920 novel *Main Street*. Lewis's protagonist, Carol Kennicott, moves from metropolitan Saint Paul, Minnesota, to the fictional Gopher Prairie and finds herself unable to attain the same range of goods available in the city. "When she did contrive to get sweetbreads at Dahl & Oleson's Meat Market the triumph was so vast that she buzzed with excitement and admired the strong wise butcher, Mr. Dahl," Lewis wrote, affirming the popularity of the trusted meatman.[30] Yet interactions with salesmen in the early twentieth century were clearly contested affairs in which women took pride in their own skills in negotiating prices and assessing different goods. Historian Tracey Deutsch has argued that the rise of supermarkets, where shoppers anonymously browsed and selected from shelves and coolers, was in part driven by retailers' concerns about the costly and labor-intensive nature of providing patrons with personal attention.[31]

While meat was certainly affordable to most but the poorest Americans, the quality and cut were highly variable, according to one's budget. At "bargain days" at a market on New York's Hester Street, the progressive social reformer Jacob Riis observed that the "great staple" in "Jewtown" was "frowsy-looking chickens and half-plucked geese, hung by the neck and protesting with wildly strutting feet even in death against the outrage.... Half a quarter of a chicken can be bought here by those who cannot afford a whole."[32] Yet Riis was writing in 1890. By the 1910s the Pure Food and Drug Act of 1906 had ameliorated some of the worst excesses of animal slaughter and preparation. Cans containing food were indeed less likely to oxidize in storage or to swell out of shape with a buildup of gas than had been the case at the turn of the century.[33] In spite of this, the basic connection between poverty and poor-quality food remained fundamentally intact. A 1941 survey of housewives in Des Moines found that only 2 percent of weekday evening meals were poultry based, whereas beef was served in 35 percent of meals, and pork or bacon 24 percent of the time.[34] Sunday dinners were of greater importance, with 15 percent reporting to serve poultry, which still compared unfavorably to the 83 percent of beef or pork meals served on the same occasion.[35]

For many observers, prewar American dining represented a depressing state of affairs. Johns Hopkins University nutritionists McCollum and Simmonds expressed concern over long-standing cultural expectations in *The American Home Diet* in 1920. "Due regard for appetite and customary food habits has necessitated the inclusion of meats in one form or another more frequently than physiological need will justify, but it is recognized that to ignore deep-seated psychic demands would defeat the purpose of the authors," they noted in their preface. With a growing scientific understanding of the significance of vitamins and minerals, McCollum and Simmonds feared that many adults were "taking too much of their food in the form of meat, bread, potatoes and sugar," a diet that they judged was poor for the bloodstream and lacking in nutritional essentials.[36]

In spite of America's polyglot of different international culinary traditions, newspaperman and prolific critic Henry Louis Mencken complained that they had been diminished by "the national taste for bad food."[37] Who was to blame for this? He held the English and their early influence upon the Americas to be partially responsible. "The badness of English cooking is proverbial all over the world," he explained. "I suggest that it may be due, at least in part, to two things, the first being that the English have a Puritan distrust of whatever is bodily pleasant, and the second that it is practically impossible to grow good food in their country." It was not that they were unaware of what good food was. Englishmen traveled the world. Rather, it was that they "prefer to be uncomfortable, and think of their preferences as heroic," he said, and "when they are at home they take a gloomy stubborn, idiotic, delight in eating badly."[38]

Though chain stores were in the ascendance and the cause of growing angst among many small shopkeepers, Mencken would berate a trend toward uniformity in dining, a strange portent in the absence of a chain restaurant industry. In 1927 he observed that "what ails our victualry, principally, is the depressing standardization that ails everything else American.... But in America the public cooks have all abandoned specialization, and every one of them seems bent upon cooking as nearly as possible like all the rest. The American hotel food is as rigidly standardized as the parts of a Ford, and so is the restaurant meal."[39] Historian Harvey Levenstein reached a similar assessment in 2003, describing a "revolution of declining expectations" in the 1920s in which middle-class interest in cooking and dinner parties took second billing to "bridge, mah-jongg, dancing, and other parties."[40]

Others charge that cost was a more prohibitive factor than lack of individual creativity. Marc Levinson argues that the high price of food as a proportion of household income, the product of convoluted and inefficient supply chains, combined with the timely labor of shopping for fresh items on a near daily basis to limit the dietary options of many American families.[41] Even for immigrants who wished to keep the culinary traditions of the "old country" alive, the changes that took place in the retail business in the prewar decades made it ever more difficult to do so, as both independent ethnic retailers alongside thousands of traditional "mom and pop" groceries were replaced by chain stores.[42] Between 1900 and 1929 the number of stores operated by chains of four or more outlets in twenty-six lines of business increased from thirty-three hundred to just over ninety-five thousand, according to a Federal Trade Commission report.[43] Chain stores had an outsized influence in food sales, compared to other areas of the retail trade. The Department of Commerce indicated that by 1929 chains accounted for 32 percent of food sales, and by 1933 this was as high as 38 percent.[44] The 1939 Census of Business revealed the continuation of this trend. Of the 131 different chains that were made up of at least 100 or more stores, 40 of them were in the food sector, by far the largest category of chain store.[45] For Levinson the "creative destruction" of the Great Atlantic and Pacific Tea Company, the most dominant of the chains, represented a boon for consumers, transforming "the humble, archaic grocery trade into a modern industry" and offering a consistent and affordable supply of reliable and popular market-tested goods.[46] Stores like Piggly Wiggly, the first to open an effective self-service model in 1916, similarly aided consumers by abolishing what many considered to be a slow and dated system in which store clerks waited upon lines of customers.[47]

As the 1930s came to a close, southeastern and mid-Atlantic farmers, ravaged by years of depression, felt little obeisance to tradition. By embracing the most efficient breeds, battery housing, and what many would consider to be inhumane feeding practices, they stood ready to remake the lived environment of poultry, transforming a sideline enterprise into an efficient and scalable operation. Could a predictable and uniform Fordism of poultry meet the increasingly standardized expectations of chain store retailers and provide variety to uninspired American diners? The descent of Europe once again into total war and the ensuing needs for massive agricultural assistance would put this burgeoning industrial model of production to the test while lifting the United States out of depression through the construction of a new economy that was increasingly based on widespread consumer purchasing power.

"A Great Volume of Fowl"

World War II represented a great boon to the emerging class of poultrymen; the war was a government stimulus that offered guaranteed contracts at stable prices for as many chickens as farmers could muster the means to produce. With the war's commencement in 1939 and U.S. entry at the end of 1941, farmers would once again be called upon to provide sustenance for the soldiers and sailors of the American military and its Western European allies. If coastal shipyards and Detroit auto plants were to build the "arsenal of democracy," American farmlands were required to be its granary, orchard, and ranch.

The speed and flexibility with which poultry flocks could be expanded in size, raised, and brought to market made them an increasingly important element of the wartime food economy, a role that would remain undiminished by the war's conclusion. With the establishment of the Office of Price Administration (OPA) in 1941 and then the War Food Administration (WFA) in 1943, the federal government took decisive action to control inflationary pressures and to attempt to ensure the even distribution of scarce commodities. In April 1942 the OPA rationed and established a ceiling on the price of beef. Red meats were highly sought after by military procurers, while fowl was intended to serve as a substitute on the home front. Public advertisements encouraged consumers "to eat more Poultry and Conserve Beef and Pork for the Armed Forces."[48] With poultry prices continuing to climb, by December the OPA had set a price for broilers at thirty-nine cents per pound, to the dissatisfaction of many farmers.

Poultrymen and their allies would relentlessly lobby the OPA in protest of these price caps for the duration of the war, resentful that they were unable to take full advantage of escalating wartime prices and describing in beleaguered terms what was, with the benefit of hindsight, a period of extraordinary growth for the industry as a whole. "On December 18, 1942 the O.P.A. issued a ceiling law consisting of 22 pages of complicated, unworkable and unenforceable regulations which left two alternatives to the midwestern poultry processor," wrote Chester B. Franz to the St. Louis Chamber of Commerce in March 1943. "The first alternative was to discontinue operations and the second was to break the obviously unfair law," he said. "There is, under the ceiling, little, if any, incentive to remain in business," Franz sadly concluded.[49]

Complaining of the costs he had expended upon fuel to keep his hens warm during a month that had been "the coldest we have had in this section for years," Theodore W. Henrichs from Lisle, Illinois, wrote to the *Chicago Tribune* that the ceiling was preventing him from defraying these additional outlays. "At present there is no inducement to raise poultry, because of the ceiling on poultry meat," he charged.[50] Other farmers balked at the inflated costs of chicken feed.[51]

In 1944 the WFA redefined the role of poultry in the wartime food chain when it began to place large orders for the use of bases in the United States and overseas, requisitioning supplies from storage facilities that had been intended for hotels, restaurants, and dining cars. Soldiers were to receive a Sunday chicken dinner twice a month, the WFA declared.[52] The OPA's Poultry and Egg Procurement Board reported in May 1944 that the army was calling for a "great volume of fowl which is needed for hospitals, where it can be utilized for stewing and fricasseeing."[53] The army's purchases of canned poultry in the first half of 1944 were so great that the major who was coordinating purchases with the Poultry and Egg Board decided not to purchase any more in the third quarter beyond what had already been committed to in earlier contracts.[54] Processors were encouraged to instead increase the preparation of frozen poultry. This too presented challenges as the army searched for sufficient capacity in private storage facilities. The board's Subcommittee on Freezer Space found a wide array of products that did not need to be frozen, such as cans of sterilized meat and cooking apples for bakeries. "Flowers take up considerable space in storage facilities over the country," they reported, while owners of large storage plants were attempting to negotiate higher prices.[55] Citing a "storage premium," the OPA increased the price ceiling on poultry by two cents in April 1944 to forty-one cents per pound, a modest recognition that farmers' challenges might be exaggerated but were not entirely fabricated.[56]

Nonetheless, the OPA was careful and deliberative in its attempts to foster greater production while controlling inflationary pressures. The administration's price controls were based on extensive examinations of farming costs, even though agents were also often stifled in their field studies by poor bookkeeping. In November 1943 Joseph McGowan visited the Polo Produce Company in Chicago, a purveyor of live, dressed, and eviscerated poultry, and returned a telegram to the OPA reporting that the company maintained no purchase records segregating its different providers. There were no records delineating whether sales of eviscerated birds had been processed on site or were already prepared upon arrival. "No attempt made to keep cost records," McGowan observed.[57]

At another processor in Gainesville, Georgia, Joseph Montgomery reported:

"Company's 1942 plant records on 1942 tonnage handled in transfers, etc. very incomplete. So far have compiled about twenty five percent of plant volume, search of balance in progress."[58] Regardless of such obstacles, the OPA, where possible, compiled detailed accounts and calculations that indicated that for poultrymen, wartime provided a successful and rewarding market in spite of the periodic limitations upon available grain. Price controls may have elicited voluminous complaints, but no agents or journalists appear to have encountered business failures—in significant contrast to a decade earlier during the Depression, when bankruptcies of farms and businesses were pervasive—and farmers needed only minimal encouragement to increase the production of a commodity they claimed was unprofitable.

In responding to Congressman David J. Ward, Democrat of Maryland, administrator Prentiss Brown noted in September 1943 that "the operations of Army requisitioning of live poultry in the Del-Mar-Va area have been given serious study in the past few weeks." Brown informed Ward of the OPA's imminent increase of the price ceiling but also observed that as of mid-August the Bureau of Agricultural Economics, an office of the USDA, had found "the Maryland average farm prices of chickens was 21.7 percent higher than a year ago."[59]

Where possible, farmers would often sell products at black market prices that were in excess of OPA limits. These sales led to occasional crackdowns by OPA enforcement officers. In August 1943 the *New York Amsterdam News* reported that poultry dealer I. Drucker from Harlem was being fined twenty-five dollars and sentenced to two days in jail for selling chickens at forty-four cents per pound, five cents above the regulated price. Fined fifty dollars for two code violations, which included charging twenty cents for plucking a fowl and then not doing so, Morris Feldstein was among ten other men penalized as part of an "intensified drive by OPA authorities of price ceiling violators in the Harlem area."[60] The black market was considered so extensive on the Delmarva Peninsula that in 1943 the army established checkpoints to monitor trucks driving north to New York and Philadelphia amid growing concern that the Procurement Division of the Quartermaster's Corps could not fulfill its poultry orders.[61]

The rapid upsizing of flocks says a lot more about farmers' approach to the wartime agricultural economy than their individual objections that they could not maximize profits after more than a decade of hardships. The USDA reported that the number of chickens populating farms increased by 36 percent from 418 million in 1941 to 576 million in 1944, even as feed prices shot up by 60 percent in the same period.[62] In 1942 exports skyrocketed by 700 percent to twenty-four million pounds, up from three million the year before.[63] Commercial broiler production increased nationwide, but it was in the

South Atlantic states that this growth was most aggressive. Whereas 50 million birds had amounted to a $25 million market in 1939, by 1943 148 million broilers returned $124 million to the region. This amounted to 62 percent of national output.[64] "The poultry industry has carried on magnificently during this emergency . . . and no doubt will do its utmost to produce the additional meat," read a USDA statement in 1943 in which the secretary of agriculture encouraged further increases. Farmers met this plea.[65]

Massive expansions in American poultry production were not merely the product of patriotic fervor, as the apparent extent of black market sales, impossible though they may be to quantify, would appear to indicate. Delmarva historian William H. Williams argued that the federal government was also committed to facilitating the growing poultry business, in 1944 building a prisoner-of-war camp close to Georgetown, Delaware, in order to provide additional labor in hatcheries, processing plants, and feed mills. A. Eugene Bailey, a manager at the Swift facility in nearby Salisbury, Maryland, recalled, "We couldn't have run the plant without them."[66]

Besides the provision of auxiliary labor, the new class of upstart poultrymen, among America's wide variety of different agriculturalists, benefited from the U.S. government's unwavering investment in scientific research and development. Large and increasingly specialized agricultural producers continued to be treated as an exceptional form of private sector enterprise, employing the rhetoric of traditional family farming and rural community even as they aggressively absorbed dwellings that had not survived the Great Depression and adopted a more corporate approach to business. They benefited from the continued power and influence of what was known as the "Farm Bloc" within the U.S. Senate, the disproportionately powerful representatives of sparsely populated rural states, a cross-party coalition that would ensure the preservation of New Deal–era support payments and a large and well-funded USDA that promoted the agricultural sciences and the marketing of American goods overseas. There were no strings attached to USDA research. "Agricultural scientists work mostly in public institutions; only a few are supported by private industries or groups of farmers," observed Charles E. Kellogg, the head of the USDA's Soil Survey in 1947. "This is because farming is mostly carried on in small units that would find it hard, even in combinations, to undertake research, and because most problems of agriculture involve so many skills that even a group of minimum size for effective work requires considerable land, buildings, and equipment," he explained. This progressive mission to provide the means of abundance to small yeoman farmers was important, Kellogg stressed, "because we should know by now that no group can be secure while others are without confidence and hope."[67]

Poultry was among the many sectors of the agricultural economy to substantially benefit from the refinements in methodology and breeding that had been developed under the auspices of the USDA. In 1943 OPA administrator Chester Bowles responded to a petition forwarded to him by the conservative Republican senator from Ohio, Robert A. Taft on behalf of the Northeast Battery Broiler Producers Association. Like so many other entreaties to the OPA, the trade association called for the price ceiling on poultry to be raised. While Bowles politely rebutted the petition, he nonetheless saw fit to praise the work of battery producers. "There are very few people in the industry that could honestly tell the difference on sight between battery grown and farm grown poultry," he observed. "I am sure the consuming public would be definitely unable to distinguish the difference."[68] Removed from natural light, space to roam and forage, and interaction with other birds, the new chicken was considered practically identical to the vulnerable insect-ridden farmyard hen.[69] Battery chickens were now, Bowles wrote, "more or less a factory proposition."[70]

The acute needs of global war had changed the face of U.S. agriculture in the late 1910s. Even in the decade of bull markets that followed World War I and the rising tide of American prosperity, growing consumer demands had not been sufficient to keep pace with domestic agricultural output. Yet as World War II reached its devastating atomic final act, history would not repeat itself as the United States sought to assert its new role as a superpower in a world razed to its very foundations. Abundant American harvests would take on a growing political significance in European and Asian nations with broken farmlands depopulated of young men by years of bloodshed. In the United States, twelve years of progressive Democratic governance had reshaped the national economy, creating previously unprecedented levels of consumer spending power for wage-earning families. The prosperity of this new postwar economy opened up a new realm of purchasing opportunities and a favorable environment for what would in time be referred to as "agribusiness."

The Making of Giants

"Walk into a Holly plant and you move into a unique world after you leave the eviscerating room," *Broiler Industry* magazine observed in 1968. In order for Holly Farms to be able to process sixty thousand chickens an hour, "nearly everything had to be designed from scratch."[71] From a plant in Wilkesboro in the foothills of the Blue Ridge Mountains that processed eight thousand birds per day, the company had grown in twenty short years to become the largest vertically integrated processor and marketer of broiler chickens in the world, accounting for 7 percent of total U.S. production.[72] (Here, the term "integrated" refers to control of all aspects of production, from the supply of chickens and feed through the distribution of finished poultry products.) Among the company's largest customers were Kentucky Fried Chicken and the U.S. Department of Defense, which shipped Holly birds to military bases in West Germany.[73] The firm accounted for a significant share of the nine hundred million pounds of American-raised poultry consumed by the U.S. military in the 1960s.[74] When the Wilkesboro facility expanded its capacity of eight thousand birds per day to twenty-five thousand, it became the planet's most prolific poultry plant.

Starting with a Model-T truck in the 1920s as a buyer and seller of chickens and eggs, Charles Lovette built one of the first large broiler houses in the northwestern Carolinas in 1926. He continued to grow the family business, employing seventeen-year-old Fred as a truck driver in 1942, until the C. O. Lovette Produce Company was renamed Holly Farms in 1952.[75] From the 1950s to the 1980s, the Lovettes' company, under the stewardship of Charles and then Fred, developed a highly respected reputation among their contemporaries in the chicken business and with major clients in the supermarket and restaurant sectors, their company synonymous with innovation and scale. Holly Farms brand chicken could be found on the shelves of Safeway stores on the West and East Coasts, with store-branded options produced by Holly Farms available in even more retail outlets.

Before Holly Farms' increasingly conspicuous operation had been established, Wilkes County, North Carolina, was most widely known for two activities: the production of moonshine and stock-car racing. They were not unrelated. As historian Daniel S. Pierce has described, it was in the transportation of illegal liquor that many early racers acquired their aptitude behind the wheel. The profits from liquor sales, in turn, were invested in and even laundered through racetracks. NASCAR champion and Wilkes County native Benny Parsons observed, "There was nothing to do in the mountains of North Carolina back in the thirties, forties and fifties. . . . You either worked at a hosiery mill, a furniture factory or you made whiskey."[76]

Social critic Vance Packard wrote a profile of Wilkes County, which was rarely the subject of national attention, in the *American Magazine* in 1950, describing it as the "Moonshine Capital of America" in an article that paid the area few compliments.[77] Even once poultry had taken off as a profitable economic pursuit, the connections to liquor remained strong. Charlie Felts, the son of a moonshine producer, recalled in a 2011 interview that some farmers hid stills within chicken coops, the hens a convenient disguise for the farmers' primary source of income.[78]

The mountainous topography of western Carolina had always been unsuitable for plantation agriculture, and the recorded white population of Wilkes County had remained upward of 90 percent since at least 1790. By 1970 African Americans represented just 5.1 percent of a population of 49,000.[79] This was also an area of considerable deprivation. More than 50 percent of those over sixty-five lived below the poverty level compared to 24.5 percent nationwide, as did nearly one-quarter of children, 10 percent more than the national average. While very few people were officially registered as unemployed, educational achievements were quite sparse. Wilkes had a 28 percent high school dropout rate, and only 3.8 percent of the county's residents had made it through a four-year college degree.[80]

In the 1950s and 1960s Holly Farms acquired plants in Hiddenite, twenty miles south of Wilkesboro, and Monroe, which was south of Charlotte and close to the state line, as well as Richmond and Temperanceville in Virginia. The company also raised its profile across the South while reinforcing its Piedmont identity by becoming one of the first nonautomotive companies to make a significant sponsorship commitment to NASCAR. As the official backer of Wilkes County's own Junior Johnson and his Ford team, Holly Farms' yellow and red colors were consistently on display as the company's profile grew. Its association with racing remained close for thirty years.[81]

Charles Lovette's company sought to lead the poultry business into an era of preeminent rural power by tightening Holly Farms' control over the supply chain, situating processing plants in remote locations from which they could cultivate local farmers to raise the company's chicks and create a level of supply to match the capacity of their ever more sophisticated disassembly lines. Farmers were paid to feed a specified diet to the company's selected breed of chick and to maintain an optimum environment in terms of ventilation, cleanliness, and temperature, then deliver chickens at a sufficient weight in accordance with a prearranged schedule. By the early 1960s, contract production accounted for around 75 percent of broiler production, with only 5 percent raised on independent, nonintegrated farms.[82]

The demands of integrators upon their contractors to invest in new facilities and equipment in order to remain on good terms and the indebtedness that these demands have often required have been well documented.[83] While agricultural scientists stressed the effectiveness of financial bonuses as an incentive toward greater efficiency on the part of contractors, the carrot and stick of rewards and debt were not quite enough for Holly Farms.[84] So they designed a bigger stick. In the 1960s they devised the "Zone Plan," a data-based method of monitoring and promoting efficiency among the "Holly Farmers." All contractors providing for the Wilkesboro plant had to be located within a fifty-mile radius, a circle that was then divided into eleven zones, each consisting of around nine hundred thousand birds, which amounted to around forty-five or fifty farms. Birds were raised on eleven-week cycles, which included a two-week break during which sheds could be sanitized. Farmers within each zone would receive weekly visits from company servicemen, who could troubleshoot problems and bring the assistance of pathologists if needed.

The defining feature of the Zone Plan was a scale whereby farmers were assessed on the basis of their efficiency and then ranked against one another on a leaderboard. Their position was determined by their ability to keep costs down and maintain low mortality rates. The top 25 percent of farmers in each zone over an eleven-week cycle received bonus payments. The bottom 25 percent received a visit from a poultry specialist, who would advise farmers on ways to improve their operation and reduce expenditures. Farmers could even be sent to company headquarters in Wilkesboro to receive further education using slide shows and film projectors. On the basis of this assistance, farmers were expected to show an improved performance. If a farmer appeared in the bottom quarter for a second consecutive cycle, then he would enter a trial status with the following batch of chicks. Upon a third consecutive period in the lowest quarter, the farmer would receive the punishment of exclusion for the following cycle, and his sheds would stand empty.

"Holly Farms management feels that if they hit [a farmer's] pocketbook, he may straighten out," reported C. Howard Smith in *Broiler Industry*.[85] While we do not have records of farmers' experiences contracting for Holly, it seems reasonable to surmise that for many, a three-month span during which a farm was absent of economic activity could be enough to sink it if there were no other sources of income, a greater possibility in an era of increasingly specialized agriculture. Farmers had indebted themselves to banks in order to purchase the equipment and set up as a Holly Farms grower. This was not unusual in and of itself in that agriculture always operated as a credit-based business. If the farmer was still standing after an eleven-week break, then he had one further chance to rank among the top three-quarters within his zone, or he would be dropped as a Holly Farms grower entirely. "In its quest for lower production costs, Holly Farms will experiment with anything that shows promise of success," Smith wrote, clearly impressed at the inventiveness of the system.[86] "Concentration on the 'zone plan' applies more effective coordination of all elements of procurement, service and supervision. Holly Farms tries to keep it as simple and direct as possible," he concluded, "and finds that it is tremendously effective compared with its previous grow-out system."[87] The distinction between an absolute and relative gauge of performance is important. Rather than asking farmers to meet a minimum threshold of efficiency, Holly

Farms presented them with a moving target that could vary from cycle to cycle. A farmer could incrementally improve his operation month after month and still find his position in jeopardy if others located within the zone did likewise.

It is unclear to what degree Holly Farms suffered from problems with slovenly growers. Some farmers are greater masters of their vocation than others. Yet the Zone Plan increased the risk borne by the farmer and institutionalized a mechanism whereby the company could weed out the least productive facilities. As farmers raised greater numbers of chicks in a confined space, they risked ailments like Newcastle disease, a virus that was transmissible between both birds and workers and potentially fatal to the flock. Similarly, the liability involved in producing large quantities of fecal matter and the environmental hazards presented by chicken shed runoffs were entirely the farmer's responsibility.[88] In creating this significant new modification within the structure of poultry production, Holly Farms began the process by which large integrators would increasingly exert their leverage over smaller contract farmers and introduced a forerunner to a competitive "tournament" model that Tyson Foods would later master, where mandatory upgrades to equipment and infrastructure left contractors negotiating a treadmill of monthly debt repayments.[89]

Capital expenditures on automation quickly gathered pace in the poultry industry in the 1960s, with the average increase in investments growing at 4.6 percent per year between 1963 and 1984, greater than the 3.2 percent average for industry as a whole.[90] A special feature in *Broiler Industry* in April 1968 showcased Holly Farms' modern production line at the Wilkesboro plant and presented a fashionable workforce largely made up of white women (see images 5, 6, and 7). Within this environment, the late 1960s was a period of impressive growth for Holly Farms. In 1968, then worth $20 million, Holly Farms merged with cash-rich Federal Compress and Warehouse, a Memphis-based cotton storage company that owned eighty-four warehouses and a couple of milling companies with operations spanning the South and the Midwest.[91] Federal, now renamed simply Federal Company, had sold its warehouse properties to New York investors and followed its purchase of Holly Farms with the acquisition of Halbert Incorporated of Bronson, Texas, a diversified poultry company that owned six subsidiaries, all in East Texas. These included three processing plants in Center, a feed mill and a feed dealer in Nacogdoches, and a hatchery in Hemphill.[92] The three plants in Center—Sabine Farm Products, Eastex Poultry, and Chubby Chickfried Chicken—were converted to the Holly Farms brand and stretched the company's access to coastal markets from the Atlantic to the Pacific.

IMAGES 5 AND 6. In the packaging area at Holly Farms' Wilkesboro plant, workers cut and then tray chicken parts on parallel production lines that operate in opposite directions. From *Broiler Industry*, April 1968.

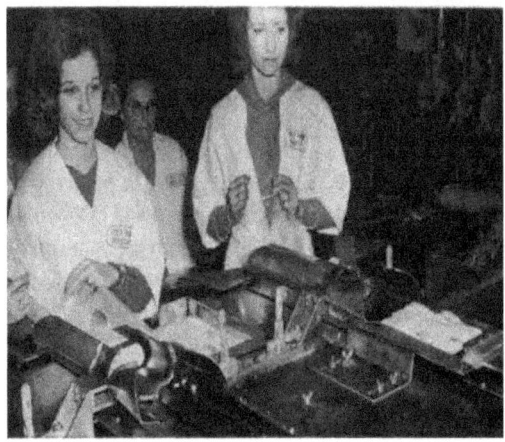

IMAGE 7. Holly Farms workers slide trays into heat-sealed plastic bags. In spite of the workers' apparent comfort in these publicity images, the machine in question could operate at a speed of up to forty units per minute, a pace that would seem relatively modest by the standards of later decades. From *Broiler Industry*, April 1968.

Expanded ownership across the different stages in the production process and substantial cash reserves contributed to making Holly Farms America's leading poultry company by the mid-1970s. Its overall capacity to run through 110,000 birds per hour, or 4.4 million per week, was double that of Perdue Farms, a company limited mostly to the East Coast market, and 50 percent greater than Tyson Foods. The only poultry company to come close to Holly Farms' scale was Gold Kist, a giant cooperative based in Georgia. Swift and Armour, historically the most famous names in American beef and pork, were still large companies, with the latter owned by Greyhound, but they were no longer industry leaders, as their centralized processing model had been surpassed by the "rural industrialization" of red meat packers such as Iowa Beef Processors (later IBP and even later the core of Tyson's beef operation), Missouri Beef Packers–Excel, known as MBPXL, and Monfort.[93] Where Swift and Armour had moved livestock by rail to and from unionized urban slaughterhouses in Chicago and Omaha, IBP and the new generation of meatpackers operated out of small towns and depended upon fragmented labor markets and interstate trucking.[94]

With greater access to financial assets than ever before, President Fred Lovette invested in capital resources that would allow the company to consolidate its advantage and alleviate its labor demands. He made his motivations very clear in 1973 when pushing for USDA approval of further methods of mechanization, including imported automatic eviscerators from Marel, a renowned equipment manufacturer producing in the Dutch town of Boxmeer, which were "superior to anything we're using in certain areas of our plants." Lovette continued: "It looks to me like this will replace at least half of the hand drawers on the line, and also remove the skill from the job. . . . And, of course, a machine can be there every Monday morning," he quipped.[95]

Holly Farms workers were invariably there on Monday morning too, but Lovette wanted to ease competition with other employers. "We're faced with a helluva labor problem," he complained. "We pay the best wages here in Wilkesboro, for example, but we have a good Chamber of Commerce too. What used to be an excellent labor market now is shared by hosiery, mirror and furniture factories." He went on: "When we built our plant in Temperanceville, Va., we had an excellent labor pool. Then other plants come in and made the situation tight. It seems to be that way all over." With a range of additional equipment, including the Dutch eviscerators to remove the animal's sexual organs and a new device that would extract lungs, Lovette believed three people could be removed from each of the twenty-six production lines across the company. "The idea is not to do away with jobs," he continued, "but to get jobs done for people we can't find." Saving $6,000 per person, he contended, the company could reclaim $468,000 per year and eventually go on to eliminate as many as 150 jobs in total.[96]

Holly Farms pressed forward with creativity and foresight in the implementation of new production methods and the preparation of new product lines designed to suit the changing expectations of 1960s family cooking. While others were trying to perfect fried chicken in a can, in 1964 Holly Farms began marketing chicken delivered to retailers chilled instead of frozen in ice.[97] Upon slaughter and defeathering, fowl would pass through a thirty-two-degree bath, adding only 5 percent moisture and lowering the birds' body temperature. They then underwent a forty-five-minute conveyer belt ride in a thirty-four-degree cooler during which the water content was substantially reduced as the carcass was wrung dry.[98] The basic incentives were very simple: transporting frozen birds involved driving ice across the country, meaning additional weight and capacity. If the ice and water content of the bird could be reduced, then the shipping cost per pound of meat would similarly fall. At the same time, the method contributed favorably to Americans' increasing desire for greater flexibility in their cooking patterns by purchasing chicken parts separately. "Holly has defied every rule in the book," *Broiler Industry* wrote without irony. "It wrung moisture out of its chickens when industry practice has been to add water, so much so that the government now imposes a ceiling of 12% moisture added by processing (8% if frozen)."[99]

Holly Pak, as the company referred to its new method, was employed in the preparation of both whole birds and selected cuts. The fresh bird contained significantly less water, but it was not bone dry. It retained 2 percent water content and remained tender as it was placed on Mobilfoam trays and sealed with stretchable poly bags.[100] Unlike frozen chicken, the meat would dent when touched before returning to shape. Hermetically sealed Holly Pak chicken was found to have a lower bacterium count than frozen chicken due to the minimal time spent exposed, and it did not drip when the temperature changed and the ice melted, reducing the risk of cross-contamination.[101]

Retailers would take some convincing that it was worth switching from frozen to dry-chilled chicken and accepting the costs of altering their storage and display facilities in order to accommodate it. Some chains tested it in certain stores and compared the results with ice-packed chicken. "Usually, they will find that even by traditional standards of percent of gross sales, they'll do no worse than on ice pack, if they'll give it a full 60 to 90 days' trial," explained marketing director Bob Montgomery. "It takes that long, in most cases, for volume to build up from a different mix to overcome the fact you're not selling as many whole birds and quarters."[102] Rather than cutting, wrapping, and pricing cuts of chicken for customers at a meat counter, Holly Pak products could simply be lifted from a crate, placed into coolers, and conveniently restocked. Holly could prelabel chicken packages, listing the name of the cut, the weight, and the expiration date. If supermarkets required products under their own in-house label, then Holly Farms was happy to accommodate them and package accordingly.[103] Holly Pak products would then have a shelf life of about five days before they needed repackaging.

Transferring the evisceration of chickens from the blades of a highly skilled butcher at a meat counter to a production line where workers only had to master one task suited both retailers and poultry companies. In addition to being able to reduce labor costs, retailers removed the responsibility for quality control from their own employees. "Everything is made or lost on that three feet between the retail counter and the customer," argued Francis Garvin, who would succeed Fred Lovette as president of the company. "We knew it but we didn't work hard enough at it. We had to get out there in the aisle, so to speak, and get the consumer involved."[104] Holly Pak products were sold to retailers at a higher price, but the ease and versatility they provided would be encouraging to consumers, who were increasingly uncertain about how to dismember chickens themselves. "Holly Pak is the finest deal offered us since eviscerated chicken replaced New York–dressed," exclaimed the merchandising manager of a top ten chain, referring to the earlier innovation whereby the head, feet, and entrails of plucked carcasses were removed. "We're pushing it into all of our stores," he continued, "15 to 20 stores at a time, as fast as logistics and store education will permit."[105]

The Rise of Tyson Foods

Beginning in the 1970s, a significant evolution within the poultry industry was under way. In 1970 thirty-four firms were responsible for 70 percent of American broilers, but among the top six producers only two considered fowl to be their core area of competency: Holly Farms and Gold Kist. The remaining four were large and diversified corporate conglomerates that had spread their risks in the postwar decades by assembling unrelated industries, a growth strategy that allowed them to work around an active federal antitrust division.[106] These included Ralston Purina, an animal feed and pet food specialist; Swift and Wilson, both of which were old-time Chicago red meat packers; and Pillsbury–J. M. Smucker, purveyors of flour, baking mixtures, and spreads. Campbell Soup was the fifteenth largest poultry producer.[107] The arguments of business strategists such as former Avis president Robert Townsend grew in influence, venturing that the large multi-interest corporations had become lackadaisical and unprofitable, guided by administrators rather than creative leaders.[108] Corporations should focus upon their core areas of expertise and depart from those where they did not hold a competitive advantage that positioned them to generate above-average returns.[109] This was a general critique that was not directed specifically toward food processors or agribusiness, but both would be impacted by the new approach to corporate ownership that would follow. Companies that were narrowly focused on monopolizing and vertically integrating the meat and poultry industries stood to be beneficiaries.

Over time, many of the multi-interest conglomerates would gradually divest themselves of their interests in the poultry industry. By 1985 Tyson Foods, tenth in 1970, would be the biggest integrated poultry processor in the world. Tyson's ascendance was less the result of innovation and more the consequence of access to capital and an aggressive approach to using it. Don Tyson, president and son of company founder John, fully acknowledged that it was Fred Lovette at Holly Farms who had influenced him to go in the direction of chill-dried, prepackaged chicken, leaving behind the ice-packed product. "He convinced me 11 years ago to go that route," Tyson recalled in 1982. "He was smart, too. He knew that if there were two of us in the field, we'd both sell more because buyers would have another supplier," he added.[110] Through the early 1980s Tyson acquired large and small operations as he grew the business. In 1984, fifty years after the company's founding, Tyson beat out Archer-Daniels-Midland to purchase Memphis-based Valmac Industries with its substantial Tastybird Foods division for $70 million, ranked months before as the fifth largest processor in the United States.[111]

"We're chicken folks, nothing else," Tyson told the Associated Press as the company acquired Poultry Specialists from grocery giant Sara Lee in 1985. "We ride all the health trends," he went on to say as the company sought to deepen its relationship with Burger King.[112] Sara Lee, like Ralston Purina, Pillsbury, Quaker Oats, and other publicly traded multi-interest corporations, often took the strategic approach of divesting its poultry operations when faced with the difficulty of explaining fluctuations in earnings to stockholders. ConAgra decided to remain involved in the poultry industry: it purchased Armour from Greyhound and acquired 50 percent of Swift, thereby taking control of the two most famous old names in American meats.[113] Toward the end of the decade, Tyson reversed its approach to red meats, diversifying into pork and seafood processing, but it was in 1989 that the company, now running revenues of nearly $2 billion, would acquire the jewel in its crown as the king of American poultry.[114]

In October 1988 Tyson attempted a hostile takeover of Holly Farms, by this point the fifth largest poultry company in the United States, with $1.6 billion in sales in the previous year.[115] The Wilkesboro firm was coming off a bad couple of years. No longer considered the great innovator, it had entered late into the production of further processed fast-food products, preferring to focus upon fresh supermarket chicken, an area of the market that had been hurt by consumer concerns over salmonella. At the same time, the company's direct entry into the restaurant business, a partnership with Safeway that situated Holly Farms branded diners in supermarket parking lots, had ultimately proven to be less than successful, the final location closing in 1986.[116]

Holly's board of directors resisted Tyson's move and sought to enter an agreement with ConAgra, the nation's second largest poultry producer, reaching what they believed would be a favorable ratio of exchange for company stockholders while maintaining the integrity of the company. "This transaction provides our stockholders with significantly higher value than any other available alternative and also gives them the opportunity for even greater value in the future as stockholders of ConAgra," said president and CEO R. Lee Taylor II in November. "I believe our management teams will work well together in a way that will benefit Holly Farms' employees, customers, suppliers, and communities," he asserted.[117] Tyson sued and sought to invalidate the agreement in court in Wilmington, Delaware, and then returned in 1989 with an improved offer to Holly Farms' stockholders.[118] While the Delaware court ruled in Tyson's favor on the grounds that the proposed merger did not give stockholders the opportunity to consider both offers, Holly Farms executives scrambled to seek an injunction of their own, fearing that Tyson would find a way to persuade ConAgra to withdraw from negotiations.[119] Tyson offered seventy dollars per share, up from its original offer of forty-five dollars on what was then forty-three-dollar stock. Shareholders rejected the second attempt to merge with ConAgra and instead finalized the deal with Tyson.[120] Don Tyson stressed the patience that had been required. "If it hadn't been such a perfect fit, we would have gone off. But it was such a perfect fit with our company, product-wise and geographically," he said as the company added Holly Farms' nine plants to its own thirty-two, twenty-two of which were in Arkansas, and extended its market share to 25 percent.[121] Seeking to further elaborate on the match between Tyson and Holly Farms, he explained that "it was like dating the high school cheerleader. I thought she'd never say yes."[122] Coming less than a year after the $25 billion leveraged buyout of R. J. Reynolds–Nabisco, a famously poor fit between the traditional Winston-Salem-based cigarette maker and the faster-paced Chicago biscuit brand, Tyson's stress on compatible company cultures was prescient.[123]

The company that had greatly influenced the way Americans purchased chicken had disappeared as a distinct entity and was absorbed by Tyson. "I am

TABLE 1. Poultry industry concentration, 1980, 1984, and 1989

	1980	1984	1989
4 LARGEST FIRMS	23%	34%	45%
No. of plants	34	41	76
8 LARGEST FIRMS	39%	52%	60%
No. of plants	60	68	105
20 LARGEST FIRMS	66%	73%	80%
No. of plants	104	105	156

SOURCES: "Nation's Top Broiler Firms," *Broiler Industry*, December 1983, 22; "Nation's Top Broiler Firms," *Broiler Industry*, December 1985, 18; David Amey, "Nation's Top Broiler Companies," *Broiler Industry*, December 1989, 52.

a fun guy," Don Tyson told Holly Farms employees in Temperanceville, Virginia, in 1989, reassuring them that layoffs were not on the horizon.[124] Nonetheless, one of the new king of poultry's first orders of business was to merge the two companies' transportation divisions and declare invalid a successful union election of Teamsters Local 592 among Holly Farms drivers that had taken place just months before.[125] Around one hundred workers, drivers, feed mill employees, and chicken catchers refused to work under new conditions that they felt had been imposed upon them; they were eventually fired. This case would finally be settled six years later when the U.S. Fourth Circuit Court of Appeals in Richmond ruled 2–1 in the Teamsters' favor, validating an earlier decision by the National Labor Relations Board (NLRB).[126] "Every change in corporate ownership cannot raise the specter of disruption in the labor relations of the company being bought or sold," wrote Judge Francis Murnaghan, a Carter appointee, in March 1995.[127] Tyson appealed the decision to the Supreme Court, at the same time contending that the live-haul crew constituted agricultural employees under the terms of the Wagner Act.[128] While the justices upheld the circuit court ruling, they agreed to hear the second part of Tyson's challenge. The Supreme Court distinguished between truck drivers and forklift drivers yet ultimately held that both were nonagricultural employees.[129]

With the Holly Farms takeover, the Arkansas firm stood as the unchallenged leader of the industry, unimpeded by the Department of Justice's Antitrust Division, producing around seventy-eight million pounds of ready-to-cook chicken per week to ConAgra's thirty-two million.[130] Within five years Tyson would claim to be supplying ninety of the one hundred biggest restaurant chains in the United States, as well as numerous schools, hospitals, and hotels, while exports would more than double to 8 percent of its overall sales during the same period.[131]

These changes in the industry had been anticipated for decades as processors had sought to dominate growers, hatcheries, and feed companies. "I predict that, in four years, 25 operators will control 75% of the nation's production," said Arkansas Valley Industry's Harold Snyder in October 1960.[132] Between 1960 and 1977, the number of poultry firms fell by nearly 40 percent.[133] As table 1 indicates, industry consolidation continued apace throughout the 1980s as broiler companies sought to create economies of scale and produce on a level sufficient to meet the needs of the large retail and restaurant chains. Their custom was essential for survival in an age when local independent venders were no longer enough to live on and company brand goods were stocking many shelves.[134]

Furthermore, publicly traded poultry processors and meatpackers were subject to pressure to merge from Wall Street investors who stood to gain from sizable transaction fees with every new merger and acquisition. Returns on equity were steady but below industry averages as grain prices continued to fluctuate, although these affected beef and pork prices more than poultry, with the chicken of the 1980s presenting a superior feed conversion ratio.[135] With major restaurant and supermarket chains giving greater returns on stock, investors contended that greater scale on the part of poultry companies would redress the balance of power. It was within this environment that Tyson was able to consistently outperform the food industry average of returns on equity.[136] With the introduction and rapid proliferation of checkout scanners and computerized tracking of inventory and sales, an informational imbalance had been created whereby grocery chains such as Walmart knew more about the demand for certain products than the manufacturers themselves. As large-scale retailers developed the power to demand great flexibility of producers and drop them if their needs could not be met, they were also able to leverage wholesale prices downward.[137] "Suppliers will never say they pay to get onto the shelf," said retail analyst Steven Mandel of Goldman Sachs, "but it just depends which form the money is coming in."[138]

In the decade from 1975 to 1985, more than five thousand companies were acquired within the food industry as the relationship between producers and retailers continued to evolve.[139] "Until some fast-food chain makes a tender offer for General Motors or until the Reagan Justice Department approves a merger of Coca-Cola and Pepsi, who can imagine a piece of takeover news that would amaze us anymore?" wrote journalist Robert Reno in 1987, indicting what he saw as the Reagan administration's relaxed attitude toward monopoly power.[140] With beef prices leveling off and agricultural prices stabilizing, food companies had become a hot commodity on the stock market. "Once among the most neglected entrees on the Wall Street takeover menu,

[they] have become the main course," observed Terry Bivens of the *Philadelphia Inquirer*.[141] Considered steadily and consistently growing investments that benefited from federally subsidized raw materials, tobacco giants Philip Morris and R. J. Reynolds both sought to modify the balance of power between major producers and retailers through two of the largest mergers of the 1980s, with General Foods and Nabisco, respectively. Tobacco and food products served different purposes but could largely be found in the same retail outlets.

While some critics charged that the Reagan administration's approach to antitrust action was one of laissez-faire, analyst Martin Sikora argued that the 1980s represented a shift in emphasis away from scale or market share with a greater aversion toward pricing domination. This was in line with Reagan's Executive Order 12,291, issued in February 1981, which outlined a cost-benefit analysis approach to regulation. "Regulatory action shall not be undertaken unless the potential benefits to society for the regulation outweigh the potential costs to society," read section 2(b) of that order.[142] Nevertheless, as the administration cut the budget for the Antitrust Division by 12 percent in its first year in office alone, Sikora agreed that this alteration in philosophy at the Department of Justice amounted to a "catalyst" that encouraged the historic wave of company mergers and acquisitions.[143] Robert Reno was left to conclude that "you show the Reagan administration a free market gone insane and it'll see an apple pie every time."[144]

As the poultry industry adjusted to the growing demands of American consumers, U.S. poultry companies, southern in both their character and their geography, were increasingly subject to their shareholders' expectations. With food companies a rising commodity on Wall Street throughout the 1980s, corporate boards divested of interests that fell outside their core mission as they aimed to streamline operations.[145] As companies such as Sara Lee, Quaker Oats, and Pillsbury all exited the poultry sector, one processing plant after another was available to existing industry leaders that had access to capital resources. None had greater access than Tyson Foods, and none was more aggressive in its expansion, which culminated in 1989 in the hostile takeover of Holly Farms.

By the 1990s the poultry industry had reached an age of maturity, and its marquee brands had taken their place alongside the giants of the American business class. Trailing in the wake of companies such as Tyson, Pilgrim's Pride, and Perdue were hundreds of small and medium-sized aspirants, primarily southern-based competitors seeking a slice of the action. The demand for chicken products from consumers simply grew and grew. In 1960 Americans consumed an average of twenty-eight pounds of chicken per year. By 1990 consumption had reached sixty-one pounds and averaged seventy-seven pounds just a decade later.[146]

After broilers were placed on a consistent regimen of antibiotics, output continued to grow in size and number so that the chicken of the new millennium would have been almost unrecognizable to the farmer of the 1950s.[147] In 2014 poultry scientists raised three strains of broiler, from 1957, 1978, and a 2005 strain known as the Ross 308. After twenty-eight days, the 1957 and 1978 strains weighed 316 grams and 632 grams, respectively. By the fifty-sixth day, they weighed 905 grams and 1,808 grams. The Ross 308, by contrast, weighed an astonishing 1,396 grams after twenty-eight days and 4,202 grams after fifty-six, more than four times the weight of the chicken of the 1950s, although it was subject to endemic health issues affecting the bird's bones, heart, and immune system.[148] While environmental and dietary factors did play a role, poultry scientist Gerald Havenstein found that between 85 and 90 percent of this shift was due to genetic selection on the part of commercial broiler companies.[149]

The vision of Depression-era poultrymen such as Charles Lovette had become a reality, a global success story that transformed the American diet. Consumers demanded chicken. Some were happy to eat it every night. Even a modest income could provide for that ambition. Yet this dream had not come without its costs. It was not the Lovette or Pilgrim or Tyson families that would bear the brunt of those costs. Those hundredths of a cent had to be extracted from somewhere to create the economies that nationwide retailers required. From the perspective of the rural workforce that endured long and unrelenting shifts in the nation's growing number of processing facilities, the miracle of modern industrial poultry took on a dramatically different perspective.

CHAPTER 3

Broken Bones, Broken Laws, and the Rise of AMC Local 525

In late June 1957 a handful of workers from the Holly Farms poultry plant in Wilkesboro, North Carolina, gathered at the home of Jennie Joines, a military wife with a husband overseas who was then in her second stint with the company. They had convened to meet with Emanuel Coutlakis, an organizer from Local 525 of the Amalgamated Meat Cutters and Butcher Workmen (AMC) to develop a plan to form a union at the facility. It was something of a surprise when they were joined by their coworker Pearl Billings. Up to that point, Billings had expressed no interest in organizing against the company, but she told those gathered that she "just came down to the meeting to see what it was all about." Billings was not a master in the art of subterfuge, and she revealed that she had earlier been in conversation with Bonnie Bare, the company paymaster and the sister of owner Fred Lovette. Coutlakis extended to Billings an offer to join the union. When she declined, he told her that she would have to leave, as they were holding an organizing committee meeting for union members only. "Mr. Coutlakis told us that in his opinion Mrs. Billings was a Company stooge sent to the meeting to spy on us," recalled Alma Gryder, one of the workers present.[1]

On her way out, Billings stopped to talk to Joines's next-door neighbor Nellie Porter, also a Holly Farms employee. Porter told Joines that Billings had "asked her why she was not up to that damn union meeting." Joines continued: "Pearl Billings went on to tell Nellie Porter that she was going to Fred Lovette and tell him who was at the meeting."[2] In order to remain aboveboard, Coutlakis asked the workers for their permission to send a telegram to the company, "pointing out that we were the Union's Committee in the plant."[3] The workers agreed to this decision, and the telegram was dispatched the following morning, a Saturday.

63

Upon receiving the telegram, Fred Lovette proceeded to post it on the company bulletin board. Life quickly became difficult for the committee members. On Monday the company superintendent, Mack Nichols, approached Margaret Elledge, who had been present at the meeting. Nichols "told me to keep my mouth shut no matter what anybody said to me," Elledge said. Later on, "one of the girls that had joined the union came and told me that the girls that had not joined the union was going to beat us up Tuesday morning as we went into the plant."[4] Alma Gryder also observed signs that trouble was brewing. Just minutes after the telegram was posted, Gene Winton, a foreman, came over to her and said, "If a chicken came over there that wasn't clean he would fire me." This threat seemed uncalled for. "Gene, you know I do my work right," Gryder told him. The following day, Winton doubled down on his earlier remark. "Putting your name on that little card is going to cause you to lose your job," he warned.[5]

Later that day, Gryder took a bathroom break and passed by the bulletin board where Bonnie Bare was gathered with other managers. She heard Bare warn that "there will be a time when they get off the line that some people in here will pitch them out of here and I don't care how they do it they won't get fired for doing it." Gryder went on to explain, "Later on there was a lot of fighting in the plant that was started by some people who had the approval of the Company."[6]

Alma Gryder did not find herself on the receiving end of any violence, but the same could not be said for Carrie Johnson, Jennie Joines, and Grace Gryder. "On June 24th at the 7:30 A.M. break I was sitting in the rest room talking to the girls and Jean Bullis, another worker on the line, came and started cussing me," Johnson recalled. "I asked her what she was cussing me for. She said she heard that 'I had said someone ought to bust you in the mouth.' I said it wasn't true and after she kept repeating that I did, she finally called me 'A God damn liar' and the fight started." It is not clear if Bullis had made an independent decision to attack Johnson or if she had been encouraged to do so, but the incident appeared to be condoned. "During the fight a company foreman named Dennis Sevette stood in the rest room door and watched," Johnson said. "He did nothing to stop it."[7]

Jennie Joines suffered more severe recriminations. Whereas it had taken three days for other workers to catch up with Johnson, Joines was targeted within less than twenty-four hours. On the Saturday evening, the day the telegram was posted on the bulletin board, "two girls jumped on me in the parking lot when I started home," she said. It did not end there, though. "On Monday the 24th I went in to work and one of the girls tried to pick a fight with me.

I did not argue with her," Joines said. "That evening after we got off from work she was waiting along with others. Fred Lovette, Bonnie Bare, and all the foremen in the plant stood and watched while she beat me up and did not try to stop the fight. She beat me in the face before they parted us."[8] Grace Gryder missed a day of work with a black eye, but Joines's injuries were more serious, and she decided not to return to the plant.[9] "I went to the doctor," she said. "The doctor told me he thought I had been hit with something other than a fist. He had x-rays taken and fractured bones were found."[10]

Following this wave of assaults, the members of the organizing committee were called in to meet with Francis Garvin, the general manager of the company's three plants. "Mr. Garvin asked us what the trouble was between us workers that we couldn't get along like one big family," Carrie Johnson reported.[11] He questioned them as to what they knew about the union and told them that to get what they wanted they could have just spoken to him. "You know we can't fire you for your work because every one of you are good workers," he told them.[12] "After talking to me sometime [sic] he asked if we had it to do over again would we sign Union cards," Johnson stated. "I said I didn't know but I guess I would."[13] Others were similarly unrepentant. "They tried to get me to sign a card withdrawing from the union," remembered Margaret Shoemaker. "I refused. Then they refused to do anything about the foremen or employees who were picking on us."[14] Alma Gryder told Garvin that she had joined because "we didn't get treated fair and that the work was too hard."[15]

"He told us he would like to be able to go out in the plant and announce that we had agreed to drop the Union for the time being," Gryder explained. "We told him 'Nothing doing,' that we were the Committee and that we were supposed to stand up for those who want the Union and we didn't intend to let the workers down."[16] On Friday, August 28, 1957, one week after the original committee meeting, Alma Gryder, Jennie Joines, Carrie Johnson, Nellie Porter, Grace Gryder, Margaret Shoemaker, and several others were all laid off. For all of the conviction of the AMC's organizing committee, in almost exclusively white Wilkes County they had met opposition both in the upstairs offices and on the shop floor from fellow production line workers who were just as aggressive in their defense of the status quo and their rejection of trade unionism. Though the NLRB later found in favor of the eleven workers, the Wilkesboro union campaign was broken.

For the chicken business, 1957 was a landmark year. Buoyed by public concerns about the dangers of food poisoning and the transferability of avian-borne diseases to humans, the passage of the federal Poultry Products Inspection Act had transferred inspection responsibilities from the Food and Drug

Administration (FDA) to the USDA. Speaking to the Senate, FDA commissioner John Harvey observed that "the poultry industry has sprung up like a mushroom in the last few years" and that "the conditions are analogous to the situation we had with red meat back in 1906."[17] Whereas FDA inspections were infrequent and limited in scope, USDA line inspectors would be a new permanent fixture within the production process, akin to that which had existed in beef and pork facilities since the passage of the Federal Meat Inspection Act of 1907.

Though long forgotten and barely considered newsworthy at the time, the travails of Holly Farms workers in the same year foreshadowed the ongoing hostility that workers faced when they attempted to challenge the absolute managerial authority of poultrymen. In their pursuit of the American consumer, chicken processors were consistently willing to deploy every tool at their disposal, both within and outside the law, to minimize labor costs and exert unbridled control over their production methods. Through mechanization and accelerating line speeds, they drove down the prices at butchers' shops, in supermarkets, and then in restaurants by operating at thin profit margins in competition both with the pork and beef industries and with one another. Even as the available labor-saving devices became more sophisticated in adapting to the irregularities of chicken bodies, poultry plants remained labor-intensive facilities, each employing hundreds of workers around the clock in multiple shifts.

Many of the hazards faced by poultry workers on the shop floor remained consistent from one decade to the next, from slippery wet floors that could result in broken wrists and hips, eviscerating machines that amputated fingers, to corrosive cleaning chemicals that caused respiratory problems and burns to the skin. Sharp knives and scissors caused innumerable inadvertent cuts and incisions, but blades worn blunt through heavy use demanded the application of greater pressure, leading to skeletomuscular conditions that would linger for years, often exacerbated by perpetual dampness and cold. The risks could be even greater in a poorly maintained plant that was plagued by old and faulty equipment and that exposed workers to moving blades and electrical wiring.

When poultry workers decided to act collectively, they often found themselves outmatched by employers and their political allies across the "broiler belt" in northwestern Arkansas and northern Georgia and up the Delmarva Peninsula of Delaware, Maryland, and Virginia. Yet nowhere were these adversities more dramatically illustrated than in North Carolina, a state that prided itself on progressive investments in education, science, and technology but where unionists and company supporters repeatedly clashed in violent confrontations akin to the union-breaking campaign in Wilkesboro in 1957.[18]

This chapter explores episodes at three different poultry companies in North Carolina, each of which, in very different ways, brings to light the violent fate of poultry workers in their respective eras. AMC Local 525, a union that for more than two decades struggled to gain a foothold in the state's rapidly expanding poultry industry, plays an important role in this story. Frequently thwarted by Holly Farms, the state's most prominent poultry company, Local 525 doggedly continued to gather food service workers throughout the 1960s and managed to win a signature election victory in 1965 with the predominantly Black workforce at Gold Kist in Durham, one of the larger companies in the United States. Although the union established job security, seniority rules, and a modest but significant benefits package through collective bargaining, its economic gains were outstripped by the inflation of the 1970s. Growing tensions between the union leadership and a mixture of both senior and younger rank-and-file workers, heightened by a radical insurgent campaign, culminated in a remarkable and almost unprecedented strike in August 1978. Though contrary to the recommendations of union leadership and ultimately unsuccessful, the 1978 strike highlighted both the limitations of union power in the southern poultry sector when the union operated at single outposts of companies with multiple facilities and the willingness of urban poultry workers in the late civil rights era to imagine something better and demand more of their employer.

By the 1980s, the AMC had merged with the Retail Clerks International Union to form the United Food and Commercial Workers (UFCW), and organized labor's presence in the poultry industry in North Carolina fell into a state of decline. With the UFCW at a disadvantage because of aggressive mergers and restructuring across the meat-producing sectors of the food economy, workers on poultry lines in rural towns found themselves short on champions. With North Carolina's light-touch approach to regulation among the state's main selling points to prospective investors, small operators were willing to cut corners in an approach legal scholar Marc Linder referred to as "throughput über alles" as they attempted to keep pace with the industry leaders and claim a stake in the exploding market for fast-food and processed frozen chicken products.[19]

A half-century of poultry industry growth would be punctuated by an almost incomprehensible industrial disaster and an avoidable act of industrial manslaughter at Imperial Foods in Hamlet, North Carolina, in 1991 when twenty-five workers, mostly African American women, died in a factory fire, unable to escape through locked exit doors. Imperial Foods fleetingly brought national attention to the workers who bore the costs of the modern American food system. Yet if the 1980s had been the era of deregulatory ascendance, by the 1990s the wisdom of a "small government" approach to occupational safety was triumphant, and even vivid tragedies could not slow the aggregation of power in the hands of private managerial authority. Ultimately, poultrymen almost always had their way, rarely hindered by an obeisance to any kind of law. The structure of disincentives designed to maintain safe workplaces, freedom of political association, and rights to representation and even to deter acts of individual physical brutality was, when applied to the postwar industrial poultry sector, simply built to fail.

Sharp Can Be the Holly

By the turn of the twenty-first century, many veterans of the labor movement, acutely aware of the sorry conditions in poultry plants, which were periodically captured on hidden cameras wielded by animal rights activists, had grown wary of attempting new union organizing campaigns, considering them costly and improbable ventures. Expectations had not always been this modest, though. In the 1950s and 1960s, AMC Local 525, established as a statewide outpost in 1944, organized and educated poultry workers in North Carolina towns in an ongoing battle to shape the character of an industry that was still in its infancy.

While Jennie Joines, Carrie Johnson, and their colleagues in Wilkesboro were attempting to gain a foothold in 1957, John Russell, a representative of the international union and later president of the local, was simultaneously organizing workers at another Holly Farms plant in Winston-Salem. Local 525's campaigns elicited early signals of the rigor with which poultrymen would fight to retain their unquestioned control of their facilities. Russell saw signs of growing discontent among Holly workers, many of whom were compensated as little as two dollars per hour. If they missed work because of sickness, then their pay was cut to the legal minimum of one dollar per hour the following day. If a worker was as little as a minute late, they were docked an hour's pay yet still required to work the hour in question.[20]

When workers walked away from the production line and went on strike in Winston-Salem in 1957, central to their concerns was the notion that they were not afforded the respect that they were entitled to as women. Foremen were accustomed to using bad language without regard for female employees, freely entering the women's dressing room at any time, and firing anyone who answered back on the grounds that they were "sassing."[21] The level of violence directed at workers and organizers quickly escalated. Union supporters contended that the company was responsible for "prevoking [sic] of fights in plants by stooges—2 women beaten up." In addition to customary tactics such as spying and assailing the union in the press and on the radio, "stooges framed up charges of assault with a deadly weapon against seven strikers" at the Winston-Salem plant. Two days after the AMC had gone on strike, the Teamsters responsible for transporting Holly Farms chicken struck too. The company filed a nine-million-dollar suit against the truckers, and "threats [were] made to dynamite the houses of Teamsters." These threats were taken very seriously by both unions. The AMC reported that the company, or presumably "stooges" acting on its behalf, "thru [sic] dynamite at meetings."[22]

In July 1957 John Russell sent a telegram to the sheriff of Wilkes County to report similar experiences. "Urge your office investigate dynamiting of peaceful Union Meeting held by Amalgamated Meat Cutters and Butcher Workmen of North America in North Wilkesboro, North Carolina on July 3rd, 1957," it read.[23] This telegram failed to elicit an investigation, so Russell contacted the Department of Justice in Washington, D.C. John J. Schauer, chief of the Organized Crime and Racketeering Section, sent an uninterested response referring Russell to the Asheville office of the FBI. "The information contained in your telegram is not sufficiently detailed to enable us to determine whether a violation of a federal criminal statute is involved," the letter read perfunctorily.[24]

No investigation ever took place, and Local 525 was unsuccessful in its Holly Farms campaigns of the late 1950s. The local redoubled its efforts a decade later because the company was simply too large to ignore. The union obtained enough signatures to schedule an election in December 1970 at the Holly Farms plant in Monroe, a small town of around eleven thousand people twenty-five miles to the southeast of Charlotte. Monroe had a dubious history and an active Ku Klux Klan. The birthplace of conservative senator Jesse Helms, Monroe was the setting in 1958 for what became known as the "Kissing Case," in which two young African American boys were charged and issued lengthy sentences for rape after they were kissed by a white girl. The Holly Farms plant in Monroe, which was a more racially balanced town than Wilkesboro, was reliant upon African American women to meet its workforce needs.

While there were fewer acts of direct violence than there had been in 1957, Emanuel Coutlakis wrote to international president Patrick Gorman that "the company put on a vicious campaign in Monroe against the Union in the course of which thirteen people, practically our entire committee, were fired."[25] These included Louisiana Robinson, in whose home the committee had been formed. Robinson was fired for chewing tobacco while working on the line, a practice that was said to be very common in the plant. While Robinson denied the charge, she also claimed that supervisors had told her she could chew as much as she wanted as long as the USDA inspector did not catch her.[26] When supervisor Spencer Jennings was asked by a colleague what had warranted the discharge of committee member Daisy Allen, "he said that you might take this damn shit, but I'm not going to have this damn shit. Because I'll fire every damn body in this plant and there won't be a damn soul left but me."[27]

In Monroe, Holly Farms courted Black ministers in an attempt to gain additional leverage against the union. Organizer Cornelius Simmons wrote to union leadership with incredulity when reporting a dinner being held at a Jim Crow restaurant. "The Bowman's Restaurant is a place where several demonstrations took place and where several were beaten, arrested and I am told at least one was shot," he wrote. "And today no Black people eat at this place, yet Holly Farms is inviting the Black leaders to be their guest at this place and to further remind them of slavery they are to have lunch in the Confederate room," he went on. Bowman's had "a Confederate emblem on the outside near the door." Simmons summarized, "They think all Black Ministers and other leaders will sell their souls for a chicken leg."[28]

Local 525 filed charges of nineteen unfair labor practices against Holly Farms and repeatedly forestalled the union election. "Our organization, as you must know, is not a trigger-happy group so far as strikes are concerned," Patrick Gorman wrote to Fred Lovette, emphasizing the relatively conservative credentials of the AMC. "But, I was wondering, Mr. Lovette, is it worthwhile? Isn't it better to talk the matter over and make a reasonable, gentlemanly effort to have an understanding and to enter into an agreement where the workers involved in your company seem to desire that they be represented by our organization?"[29] Holly Farms was unrelenting. When the NLRB instructed the company to rehire Daisy Allen and Local 525 sought to depict this as evidence of union strength, the operations manager, Sam Zimmerman, issued a derisive flyer to employees. "*WHY IS DAISY ALLEN SMILING*?" it began. "She was fired from Holly in 1970 and could not come back until 1973," Zimmerman wrote. "She told the government *she lost $7,605* in pay during that time—but she *got* only $1,571 from Holly," he boasted. "She don't have much to smile about, does she?" For the Lovettes, it all seemed worth it. The NLRB finally supervised an election of the 461 workers at Holly Farms' Monroe plant on a cold Friday in November 1973, three years after the date that had been originally proposed. Local 525 received 33 votes, but 384 workers voted against a union. Even when interacting with a more diverse workforce, the AMC found small-town North Carolina to be a barren environment where rural workers were cautious before reneging against one of the community's largest employers. In Monroe workers delivered a clear victory for management and a validation of its methods.[30]

The defeat in Monroe was a significant setback to Local 525, but not all businesses were as incorrigible as Holly Farms, and not all North Carolinians were quite as reluctant to support unionization. The AMC had been carefully assembling a winning track record in meat departments in the chain retail sector and at red meat and poultry concerns during the late 1960s, growing from 1,064 members in 1965 to 1,849 in 1966.[31] By 1969 the local's membership stood at nearly three thousand.[32] Some of these units were very small. In February 1966 the union won an election in the Meat Department of an A&P Tea Company store in Washington, North Carolina, by a vote of eight to zero. One month later, the union lost at A&P Lumberton by twenty-nine to nine but won representation at A&P Waynesville by a vote of nine to four.[33] The union added meat departments at K-Mart in Asheville, Charlotte, Greensboro, and High Point.[34] They added members in packing houses operated by Armour, Swift, and the Jesse Jones Sausage Company, as well as at Rockingham Poultry, a smaller operator on the state's central southern border. At Rose Hill Poultry in the eastern part of the state, the local demonstrated its willingness to engage in a sustained campaign and absorb setbacks, suffering defeat twice before finally winning a union election in 1964.[35]

Gold Kist in Durham

In 1965 Local 525 won a signature victory at a poultry plant operated by Gold Kist in Durham with a workforce of around three hundred. In contrast to Wilkesboro and Monroe, Durham was a rapidly growing industrial city in the 1960s with a population of nearly one hundred thousand by the decade's end. Durham was "a tobacco town if ever there was one," wrote Paul Hoffman for the *New York Times*, and the city's Liggett & Myers plant employed around twenty-five hundred workers, who produced as many as thirty-five hundred Chesterfield, L&M, Lark, and Eve cigarettes every minute. American Tobacco, also present, was responsible for making Lucky Strikes.[36] Exploring the city's protests in the late 1960s, doctoral student Francis Stevens Redburn found working-class Black neighborhoods where "the streets were narrow, unpaved, and unlighted, the houses dilapidated, the plumbing nonexistent or in need of repair, and the rats and cockroaches abundant."[37] The city's councilmen, made up largely of white men of standing, had typically "believed that what was good for business was good for the community" and were unconcerned "with the deteriorating economic position of white and Negro labor in manufacturing."[38] Redburn noted that "these are not, for the most part, urbane and enlightened individuals."[39]

Yet Black Durham was much more than the sum of the decaying bricks and mortar described here by Redburn. By the late 1800s, Durham had already established itself as a source of pride and a locus of educated and more affluent African Americans, so much so that by 1925 sociologist E. Franklin Frazier described the city as "the Capital of the Black Middle Class."[40] In spite of the opportunities Durham provided, it had nonetheless remained subject to many of the oppressions characteristic of the Jim Crow South, and the city's elite minority was greatly outnumbered by its African American working class, often drawn in from rural areas and laboring in low-wage factory jobs. It was within and in response to this context, found historian Leslie Brown, that Black women "expanded their public roles beyond functional laborer and family member" by claiming and controlling spaces as their own: formal spaces in churches, clubs, and societies and informal spaces such as "porches, kitchens, gardens, and walkways of the neighborhood."[41] By the 1940s and 1950s, African American women's organizations were at the forefront as the city's Black Freedom Movement grew in strength and influence.[42]

Though the largest occupation for Black women remained domestic service, many sought greater independence in the tobacco plants, even though they were excluded from the better-paid positions and regarded as of secondary importance by the Tobacco Workers International Union.[43] Within the active and politically charged context of civil rights–era Durham, Local 525 found a receptive audience with the working-class African American workforce at Gold Kist in 1965. The union campaign was sandwiched between two periods of heightened Black community mobilization: a successful movement to desegregate public accommodations in 1963 and sustained demands for improvements in substandard public and private housing between 1966 and 1968. Guiding union organizers to workers' homes for evening visits, Laura Green, an employee since 1956, had still exercised significant caution, recalling that they had driven around in a hearse "so that people didn't know who we was." Besides addressing fundamental issues of vacations and paid leave, the union gained support from a sense of disempowerment on the shop floor. Women working rigorous and fast-paced line jobs for extended periods of time found it difficult to receive relief to visit the restroom. When the line broke down due to mechanical error pay was docked for the duration of the stoppage. Workers' concerns were often met with indifference. Then there were grievances that were nonetheless indicative of a general sense of disrespect, such as the company's refusal to take messages and notify workers when they were on the production line. "I knew a lady her house had caught fire and she was working," Green said. "They called her to explain but she couldn't go to the telephone and nobody didn't even tell her." She did not learn that her house had burned down until she returned home.[44]

Though the union was able to negotiate a contract quite rapidly and gain two weeks of annual paid vacation, winning changes on the shop floor proved to be an ongoing struggle in the face of intractable managers and supervisors. Elected by her peers as the chief steward, Green felt that Local 525 left her ill-equipped to enforce workers' demands. She wrote to Russell in August 1965 asking for further training and for him to meet with them. "The foreman is now saying you said do like we were doing before the union," she wrote.[45]

Three months later, having received no response, Green wrote again, appealing to Russell, "You have got to come here and straighten these people out. If you don't the whole thing is going to collapse and these people aren't kidding. We are paying too much money each month not to get any more benefits out of the contract than we do." Green explained that workers remained upset about the ongoing unavailability of restroom breaks. "They don't use the regular relief with the exception of the men, especially in the eviscerating room. They are using discriminatory practices as far as we are concern [sic]," she asserted. "We have been visiting other plants that are in the same Local 525 and their relief is altogether different from ours," she continued. "We would like to know why we are not getting the same benefits as the rest of plants."[46]

Breakdown pay remained a serious issue. Workers had been paid for a forty-five-minute breakdown on November 8, but when the same problem recurred for two hours the following day, workers were not compensated for their time. Referring to the plant manager, Green wrote that "he also said that he was going to call his lawyer and whatever he said about it he would do just that, but if his lawyer said not to pay he would let you and the lawyers fight it out." She summarized the situation: "This contract is messed up somehow and they use every trick in the book. They try everything they can not to abide by these rules and regulations of the contract. They know we don't understand it and they don't either but they are trying all they can to make fools of the stewards and all."[47]

In the ensuing years, John Russell developed a cordial working relationship with the management of Gold Kist Durham, exhibited in the friendly and familiar tone that inhabits the lengthy record of correspondence between the union office and the company. Stewards such as Green grew in experience, and jobs at the plant remained challenging, but they represented a stable form of employment that was free from arbitrary and unjust dismissals. In spite of the incremental improvements provided by union representation, relations between Gold Kist workers in Durham and the local leadership, situated over two hundred miles away in Asheville, remained uneasy. By the early 1970s, a period of rising inflation, the pay raises provided by the union contract were failing to keep pace with the growing costs of living. In 1971 the average hourly manufacturing rate was $3.68 in the rest of the United States but $2.64 in North Carolina.[48] As of 1971 the base rate for starting employees at Gold Kist was $2.35 per hour, increasing to $2.50 after their first year with the company. Certain job classifications provided incremental pay above the basic rate. A knife sharpener received an extra nickel, a foot cutter eight cents, a bird hanger fifteen.[49] This was greater than the $1.60 federal minimum wage but nonetheless modest. The 1974 contract between the two parties included two weeks of paid vacation after three years, three weeks after twelve years, life and health insurance, and the continuance of what was primarily a Monday through Friday schedule with the provision of time and a half if employees were called in on a Saturday and double time on a Sunday.[50] Incremental increases of ten, twelve, ten, thirteen, and eight cents in successive years amounted to a fifty-three-cent across-the-board raise over the duration of the contract.[51]

This didn't impress recent hire Karen Walker, a New Jersey native who had spent two years at the University of Cincinnati before dropping out and returning to the East. Walker was a member of the Marxist-Leninist Progressive Labor Party (PLP), a group formed by members of the American Communist Party who had grown disaffected with Khrushchev-era politics in the USSR and had taken inspiration from the rise of Maoist China. By 1970 the PLP had distanced itself from China too, lamenting the cessation of the first phase of the Cultural Revolution in 1968, one of the "four great revolutions [to have] marked the forward thrust of humanity."[52] Over the course of four years, Walker engaged in a creative campaign that was initially directed at Gold Kist but that in time evolved into a challenge to John Russell's stewardship of the union. The campaign was a critique of the bureaucratic and incremental change wrought by the AMC's established brand of unionism and the Old Left, and it was not unlike that leveled by other radical activists who entered industrial occupations.[53] While the workforce at Gold Kist expressed limited interest in the particular model of revolutionary politics offered by the PLP, in a city with a recent history of social protest, Walker's DIY *Meat Cutters Workers Action Movement (WAM) Newsletter* found an audience among employees who had never had a reason to trust Durham's business-oriented political leaders and whose confidence in the Asheville office had already eroded.

For Walker, who was initially deployed to the plant's line of Kentucky Fried Chicken products, the 1974 contract was the first sign of the union's trepidation. "A Quarter?!" read the headline on the front page of the *WAM Newsletter* of July 18, 1974. The article asserted that the union had entered negotiations with the demand for an immediate forty-five cents more upon the base rate of pay and a cost of living adjustment but had settled for twenty-two cents over the first year with few signs of resistance. In the first union meeting to discuss the contract, forty-nine of fifty members voted for endorsement; however, the second meeting, at which Walker was present, was more contentious. She claimed that Russell labeled her "cock-eyed" and "an agitator who wanted to strike just to be striking." By the end of the meeting, fourteen voted against the contract, and only three voted in favor of it. Providing an "inside view" of the contract-making process, Walker explained in the newsletter that "we were sold-out by our union leadership and two people in particular hold the main responsibility for this—John Russell and Pete Leake," the union's business agent. "It's funny how they happen to be the only two people who don't have to work for our lousey wages." Did Russell and Leake do all they could have? "The negotiations were a game—a real joke. The whole deal could have been wrapped up in an hour—but that wouldn't have looked good. It had to look like each side was 'bargaining hard'—sweating it out right up to the deadline."[54]

In more than one article, Walker framed work at Gold Kist within the broader dynamics of gendered and racialized economic inequities. Over the past year, "workers have been speeded up and laid off," while "our wage increases (and more) have been lost to inflation."[55] After reporting that Gold Kist placed 266 in the Fortune 500 for 1974, she pointed out that the five hundred companies accounted for 79 percent of all profits in the United States at the time, adding that "Gold Kist is hanging right in there," with $572,982,000 in sales. She then compared Gold Kist workers' situation with that of another plant everyone was familiar with. "Right above Gold Kist on the list is Liggett & Myers (#264) with $582,797,000 in sales. Practically the same size and yet the lowest paid worker at the Durham L&M plant makes more than the highest paid worker at our plant!"[56] Early WAM newsletters also situated Gold Kist in the context of the state economy: "At Gold Kist our wages are way behind those of other union workers in North Carolina; and North Carolina workers have the lowest wages in the country."[57]

"They thought the victory had been won by pure virtue of getting it organized," Walker asserted forty years later, describing her conflict with Local 525 leadership. Russell and Leake were the "upper management of the union," she argued, "and they were proud of all the unions they had." Nevertheless, "it wasn't a thriving, living thing where you continued to build a base with these people and fight for more at all. It was: 'it's done, we're just going to keep nurturing this thing along and keeping it alive.' That's where the differences were," she said.[58]

Though Laura Green had an uneasy history with Russell and Leake herself, as 1974 proceeded into 1975, she regarded the growing popularity of Walker's newsletters with increased concern. Green remained the elected chief steward and was also a killer on the shop floor, slicing the necks of chickens that had been missed by the mechanical knife. "I just always remember her coming out with this thing wrapped around her head and a garbage bag on her splattered with blood," Walker observed.[59]

Green repeatedly wrote to and called the Asheville office requesting instruction. "If you have any thing to say what we should do or say you can let me know," she wrote in December 1974. "She's trying to get our people to join W.A.M.," she added.[60] A month or so later, Green's level of agitation had clearly increased. In late January 1975 she left a message for Russell that was marked "Urgent," underlined twice in red ink by whoever received the call. "Laura Green called 1/23/75 said it is imperative you call her at home ... or at the Gold Kist plant, she says Karen Walker is tearing up the union," the message explained. "I don't know where our union is going if something isn't done about this," she lamented.[61]

Even as Karen Walker continued to photocopy and widely distribute homemade radical newsletters on blue, pink, and yellow paper, Gold Kist did not fire her but in 1975 moved her to the position of drawhand, the burdensome job of removing the bird's viscera. Reaching into the chicken, "you have to be between the rib cage and the gut and reach all the way down to the very neck of the bird where between your fingers you get the esophagus," Walker described, illustrating the movement with an awkward downward twisting motion. There is then a technique for pulling the viscera out. In order to do so, "you can't break the esophagus. You have to stretch the esophagus and pull all of the guts out, and they're splayed over the side of the chicken." Still, some chicken components ended their lives as projectile weapons. "We had great gall bladder fights," Walker recalled.[62]

The job was both delicate and physically grueling. "I'd go home and soak my hands," she said. "My hands were so in pain from doing this, and you'd do both, you had to be good at both hands eventually or else you'd kill yourself." Some drawhands would really take pride in their mastery of this difficult job and offer to cover coworkers' bathroom breaks without a substitute. "Some of the younger women would say 'I got yours, just go,' and so they'd pull every chicken," rather than the usual procedure, which was to pull every other one. "I always thought, you're fools. You're going to kill yourself. This feels good, you're really good at it, but there's going to be a price to pay for this."[63]

A 1989 study conducted by OSHA and the Georgia Institute of Technology into the ergonomics and industrial hygiene at two undisclosed poultry plants validated Walker's experiences and laid bare the growing legacy of physical damage borne by poultry workers. "Employees who draw and present the viscera ('draw hands') in the Evisceration Department have the highest upper-extremity discomfort level and every person interviewed from this job reported frequent pain and numbness in the hands at night," the report read.[64] Late in 1975 Gold Kist introduced a new machine that simplified the drawing process, but it was also designed to increase the speed of production, leading the union's business agent to report to Russell that "most complained that it was too fast and that they could not keep up with the machine."[65]

By 1977, Gold Kist was finally ready to move against Walker's newsletters, some of which had become more inflammatory than they were strategic. On March 31 she was issued an official warning from the personnel division. "You have engaged in efforts to inspire or incite other employees to commit an act of assault involving Mr. John Russell, President of Local Union #525, by your telling them that, quote, 'we need to put our heels where they will do the most good—RIGHT ON HIS ASS—the next time he shows his face at Gold Kist,' end quote." The company's warning continued. "Mr. Russell has a contractual right to visit or be in our facility as an authorized representative of the Union," Walker was instructed. "You are not to engage in such acts as encouraging assault on visitors to our plant in the future," the notice read.[66] Walker was finally dismissed on June 29, 1978.[67] What was the final straw? It was not dramatic, but it concerned, as usual, the distribution of leaflets. Walker recalled, "They said if you pass it out one more time you'll be fired, and of course I passed it out again, but I kind of knew I was going to be fired."[68]

Even though Green had questioned Walker's renegade campaign, there were areas in which she and others maintained doubts about the resolution of the Asheville office, doubts that would be articulated as the union approached the next round of contract negotiations, which were set for 1978. The membership of the union had evolved too. Gold Kist had introduced a second later shift in January 1976 to meet the growing demand for poultry products. Older workers largely opted to exercise their seniority and remain on the early shift, making way for a younger but still predominantly African American workforce in the evenings. Questions relating to the evening shift were among the bones of contention between union members in Durham and John Russell's leadership.

In April 1978 a group of more than thirty union members, including all of the elected departmental stewards, signed a letter authored by secretary Barbara Green to the AMC's international president in Chicago, Harry Poole, requesting the dispatch of an outside contract negotiator and an investigation of Local 525. Highlighting their continued efforts to sign up members and the unit's impressive rate of dues payers, the workers stated, "We know that our Business Agent, Pete Leake, and our President, John Russell, are not servicing our unit and are not representing us fairly. We have lost confidence that they will bargain for us in good faith." Twice that year Leake had called meetings for union members and then failed to attend. "We stood out in the street for close to an hour waiting for Pete to show up with the key to the union hall. We then gave up and went home."[69]

Workers similarly felt betrayed by negotiations in 1975 concerning the evening shift. "Instead of negotiating a second shift premium pay at that time, Russell agreed with the Company 'that should a second shift be created, premium pay for second shift would be discussed.'" Barbara Green continued: "Russell has been a negotiator for too long not to know that a 'discussion' over such a benefit gave us no power to win anything." The company had decided against it, "so for two and a half years, Gold Kist is one of the only plants around, both unionized and non-unionized, that does not pay its second shift a premium rate." In spite of insisting that "we will not be satisfied with your writing a letter or making a phone call to John Russell to ask him about the situation," there is no evidence that the international responded to the complaint in any form.[70]

Faced with the growing strength of powerful poultry operators such as Gold Kist and a workforce facing a nearly 8 percent rate of inflation, Local 525 leadership had become untethered from many of its most active members, underestimating their growing alienation. In July 1978 the contract negotiating committee agreed to a pay increase of eighty-five cents per hour to be implemented over the next three years and improvements in medical, maternity, and surgical benefits, described by Russell as "excellent improvements in insurance."[71] While some considered eighty-five cents to be acceptable, there was a growing consensus that nine days of paid leave every year were insufficient, and the complete absence of paid sick days, even for workers injured at work, was even more unacceptable. Gold Kist's representatives rejected the idea, claiming that any allowance for sick leave would inevitably be misused and amounted to an extension to the nine days that the company already provided. At a union meeting in late July, Local 525 members decided this was the hill on which they intended to make a stand, rejecting the contract and then voting to strike by a margin of 109 to 55.[72]

In a letter to the international, Russell explained that while the strike mood had been building, it "could have still been avoided if there hadn't been an unprecedented gang up of Progressive Labor Party members, Maoists, Revolutionary Socialist Youth, Commission Against Racism (CAR), TUEL's, TILIS, Communist Workers (M-L), League for Peace and Democracy, Revolutionary Workers Party and several other smaller groups aligned with the ultra left. These groups have infiltrated, to one degree or other, the unions in tobacco, textile, hospital, machinery (IAM) [International Association of Machinists and Aerospace Workers], paper, American Federation of State, County and Municipal Workers and probably a few more I don't know about." In Russell's eyes, this illegitimate collection, uncharacteristically unified in their purpose, if we believe his assertion, had misled members of Local 525. "They couldn't have got this over if there hadn't been a full mobilization for the meeting on the second shift and less than decent mobilization on the first shift," he wrote. "The second shift is a hotbed of young blacks recently hired by the Company. The first shift was older and greater seniority people, who did not turn out for the meeting because they thought acceptance was a foregone conclusion."[73]

Once the strike vote had taken place, union leadership established a strike committee "in order to get more good people in key positions" and "take the strike away from the PLP and their followers."[74] Members of Local 525 in Durham, unaccustomed as they were to industrial action, established highly effective pickets in the final week of July, reducing a plant that typically processed 120,000 birds per day down to no more than a truckload.[75] "All night long last night, some of the best fighters, men and women, did just that," wrote Karen Walker, present at the picket in spite of her termination from the company. "They kept a clean-up crew from coming in time after time. These strikers did not 'cool it' and were not 'nice.' They marched together in large numbers and *did not back down* even when the cops started to put on riot gear and threatened to arrest them!"[76] Under pressure from the company and warned that they would lose their medical coverage, union members voted to remain on strike a week later.

On August 1 Gold Kist purchased an old yellow school bus, which it used to transport replacement workers through the picket line, using the company's nearby warehouse as a rendezvous point. Not surprisingly, the bus quickly became a target for the ire of striking workers, and the rendezvous point for nonstrikers was moved from a warehouse adjacent to the plant to the Northgate Shopping Center. Concerned about the number of bricks and stones that seemed to consistently sail in the bus's direction, Gold Kist refitted the vehicle, adding a CB radio, lining the inside windows with canvas, and mounting a half-inch of chicken wire around the windshield and side windows surrounding the driver.[77]

As a series of vehicles attempted to gain entrance to the plant on August 8, they were met with growing levels of aggressive opposition from a picket that was equipped with an assortment of bats, clubs, pipes, chains, and other improvised weapons.[78] When manager James Perdue drove toward the main gate in a blue Chevy van carrying a supervisor and a job applicant, he was sighted by Joann Martin, who moved to obstruct the gate. There were conflicting accounts of what happened next: supervisor Carl Lowery asserted that she stepped aside and punched the driver's window; Martin claimed that Perdue hit the gas, and she narrowly escaped, losing her balance and accidentally striking the vehicle with a flailing arm; and Robert W. Leiner, the NLRB judge later evaluating Martin's dismissal, concluded that "the chicken game" had taken place but was unwilling to absolve either side from some measure of responsibility.[79] When nonstriker Betty Labron drove her car through the main gate, Thelma Brockington was alleged to have attempted to open the car door, and when she found the door locked, she kicked at the vehicle in frustration and uttered, "We know who you are. We'll get you tonight." Brockington, like Martin, was fired but rebutted the allegations, claiming that she had a broken toe and had been wearing slippers that day and that an abscess in her groin prohibited her from lifting her leg and reduced her to a limp.[80] A delivery driver of live haul chickens from nearby Pittsboro said that when he drove up there were "eight or ten people who were standing with rocks or bricks," and he identified another worker, Dreama Glover, who threw a "half brick or rock at the truck."[81] A "new employee" named Larry Joyner, on probation after having recently pleaded guilty to "misdemeanor larceny," claimed that he "had had his automobile hit by rocks when coming through the main entrance on Latta Street."[82]

The greatest animus, as ever, was reserved for the school bus, which was subject to a more severe barrage of rocks and bricks than on prior occasions. Like Martin and Brockington, some workers were reticent to relive the event. The discharged Geneva Poole asserted that she had only thrown two small rocks at the bus and was unsure if they had even hit the large yellow target.[83] Percy Hester and Dreama Glover were charged as being among the eight to ten who threw rocks at the bus. "To my right, I saw Percy Hester throw a brick and the window fell—glass was falling. As we turned the corner, Karen Walker threw a bottle in the right front windshield," swore Annie Mae MacLeod, a fourteen-year employee and manager of the night cafeteria who refused to strike.[84] MacLeod, perhaps the strike's most vocal opponent, told the NLRB's general counsel that Hester threatened that "if I went back to work . . . he was going to kick my black ass, fuck up my car and blow up my house."[85]

At times, MacLeod proved to be a problematic witness, despite her central location as a passenger on the school bus. She identified Annie Herring, described by Judge Leiner as "a rather elderly lady," as one of the rock throwers, disregarding her protestations that she was eighty-five feet away from the bus. Further scrutiny revealed a history of bad blood between the two women dating back to 1963, when Herring had gone out with MacLeod's husband. Charges against Herring were dismissed, and she was ultimately reinstated at the plant.[86]

After Guy Matthews, the driver of the school bus, had navigated August 8's particularly vituperative volley of projectiles as he left with sixteen nonstriking employees, MacLeod noted that they were being followed by an orange Buick with a distinctive white roof. They recognized it as the car of Walter Burroughs, a worker at the plant who was on strike. Having dropped off the sixteen, Matthews found Burroughs's car parked and deliberately obstructing the exit as he attempted to leave through the north gate. Matthews maneuvered around the Buick, which then pursued him as he headed out on the highway. Pulling up alongside the moving bus, one of the passengers in Burroughs's car, which included his wife, Anza Burroughs, and coworkers Anthony Nesmith and Lawrence Fulton, hurled a glass bottle through the passenger door of the bus, breaking one of the panes. As the two vehicles reached a stoplight and stood next to each other, Burroughs leaned out of the window and threatened, "I'm going to get your white motherfucking ass," according to Matthews. At a subsequent stoplight, close to the warehouse, Fulton and Nesmith climbed out of the car and started approaching the bus, which was once again obstructed by Burroughs's stationary vehicle. Matthews escaped this predicament by driving into the rear end of the Buick, then cutting around it to the left and running the red light, injuring Anza Burroughs in the process. Though the Burroughs party claimed not to have been following the bus, Fulton and Nesmith maintaining that they were there to help Walter wash his car, an NLRB judge later rejected their testimony on the grounds that the appearance of the police merely seconds after the accident to arrest Burroughs lent credibility to Annie Mae MacLeod's assertion that she had summoned them from a telephone at the north gate. Though a charge of disorderly conduct leveled at Walter Burroughs was later dismissed in court, both he and Anza, as well as Anthony Nesmith, were all subsequently discharged from Gold Kist.[87]

This marked the height of the unrest at Gold Kist in Durham. Following around twenty arrests and an increased police presence of around seventy officers the following day, Russell drafted in a trio of veteran organizers, including the highly respected retiree Cornelius Simmons, to manage the picket lines and disseminate the local's message. When a group of workers started to picket a nearby Kentucky Fried Chicken restaurant, the company immediately filed a secondary boycott charge, which Russell claimed he persuaded Gold Kist's attorney to withdraw.[88] Returning to negotiations in the third week of the strike, Russell wrote to the international, "We drove the outsiders off the picket line we made the pickets give up their clubs, bats, pipes, chains and other weapons they had carried at the instigation of their allies."[89] With Gold Kist in little mood to provide concessions and offering a reward of $2,500 "for information leading to the arrest and conviction of persons committing unlawful acts (such as firing shot gun blasts into employees [sic] homes, automobiles, or throwing bricks into employees homes) against Gold Kist employees & their property," Russell persuaded company management to reissue their original contract offer, an agreement that members would finally consent to, with nothing to show for their month-long efforts.[90]

Great resolve had been required to create a union presence in the food processing and retail sectors of North Carolina and achieve contracts that provided workers with a measure of job security while offering a package of modest benefits not always available in nonunion facilities. Yet when Local 525 operated as the representative of the workforce at a single facility of a large national operator, the potential leverage that it could exercise was limited at best. By the late 1970s, John Russell had developed comfortable working relationships with management in Durham and routinized the collective bargaining process, leaving him increasingly at odds with a discontented workforce that aspired to more than what was on offer.

As the 1970s transitioned into the 1980s and companies more aggressively sought to wrest away the vestiges of remaining union power in the meat and poultry sectors, scenes of industrial conflict akin to Durham in 1978 would fade into the past. Though the plant in Durham remained open until 1989, in an era of deregulation and limited government oversight, poultrymen in North Carolina and across the southern states attempted to consolidate their advantage, expand, and increase the speed of their operations in order to claim their stake in the growing market for fast-food chicken.

A Signature Disaster

On September 3, 1991, a hydraulic fuel cable came unleashed at Imperial Food Products in Hamlet, North Carolina, creating an acrid blaze that cost the lives of twenty-five workers, mostly from smoke inhalation, as padlocked fire escapes prohibited an orderly evacuation. A makeshift plant situated in a former ice cream factory, Imperial was situated in a once-noteworthy railroad town that had experienced no growth in household income during the decade of the 1980s and in which 8 percent of adults were out of work.[91] The victims, ten of whom were white and fifteen African American, seven men and eighteen women, were parents to a total of fifty children. "I lost a cousin, Elaine Ratliff," observed Ada Blanchard, a survivor of the fire and a lifelong resident of the small town. "Rose Wilkins, Bertha Jarrell, I mean basically all of them, Gail Campbell had a little boy Tony, just started to kindergarten, and Gail didn't live to see him get into first grade. Elaine had two small ones. . . . Margaret Banks had two small ones."[92]

Emmett Roe's Imperial Foods was one of many smaller companies that had taken aggressive steps to obtain a cut of the action in the growing poultry market of the 1980s. "These newer further-processing firms, *entrepreneurs*, unencumbered by the politics, size and weight of a large food organization, back up their dream with all of their resources," explained William A. Haffert in *Broiler Industry* in 1985. "Most large food companies, if one were to be honest, are a bit staid, lots of capital," he added. The insurgents were different, though. "They mortgage their houses to fulfill that dream." In entering the poultry business, they sought to be the agents of a revolution within the industry, Haffert argued, a transformation toward further processed chicken where "demand pull" was replacing "commodity push" as the defining force.[93]

Besides the plant in Hamlet, Roe had purchased Haverpride Farms in Birmingham, Alabama, in 1988, followed by an additional facility in Cumming, Georgia, shortly thereafter. The company's growth was buoyed through the mid-1980s as a contractor to Shoney's, a family restaurant chain that had cautiously but methodically expanded from 1,084 facilities in 1984 to over 1,600 by 1990, building largely through cash flow rather than loans.[94] "They were a very, very important supplier," Shoney's vice president responsible for purchasing said of Imperial in 1991.[95] Roe had found an ideal partner in the restaurant business, yet a fire in the Cumming plant on Christmas Day 1989 was followed by a legal dispute when another of the firm's retail clients, Lyle Farms, started receiving complaints about the quality of the nuggets coming out of the Birmingham operation. "Some contain soy protein isolate to lower cost, depending upon customer requests," a 1984 profile of the company had read.[96] A former employee had maligned the ingredients further. "I've seen the meat that's gone in it. I've smelled it. And I wouldn't feed it to my dog," they observed.[97]

Already in debt to its fresh poultry supplier, Imperial lost the Lyle Farms contract and by 1990 couldn't cover a $4,000 debt to the power company. It closed Haverpride, dismissing all 115 workers without notice. When it emerged that the company had stopped paying its workers' health-care benefits months earlier but had continued to withhold the money from paychecks, Roe was sued by his former employees in the Birmingham District Court and instructed to issue them $250,000 in severance pay.[98] Sinking in a sea of red ink, Roe cranked up production in Cumming and Hamlet, creating a strain on the sewage systems of the two small towns. "Your facilities' wastewater discharge has caused more problems for the City of Cumming's treatment process than all others combined, both industrial and domestic," wrote the city's sanitation engineer.[99] In Hamlet the authorities twice threatened to cut off water services to the plant, effectively closing it down, if it could not bring its sewage output in line with city limits.[100]

In the wake of the 1991 fire, business leaders quickly distanced themselves from the Roes, Emmett and his son Brad, who worked as a manager within the plant. "Stating it as clearly as possible, Imperial Foods was a 'rotten egg' or a 'bad apple,'" said Phillip Kirk, the president of North Carolina Citizens for Business and Industry.[101] The president of the National Broiler Council wrote an op-ed for the *Washington Post* asserting that "the industry as a whole should not be held accountable for Imperial's disregard for worker safety," while Monroe poultryman Clayton Loflin wrote to the *Raleigh News & Observer* to request that the newspaper stop referring to Imperial as a "poultry processing plant," given that the company "bought, cooked and resold poultry products." Loflin went on: "It could just as easily have been cooking fish or french fries when the tragedy happened. A more accurate description of Imperial Food Products would be 'food processor' or 'wholesale restaurant.'"[102]

While there were elements of danger and disregard across the poultry industry, Imperial was outstandingly haphazard in its day-to-day practices. Workers who found their way to Roe's doors often did so because the five dollars per hour offered was marginally more than the few other options in the area. The 1980s had not been kind to Richmond County; a workforce of fifteen hundred at the CSX Transportation freight yard had been reduced to about five hundred.[103] In 1990 the North Carolina Radioactive Waste Management Authority proposed Richmond as a possible site for cooling pools to situate spent fuel rods, but the county rallied and rejected the idea of a nuclear waste dump.[104] "I went to the unemployment office, all I got was Imperial," remembered Ada Blanchard. "I couldn't stand the smell of chicken, that fresh chicken and so that made me sick on the stomach, to smell that horrible smell was just terrible and I didn't think I was gonna make it. I was wanting to give up on it but my mother told me not to, she said 'Ada, you can do it, you can handle it,' and I had to handle it for my children if I could feed them," she added. Blanchard persisted in the job.[105]

Scrutiny of potential hires was minimal, and so was the training. "If the references looked good and the dates were correct and all, you know, if everything jibed, so to speak, I wouldn't go into so much reference checking as I normally would with somebody else," one of the front office staff explained.[106] For a stretch of time, new workers would be handed formal written guidelines outlining their employment, "until our copier broke down," one interviewee recalled. Beyond establishing that open-toed shoes and jewelry were prohibited and a few other commonsense instructions, there was no systematic training program pertaining to employee health and safety. "It was not under my job description," observed the staff member responsible for the company orientation.[107]

"The first day on the job," one line worker explained to state investigators, "I was never given any instructions on what to do in the event of a fire or an emergency. No fire drills were held and I was not given any instructions on how to use a fire extinguisher." She continued: "I had worked at places before that I had been shown what to do . . . every other place (but Imperial)."[108] It was assumed that if a fire started, someone from "the supervision or lead guys or maintenance" would handle the source while the line workers escaped.[109]

While unquestionably negligent, managerial staff at Imperial found health and safety regulations difficult to comprehend and effectively implement. There was an OSHA poster on the employee bulletin board, and one of the managers wrote to the state Department of Labor requesting a copy of the code, "just to have in case something came up . . . that I could look in it." The booklet arrived, but it was never used, consigned to a desk drawer. "[Of] course, looking in it, you got to have a B.A. degree to read the darn thing," investigators were told.[110] Another member of the staff found the regulations similarly confusing. "I don't think nobody is really aware of the rules or laws or anything like that," he said. "You hear so many things you've got to have. I've heard so many things: the doors got to be a certain size. You got, you know, all this crap—and nobody can give you any kind of answer."[111] While workers expressed concern for their safety, most managers, when asked, said that they had never really countenanced the possibility of a fire. "I know that may sound a little strange. It just never crossed my mind," one observed.[112]

For poultry industry leaders, the ham-handed amateurism of Imperial Foods and its inability to even operate in a manner that protected its own long-term interests brought the whole business into disrepute. In a 1992 report, the U.S. Fire Administration, an office of the Federal Emergency Management Agency, compared the Imperial fire to a similar accident at a Tyson facility in North Little Rock that had occurred just months prior, in June 1991. Unlike in Hamlet, Tyson had a fire safety director as well as safety committees that had implemented evacuation drills and trainings throughout the life of the plant. Upon realizing that a fire extinguisher would be inadequate, the Tyson worker at the cooker in question immediately signaled the alarm, and all 115 workers were evacuated within three minutes and accounted for shortly thereafter.[113]

The Mastery of the Machine

By the 1990s, poultrymen justifiably felt that they had achieved a mastery of their craft, a grand machine that could turn chicks into chicken dinners that were so easy to prepare that they could be unpackaged and eaten within minutes. Small family firms like Imperial didn't just attract negative attention to the industry that tarnished the aluminum sheen of Tyson's and Pilgrim's state-of-the-art facilities; they lacked the sophisticated aptitude of the leading players. Being a vertically integrated poultryman didn't just mean getting the birds out the door as quickly as possible: it meant investing in political allies, in research and development, in human resources, in communications and marketing professionals, and in controlling suppliers in a network of farms.

Yet while the machine served its purpose with stunning productivity and deliberateness, it was not without its flaws, creating considerable externalities both human and ecological. As the tragedy in Hamlet unfolded, the Reverend Jesse Jackson, a civil rights leader and twice presidential candidate who had grown up not too many miles away in Greenville, South Carolina, and graduated from North Carolina A&T State University in Greensboro, repeatedly visited the small town to offer comfort to family members of the departed.[114] Invoking Imperial Foods, Jackson continued to draw attention to governmental neglect of workers' safety and to regional poverty, declaring five weeks after the fire that "Hamlet is to these economic issues of workers what Selma was to the political issues of 1965."[115] In appealing to his party with a message of racial healing at the 1992 Democratic National Convention, Jackson related the experiences of women at Imperial who had told him their stories. Before a national audience he recalled one of them telling him, "I pluck ninety wings a minute, sometimes I can't bend my wrists, I catches this carpal thing." Unable to obtain medical care, a worker was ultimately crippled, fired, and called a "lazy bitch," Jackson explained. "I said 'you are not lazy, and you are not [a] bitch, and you are not alone and a change is coming.'" He concluded, "If we keep Hamlet, North Carolina in our hearts, and before our eyes, we will act to empower working people, we will protect the right to organize and to strike, we will empower workers to enforce health and safety laws" as part of "a movement for economic justice across this nation."[116]

In this short but pointed anecdote, Jackson had identified the problem at the heart of the machine. It wasn't that it was especially liable to break down or combust. Far from it. It was that the machine rarely stopped at all while still requiring the continuous attention of hundreds of workers carrying out repetitive manual tasks. Though some of these tasks were eliminated through mechanical inventions, for decades line speeds continued to increase. While poultry plants operated at a rate of around fifty birds per minute in the 1970s, they had accelerated to ninety per minute by the late 1980s.[117] The USDA, in keeping with its broader mission, consistently supported these increases based on the logic that increased production would provide a price benefit to consumers. Besides raising the chance of contamination, faster line speeds resulted in a sharp increase in the number of recorded repetitive motion injuries (RMIs), the most common of which was carpal tunnel syndrome, an intensely painful wrist injury that can linger for years and render the sufferer unable to work.[118] The number of workers receiving compensation for RMIs in North Carolina increased sharply from 145 in 1982 to 480 in 1986. As a proportion of workplace injuries, RMIs grew from 7.7 percent to 19.8 percent over the same period.[119] Data from the Bureau of Labor Statistics, generally considered to be limited by endemic underreporting of incidences, nonetheless reflected the high concentration of this type of complaint within meatpacking and poultry processing, where 480 of every 10,000 workers were estimated to be suffering from an RMI in 1986, up from 164 in 1979.[120] Naturally, the number of poultry production workers was increasing too as demand increased; nineteen thousand in 1947 had increased to fifty-five thousand by 1968 and stood at around two hundred thousand by 1994. The rate of injuries was clearly rising at a sharper rate, though, with concerned Democratic congressman Tom Lantos warning that RMIs represented "the major occupational epidemic of the 1990s."[121]

In the face of the growing problem, OSHA pursued a series of high-profile cases against meatpackers. In July 1987 an inspection at the Iowa Beef Packers (IBP) plant in Dakota City, Nebraska, led to 620 citations issued for willful violations associated with RMIs.[122] Finding a series of irregularities and a failure to record 1,038 incidents, a Labor Department assistant secretary described it as "the worst example of under-reporting injuries and illnesses to workers ever encountered by OSHA in its 16-year history," as the government proposed a record $2.6 million fine.[123] By agreeing to initiate a three-year plan designed to improve ergonomics, IBP was later able to settle for a still substantial fine of $975,000.[124] The IBP case was followed a year later with a series of citations issued against the John Morrell Company, a meatpacker in Sioux Falls, South Dakota, like Nebraska a state under federal jurisdiction. As many as 880 of 2,000 workers at Morrell had sustained some form of RMI between May 1987 and April 1988, with an average time off of one day in 180 cases that had required surgery, considerably less than the thirty to sixty days recommended by the National Institute for Occupational Safety and Health (NIOSH).[125] "Young men and women who can no longer open a jar or lift their children are the victims of Morrell's callous, concerted indifference," said UFCW president

William H. Wynn.[126] OSHA proposed another record fine of $4.33 million but settled at $990,000, with an additional $260,000 being directed to NIOSH by Morrell, a subsidiary of Cincinnati-based United Brands.[127]

Mother of three Donna Bazemore contracted carpal tunnel syndrome working on poultry evisceration and trimming lines and won a high-profile but ultimately meager $1,200 workers' compensation claim against Perdue Farms. "Every time I'd say 'my hand hurts,' they'd give me three or four pills," she told *Southern Exposure* in 1989. "I knew what an Advil was. But these other ones had no name on them. And it got to the point that I was happy to go to the nurse's station to get piped up so I could do this work and totally disregard the pain. I didn't know what I was taking." Eventually, Bazemore could no longer squeeze her hands or zip her pants. "When I got to work, I'd get my hand bandaged," she explained. "You almost had to stand in line and wait to get into the nurse's station to wrap your hands with Ace bandages. Some women would take big bundles home and wrap their hands on the way to work. Some would buy them from stores. There are very, very few people that I know on the eviscerating line that don't have a problem with their hands," Bazemore observed.[128]

Investigations also took place in poultry. A 1990 NIOSH review of Perdue Farms plants in Lewiston and Robersonville, North Carolina, reached similarly troubling findings among both workforces, 90 percent of whom were Black and the great majority of whom were women. Operating with blunted scissors and knives and poor medical treatment, 36 percent of 174 respondents at Lewiston, a plant of 2,600, and 20 percent of 120 respondents at Robersonville, employing 550, displayed a litany of injuries, including carpal tunnel syndrome; tendonitis of the wrist, fingers, and rotator cuff; and tension neck syndrome.[129] Though Perdue had implemented some rotation of employees among tasks, a popular company proposal when faced with a proliferation of injuries, NIOSH asserted that this scheme was largely ineffective, given that most rotations were from one high-intensity position to another that was similarly demanding.[130]

The seriousness of this report was such that Perdue agreed with the North Carolina labor commissioner to institute a remedial program to improve its ergonomic practices, yet the industry as a whole would not follow suit.[131] Rather than slowing line speeds, poultrymen resolved to suppress the number of complaints, discouraging workers from seeking outside medical care and, similar to Donna Bazemore's experience, administering Bengay, bandages, and aspirin to injured workers through on-site nurses. Faced with growing concern that RMIs were affecting not just meat cutters but also supermarket cashiers, telephone operators, and the growing legion of keyboard-bound office employees, OSHA drafted new rules in June 1994 compelling employers to evaluate their ergonomic practices based on workers' compensation claims and injury logs. The rules' detractors, like the National Association of Manufacturers, which described them as potentially "the most expensive regulation ever to hit business," found newly empowered allies in the Republican majority that assumed control of the House of Representatives in 1995.[132] The Labor Department faced a unified and well-funded opposition spearheaded by Whip Tom DeLay, a former Houston exterminator who cited an EPA ban on carcinogenic chemicals that he used to purge fire ants as formative in his decision to enter politics.[133] Paring down the new rules in March so that they would only affect twenty-one million workers rather than the ninety-six million covered in the original proposal, OSHA ultimately abandoned new ergonomic standards entirely in June 1995 as DeLay threatened to cut $3.5 million from the agency's budget, the estimated cost of the new program.[134]

As a former governor of Arkansas, Bill Clinton inevitably had to do business with Don Tyson, one of the state's largest employers and a leading contributor to local Democratic candidates.[135] Whether this long-standing relationship had a bearing in the Clinton administration's unwillingness to expend political capital on new ergonomics rules is hard to say, but with a Republican Congress that was ideologically opposed to any expansion in the Department of Labor's regulatory powers, the poultry industry faced few obstructions in its continued aggressive expansion. As the African American and white populations of rural southern towns continued to erode during the later twentieth century, the industry met its growing labor needs through the establishment of extended networks of Latin American migrant workers, themselves often similarly displaced from rural work by the industrialization of agriculture in their native countries.[136] The development of migrant networks to the United States is the subject of a substantial and rich body of literature, and scholars such as Steve Striffler, Leon Fink, and Kathleen Schwartzman have explored the centrality of migrant workers within the poultry business in considerable detail, highlighting the unique vulnerabilities that these workers faced at the hands of recalcitrant employers.[137] The mobility of migrant populations and the ability of employers to draw upon extended transnational networks within Latin American communities were essential to the ongoing viability of the rural industrial model of meat and poultry production that had fully developed by the century's end. Yet migrant workers' very legitimate concerns about the potential repercussions that they could face should they raise objections to the danger and pace of work ultimately contributed to the code of silence mandated by employers and the growing legacy of physical harm and disability that resulted from extended periods of production line work within the poultry industry.

No End of the Line

In spite of the efforts of survivors, activists, and even Jesse Jackson, the disaster in Hamlet did not have the same reverberating impact upon the political psyche as the historic Triangle Shirtwaist Factory fire eighty years prior, when nearly 150 garment workers perished in Manhattan's Greenwich Village. Compared to the horrifying spectacle of young women jumping from windows eight, nine, or ten stories high, the small-town poverty of the U.S. poultry workforce was more easily set out of sight and out of mind, as it was designed to be.[138] If rural African American women experienced estrangement from the locus of state or even national politics, the demographic changes within the country's slaughterhouses in the decades that preceded Hamlet only exacerbated the marginalization of the poultry workforce. Central and South American migrants, some with documentation and others without, would exchange one form of rural poverty for another, often inhabiting makeshift housing and trailer parks and existing on both the geographical and political margins of the communities in which they were situated.[139] Carrie Johnson and Laura Green were part of workforces that at times had divided attitudes toward management and unionization, yet they shared many cultural, social, and historical experiences with their coworkers that formed a basis for periodic shop floor organization and resistance. Increasingly, multinational workforces with divergent linguistic backgrounds shared fewer commonalities with one another and with a remaining minority of U.S.-born workers, making worker organizing ever more complicated as the presence of labor unions waned across the meat and poultry sectors.

Crucially, in most cases poultry companies selected the geography upon which they would fight their battles, over time deliberately avoiding cities such as Durham and Richmond where successful union campaigns had taken place. This significant home field advantage was compounded by a deliberately limited regulatory framework and the probusiness political approach of southern states. For poultry producers, the costs of working outside the law, whether this meant employing unfair labor practices against union campaigns, neglecting occupational safety and health or environmental regulations, or purposefully recruiting vulnerable immigrant populations, could be factored into spreadsheets as merely the cost of doing business. The penalties that resulted from this cost-benefit approach to federal and state laws were

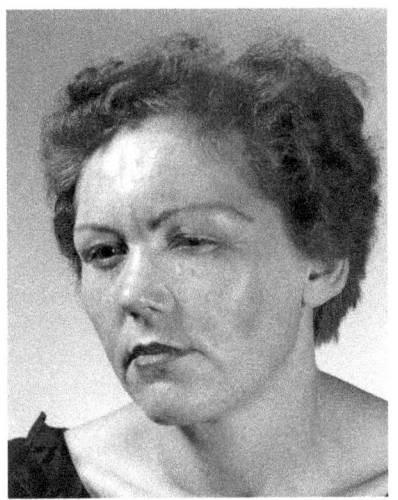

IMAGE 8. When Jennie Joines attempted to form a union at Holly Farms' facility in Wilkesboro, North Carolina, in 1957 she was attacked by two coworkers in the company parking lot. "The doctor told me he thought I had been hit with something other than a fist. He had x-rays taken and fractured bones were found," Joines recalled. Amalgamated Meat Cutters and Butcher Workmen of North America, Local 525 (Asheville, N.C.), Records, Southern Labor Archives, Georgia State University.

infrequent and modest. There was always someone from somewhere in the world prepared to try their hand on the poultry line. Sixty years after Carrie Johnson, Jennie Joines, and Grace Gryder had raised their voices and then their fists in defense of their rights at Holly Farms, the obstacles faced by poultry workers remained as consistently intractable as they'd ever been.

CHAPTER 4

The Business of Feeding People

In the second half of the twentieth century, the architecture of American dining was transformed as rising incomes, suburbanization, and automobility met a desire for greater convenience and a lightening of household chores. A heavily subsidized scientific farming sector, underwritten by expansive and capitalized agribusinesses, formed a close relationship with an increasingly powerful restaurant industry. Hand in hand, their influence permeated American domestic living, their vibrant and evocative images and designs splashed across magazines and billboards, their narratives of predictable comfort and mild stimulation spoken and sung as jingles on radio and television. McDonald's was to restaurants what Ford had been to motor cars and Levitt homes had been to housing, a democratic and respectable serving that was available to most, a fair reward for a hard-earned dollar. But McDonald's represented more than a product. It represented both a system and a model of production that was imitated at home and exported overseas. Alongside its partners in agribusiness, the company created a continental infrastructure of supply chains, concentrated animal feeding operations, and brick-and-mortar restaurants to deliver meals to Americans at their convenience. It was a system fueled primarily by what seemed for years like an unending demand for beef burgers served with fried potatoes.

Yet just as the rudimentary Model T eventually faded from favor, the limitations of Richard and Maurice McDonald's original offerings would, over time, become equally apparent, and consumers would seek alternatives. By the 1970s, many diners were embracing variations on the original theme of McDonald's, notably, Wendy's Old-Fashioned Hamburgers, created by Dave Thomas. Some consumers would turn to other fast service alternatives such as Pizza Hut and Domino's Pizza. But by the 1980s, there were new factors at play that dramatically disrupted the profit margins and the menus of the giant fast-food chains. Spiraling beef prices combined with a growing awareness that there were drawbacks associated with a heavily beef-based diet for an increasingly sedentary and office-bound population. Rising concerns about obesity and a growing vogue for personal fitness training as both an antidote and a lifestyle choice placed new demands on the restaurant industry as some consumers called into question the healthfulness of traditional fast-food offerings.

As body-conscious diners indicated a preference for menu diversity and lighter meals, the restaurant industry turned its attention to poultry, the great emerging force in American agribusiness. An industry that was decades in the making was poised and ready to offer chicken-based alternatives on the grand scale required to meet the needs of nationwide chains such as McDonald's, Wendy's, and Burger King. The restaurant industry's megalithic infrastructure of quick service food delivery, designed for the provision of beef, embraced a new partner and became a catalyst in the extraordinary growth of chicken as the central feature in the American diet. While fried chicken outlets generated increased business in buckets of legs and wings, the growth of fast-food poultry was coupled to the growing popularity of finger foods and easy home preparation. It was within this context that the products of Robert Baker's research would reach their zenith, as the Chicken McNugget, based on his earlier notion of chicken cubes, emerged as the fast-food success story of the 1980s. Debuted at McDonald's in 1983, these amazingly cost-effective offerings of further processed chicken represented an unexpected boon to both poultry companies and restaurants, spawning almost instant imitations for both competing outlets and the domestic market in frozen foods. Yet consumers' evolving demands were varied and often contradictory, able to maintain multiple conflicting ideas simultaneously. Fitness clubs and home workout equipment, casual sportswear and diet sodas were embraced by Americans in the 1980s and accompanied a growing interest in healthy eating, but the most popular chicken dishes often proved to be those with the most limited health benefits. At the same time, chain restaurants consistently found that when they increased portion sizes and reduced prices, sales invariably increased. By the decade's end, further processed chicken had found a place on the menu in the largest chain restaurants under the guise of a lighter, leaner alternative to beef, but as a central feature in an arms race of low-cost value meals, a contest initiated by Wendy's but brought to its culmination by PepsiCo, the prospective health benefits of fast-food poultry would become increasingly elusive.

The Infrastructure of American Dining

Dave Thomas was not new to the restaurant industry when he opened his first Wendy's in Columbus, Ohio, in 1969. An army chef during the Korean War, Thomas was discharged in 1953 and returned to his prior job cooking in a Hobby House restaurant in Fort Wayne, Indiana. He grilled ribs, fried chicken, and served them with potato salads, pickles, onions, and rye bread. Sometimes he cooked a ten-ounce T-bone steak for a more indulgent customer. It was in this environment that the business-minded chef observed the successes and shortcomings of a busy diner and came to understand some of the challenges associated with the quickly evolving restaurant industry. Some customers would ask for bread rolls instead of rye bread. Seeking to please diners, the owner would make rolls available. If bread rolls proved to be popular, then the owner concluded that they may as well be a permanent feature on the menu.[1] With every additional item the inventory and preparation of meals became more complicated.

The prevailing wisdom up to that point had been that customers wanted choices. It had worked wonders for Henry J. Heinz, his company slogan of "57 Varieties" inspired by an advertisement for "twenty-one varieties of shoe" that he had observed on an elevated train in New York.[2] Heinz had exceeded fifty-seven varieties in the 1930s, and his company became an international purveyor of soups, condiments, and canned vegetables. In the postwar period of rising affluence, some felt that the way to win consumers' dollars and maintain their attention was to offer a diverse array of options. Thomas's subsequent manager at the Hobby House Ranch and Barbeque in Evansville, Indiana, certainly thought so, and the menu grew longer. But as Thomas became ever more aware, lengthier menus made kitchen operations more convoluted. The variety "killed our focus," he wrote.[3]

An extensive menu was expected in full-service restaurants, but by the 1950s many Americans' eating habits were shifting. One merely had to look at the changing landscape, defined as it was by highways. Automobiles users, for whom travel times had been greatly abbreviated, increasingly expected speedier service at restaurants too. A fast turnover of customers was not just helpful; it was at a premium, a defining feature of the rapidly expanding postwar restaurant industry. Fewer items quickly dished up appeared to Thomas more profitable and efficient than a panoply of different meals delivered in an untimely fashion. Make only a few items, but make them well. Finding his way in California, Glen Bell, the founder of Taco Bell, would agree. "Don't sell everything your customers ask for," he said. "Decide what you're going to sell, then make it the best it can be."[4]

This was not the only area in which the operation could be made more efficient. Kitchens could be further streamlined if consumers would accept disposable dishes and napkins and agree to eat with their hands rather than knives and forks. Ray Kroc, the company president at McDonald's, shared some of the same insights. By the time Thomas opened his first restaurant, McDonald's was already the biggest fast-food chain in the United States. Not only was there a restaurant in every state, but by 1970 there were fifteen hundred outlets across the nation. The number of restaurants continued to grow at a staggering pace throughout the early 1970s, at some points reaching a rate of more than one new opening every day. By 1972 there were two thousand McDonald's restaurants, by 1974 there were three thousand, and by 1976 there were four thousand. As Kroc continued to branch out into international markets, he quadrupled the number of restaurants to six thousand by 1980.[5] Thomas was entering into a competitive market with explosive growth potential but clear leaders, McDonald's, KFC, Dairy Queen, and Burger King already accounting for almost 40 percent of U.S. restaurants.[6]

Like the entrepreneurs behind other fast-food chains, Thomas developed an easily identifiable aesthetic. "We put a lot of effort into designing a building that reflected the 'old-fashioned' theme while retaining modern functionality," he said.[7] It included "tables with four not particularly comfortable chairs around them" so that visitors would not stay for too long. Launching in 1969 in a period of political turmoil and at the tail end of the civil rights movement, Thomas's restaurants boasted "Old-Fashioned Hamburgers" on every sign in a font evocative of the old American West, at least in the popular imagination. An image of his red-haired and freckled eight-year-old daughter, Melinda Lou, wearing an unfashionably dated dress became the company logo. Wendy's in Columbus presented an image of simplicity and innocence as it opened six months after the bloody Battle of Hamburger Hill in South Vietnam. In branding his chain with an icon conferring the same benevolence as Ronald McDonald, Thomas demonstrated a shrewdness that would be easy to overlook, creating a nationally recognizable brand that allowed the company to draw upon high-end investors as well as the capital provided by potential franchisees.

Three years after opening the first restaurant in Columbus, Thomas began to fulfill his plan of expanding Wendy's into a national chain through a balance of company-owned and franchise-driven growth. Unlike McDonald's, which only sold licenses to franchisees to operate a restaurant at a specified address, Wendy's was willing to sell highly demanding territorial licenses that required the construction of a sizable number of restaurants within a specified region and time frame. To make this possible and to avoid some of the pitfalls associated with expansive leases and underfinanced owners faced by earlier franchise chains, the company was very selective when it came to sorting through the hundreds of applicants applying to open up a restaurant. The vice president of franchise sales, Graydon Webb, explained that they were less reluctant to contract businessmen with unproven track records and limited liquid assets. "Doctors and lawyers who want to invest money do not have the attitude and desire to do well," Webb said. Wendy's was looking for owners who would take a hands-on approach and "who can build sales." He added that, though it was not required, "many of our franchisees were self-made millionaires before they joined us."[8] The consequence of this strategy was to create a more limited pool of franchisees that owned multiple restaurants, with the ten largest owners operating over four hundred outlets in 1979.[9]

Attracting this class of franchisee helped facilitate the staggering growth of Wendy's from one restaurant in 1969 to around eighteen hundred by the end of 1979.[10] The cost of opening a Wendy's in the early 1970s averaged around $200,000 for the land, the restaurant, and its contents. By the mid-1980s, the cost had risen and could reach as much as $1 million.[11] Nevertheless, the building of fast-food restaurants was consistently and directly supported and promoted by the federal government through the Small Business Administration (SBA). Founded in 1953 during the Eisenhower administration by the Small Business Act, the SBA had a record of providing loan guarantees to many former members of the military who were attempting to open franchise operations.[12] As an agency the SBA could be the subject of political debate in determining what sort of businesses to support, as the terms of eligibility could strongly shape the interests of the pool of applicants. "The small firm contribution to innovation is widespread in such areas as instrumentation, consumer goods, and medical devices," the SBA boasted, but its issuance of loans did not really reflect this as a priority. Franchises had become eligible for both direct and guaranteed loans in the mid-sixties and since then had become consistent recipients of assistance. When relaxations were proposed for the SBA's size standards in 1981 so that smaller businesses would be able to apply, the International Franchise Association (IFA) stepped in to defend the status quo, asserting that it was "vitally interested in preserving growth opportunities for present and future franchisees." For fast-food restaurants, SBA loan guarantees were "essential to survival." What was more, the IFA saw the potential crowding of the pool by smaller companies as a threat to the rise of multiple unit operations, "which [had] allowed the franchising industry to participate in growth patterns designed to keep pace with customer demands."[13]

The independent status of franchising operations had allowed them to become major beneficiaries of SBA assistance while presenting themselves as safe investments with a very clear business model and a track record of great success.[14] Retailers of different varieties made up 30 percent of small businesses by the mid-1980s, but they made up 41 percent of SBA borrowers.[15] In the 1990s journalist Greg Critser asserted that franchise loan support had continued apace, with nearly $1 billion provided for just this purpose in 1996. Within this budget, six hundred loans were provided for fast-food franchisees, by far the largest type of franchise to benefit.[16] Restaurants had developed a clear formula for success by this point. In responding to the failure of a company that was developing an anticancer device to obtain a loan in 1995, former SBA official Jere Glover said that "if this had been a car wash or a restaurant, it would have sailed right through."[17] In spite of ever greater public health concerns over the consequences of high carbohydrate and high fat meals, the SBA, an agency subject to minimal public interest, was a key contributor in allowing restaurants like Wendy's to become a permanent fixture on highways and in strip malls.

As Thomas's operation started to pick up speed, many questioned whether the United States really needed another burger chain. Were there not enough already? Some experts argued that in the painful economic climate of the early 1970s, the market was saturated and that the major chains were going to have to take stock and be satisfied with what they had for the time being or else "pirate" business from rivals. As once-famous chains such as Victoria Station and Sambo's faltered into decline and toward ultimate bankruptcy, the onus was on franchisors to develop original concepts.[18]

In spite of these gloomy forecasts, Wendy's, Taco Bell, and Domino's were able to develop distinct and specialized niches within the market, made possible by ongoing changes in lifestyle among many Americans. The ratio of meals eaten at home to those eaten out, except for slight slowdowns in the mid-1970s and early 1990s, continued to shift in favor of the latter from 1960 to 2000. Whereas around 20 percent of meals were eaten at restaurants in 1960, this figure had reached more than 30 percent by the 1980s and stood at 40 percent by 2000.[19] As the U.S. population increased by around one hundred million people in this forty-year period and the proportion of meals eaten out doubled, the share of the total dollars spent on food increased by nearly the same proportion. In 1960 26 percent of the overall dollars that were spent on food were spent on meals outside the home. By 1970 this amounted to a third, by 1980 it was 39 percent, and by 2000 47 percent of food dollars was spent on meals at restaurants.[20]

Though Wendy's claimed to be challenging McDonald's, competition between the burger chains was not a zero-sum game. Thomas directly compared his restaurant to the market leader. "They set me up," he said. "By that I mean they gave me something to look good against." There were two things that impressed him about McDonald's, he said: "their real estate and their potatoes." But a burger that sat "sweating under a heat lamp with the ketchup and mustard already spread on it, will never be as good as one that's freshly made."[21] Thomas wanted to sell patties that were made the morning of sale, unlike McDonald's, Burger King, and Hardee's, which cooked a prepared product from frozen.

Besides making a burger that was customizable with a combination of different condiments, Thomas wanted his "Cadillac hamburger" to be bigger. His rivals were selling burgers that were a modest one-tenth of a pound in weight. Thomas offered quarter-pound beef patties in sixty-nine-cent burgers. If customers wanted more for their customized burger, they could have two patties in a "double" for $1.25 or three for $1.75. By ordering more food, the price per pound decreased. In the jargon of fast-food chains, this represented a competition over the provision of "value," as for more than twenty years Thomas continued to insist that the meals offered by McDonald's and Burger King were insubstantial "breadburgers."[22]

In less than a decade, Thomas had built the country's third largest burger chain from scratch and set in motion a commercial juggernaut, with 1,251 units nationwide by 1978, which would grow to 3,582 just a decade later, including 299 restaurants in Ohio alone, 259 in Florida, 251 in California, and 234 in Texas.[23] He had similarly transformed the nature of competition within the fast-food business. Restaurants would continue to compete over presentation, service, and real estate, but in his commitment to sell "better hamburgers than McDonald's or Burger King at a cheaper price per ounce," Thomas had introduced quantity as a new and central element of his brand's commercial appeal, a challenge to rivals that would not go unanswered.[24]

A Changing Climate

Even as burger chains were rapidly expanding across the map, there were warning signs on the horizon. In 1976, amid climbing grain prices, Americans ate an all-time record 93.4 pounds of beef per person.[25] The relationship between grain and beef prices is an unusual one. When feed costs appreciate, cattle farmers often choose to avoid paying higher prices by liquidating stock and selling it to market. This can lead to a short-term depreciation in meat prices, followed by a medium-term spike. The prices of smaller animals such as hogs and poultry have a more intuitive relationship, rising and falling with the price of feed, as stock levels are more readily adjusted.[26] Between 1975 and 1980 the number of beef cattle and calves fell by 16 percent, from 132 million to

110 million, while the average price per head increased threefold, from $159 to $502.[27] In spite of the number of broilers increasing from around 2.9 to 4.0 billion, the price per head remained relatively stable, increasing modestly from $1.74 in 1975 to $1.88 in 1980.[28] The rising wholesale price for beef precipitated a sharp ascent for regular consumers by early 1979. By April the USDA was reporting that beef prices had inflated by 33 percent over the previous twelve months, while the National Cattlemen's Beef Association reported the figure to be 42 percent.[29] Alfred E. Kahn, President Carter's economic advisor on matters of inflation and a proponent of deregulation, blamed the price controls of the Nixon administration and stated that "there is very little that can be done about the situation except to let the normal forces of the market restore the balance."[30] Kahn, also a professor at Cornell, said this just as government agencies announced their intentions to reduce beef purchases in the following year and a half.

An increase in the price of beef by thirteen cents per pound, or 37 percent, between April 1978 and April 1979 presented a clear and immediate hazard to America's legion of burger restaurants.[31] While full-service restaurants and supermarkets benefited from some measure of protection provided by their diversified range of menu items, the business models for McDonald's, Burger King, and Wendy's all relied upon a high turnover of low-cost beef. In order to keep pace with the new costs of basic materials, McDonald's started raising its prices by about 11 percent every year, beginning in 1977 and continuing through the 1980s. The economic disincentive to buy beef coincided with growing signs of consumer fatigue toward the standard burger menu. "A diet of hamburgers, French fries and milk shakes just no longer satisfies the fast food consumers," said the president of Jack in the Box in 1982.[32] Restaurant industry journalist Jane Wallace wrote, "An ever-more demanding public has tired of the concepts that once lured them to eat at new places. Themes that were considered clever have become clichés."[33]

Restaurants also had to address evolving nutritional expectations. A growing interest in running clubs and bodybuilding in the 1970s had evolved into what was widely described as a burgeoning "fitness craze" by the end of the decade in which a predominantly white middle-class population invested in health club memberships, athletic apparel, and home workout videos and equipment.[34] Southern California and its outsized national cultural influence established an image that many sought to imitate. *Los Angeles Times* reporter Alan Maltun described a new generation of fitness enthusiasts in suggestive terms after a visit to a health club in 1979: "Across the room, a blonde stands behind the registration desk as a guest signs in. Her big blue eyes follow healthy-looking males striding by—their muscles rippling under tight-fitting

T-shirts." Maltun continued: "At the juice bar around the corner, patrons with racquetball racquets dangling from their arms line up three deep for a quick energy fix. Next door in the pro shop, a cheerful, smiling saleswoman shows a customer the latest sports wear."[35]

Two years later, journalist William Overend profiled what he referred to as the "gym generation," an approach to the physique that had left Muscle Beach and Southern California and was set to spread across the country. Overend described how the "Body Temples" of the gym generation were "mirrored palaces of chrome and glass, with new miracle machines to transform long-neglected bodies into marvels of well toned flesh." The gymnasium craze could be seen in part as a reaction to the heaviness of the American diet. "We all eat better these days, the standard of living is higher, and so we all take in a lot of fat," explained Rudy Smith, the president of Holiday Spas Health Clubs of California. "If we don't burn that off, it turns into ugly body fat," he added before judiciously observing that "just watching Rocky racing up those stairs and getting stronger . . . really was one of the turning points for all of us."[36] *Rocky* was indeed the highest-grossing film of 1976, and Sylvester Stallone's icon of white redemption was just one of a growing wave of cinematic works featuring heroic muscle-bound male protagonists.[37] In a 1988 study of Americans' attitudes toward their bodies, sociologist Barry Glassner saw similar themes of redemption in the migration to gymnasiums. "Whether or not it actually improves our appearance, body work gives us something we desperately crave in this post-Watergate, post-Vietnam, post–Ollie North age," he wrote. "It allows us to feel morally pure." Though this reaction was very much situated before the backdrop of ubiquitous images of athletic bodies, for Glassner it represented a personalized need to assert self-control and a response to feelings of vulnerability on both an individual and a national basis.[38]

The exercise craze was not the first in U.S. history, nor was it the birth of the "strongman" in American culture. Yet what made the 1980s different, asserted Charles Gaines in *Esquire* in 1986, was that rather than existing as a somewhat obscure subculture, "the merchandise has sprung from the backs of comics and is *everywhere* now, being bought and used not only by the gym rat but by his parents, his grandparents, his boss, even his girlfriend." Like Glassner, Gaines connected this changing aesthetic to a deeper psychological need. "In 1980s America, muscles have come to *mean* something again: an obsession with the beauty of health and a growing impatience with having sand kicked in our face have combined to give back to muscles a national symbolic credibility."[39]

In the ensuing decade, the fitness craze expanded from its spiritual home in Southern California, where there were an estimated seventeen hundred fitness clubs by 1988, to a nationwide cultural phenomenon worth an estimated $5 billion as thousands of health clubs opened from coast to coast, ranging in size from large chain facilities to small fly-by-night hustlers looking to make a quick dollar by selling lifetime memberships.[40] Kristin, a salesperson at a health club in Richmond, Virginia, explained "the sex closing" to Barry Glassner. "That's where you tell a guy you're going to go on a date with him, to get him to sign the membership paper. Then, if he comes to collect on the date, you just blow him off. . . . Tell them you got a boyfriend. Guys don't really care, because once they get into the club there are lots of other girls, so the main focus isn't on you anymore."[41] Like any other start-ups, many gyms failed, leaving clients who had invested in long-term memberships out of pocket. As business grew, more specialized lines of enterprise emerged: health clubs that catered to women, students, and born-again Christians, as well as subsidiary industries in athletic casualwear and home workout equipment.[42] In 1988 alone Americans purchased an estimated six hundred thousand treadmills for domestic use, amounting to a $282 million market. Another $159 million and $121 million were spent on cross-country ski simulators and rowing machines, respectively.[43]

For the gym generation and before long within greater swaths of American society, corporeal shape was increasingly considered a signal of an individual's greater character traits. Whereas lean, muscular bodies indicated self-control, discipline, a commitment to self-improvement, and even virility, obesity was often assumed to indicate a moral failing on the part of the individual, inactivity, a lack of pride in one's personal appearance, and an irresponsible relationship with food. Both the fitness industry and fitness professionals perpetuated the notion that success in the form of an ideal body was attainable to anyone willing to invest their time and money into a healthy lifestyle and the optimum selection of products. These cultural assumptions had very real impacts upon individuals' upward mobility in many professional settings, as well as their sense of self in the broader social sphere, in spite of a complicated relationship with medical research on the subject of obesity, which indicated that ideal bodily weight often bore little relation to the images on magazine covers.[44]

Within this new social and cultural context, red meats quickly found themselves in an unfamiliar position. Red meat had long been considered the centerpiece of many meals, but a counternarrative developed suggesting they could be dispensed with entirely. Dr. Jean Mayer was perhaps the most influential nutritionist of the time and a scientist with an accomplished record researching body weight and obesity. In books and newspaper columns, he advocated a balanced diet consisting of the "basic seven" food groups, rejecting the "basic four" introduced by the USDA in 1956 as too broad and dismissing Dr. Robert Atkins's diet, which promoted high protein and fat consumption with a reduction in carbohydrates as "absurd" and a "fad diet."⁴⁵ Mayer warned the increasing numbers of Americans who were seeking to reduce their girth against relying on high-protein, high-fat foods for a source of caloric intake. He estimated in 1981 that the caloric content of the average American diet consisted of around 12 percent to 14 percent protein, 42 percent fat, and 46 percent carbohydrates. The fat intake should be reduced to around 30 percent in favor of complex carbohydrates, Mayer asserted. That 12 percent of additional carbohydrates should not be made up of sugars, though. In order to achieve this reduction, he recommended that the fifth group of the basic seven should be made up of "one or two servings of lean meat or poultry, fish, dried beans, peas or nuts and eggs."⁴⁶ While a diversity of dietary plans attracted individual followings, the idea of switching toward leaner meats became established in the mainstream of popular thought in the 1980s.

Beef had an image problem, a cost problem, and consequently a sales problem. "Chickens are stampeding our beef customers," exclaimed the May 1981 issue of *Successful Farming* magazine, warning that poultry consumption could overtake beef by the decade's end.⁴⁷ Cattlemen and packers were put on the defensive as chicken and beef sales headed in opposite directions. The National Live Stock and Meat Board sought to redirect public perceptions, arguing that its product was much leaner than it had been in the past. A spokesman asserted that "beef is much different than what our grandparents and maybe parents put on the table" before adding, "We're trying to overcome some misconceptions."⁴⁸ The problem was that they were not misconceptions, though, and it was very difficult to alter people's basic understanding of a product with which they were so intimately familiar, one that they dissected and consumed.

This posed a serious obstacle to restaurateurs who had accepted the McDonald's model of speedy output through simplicity. Dave Thomas remained deeply skeptical of menu diversity. "Everybody likes burgers," he asserted in the late 1970s. "We concentrate on doing only a few things, but we do them better than anyone else," he said.⁴⁹ "I can hardly stand chicken," he told *Restaurant Business* in 1978, explaining that he had sold his share in Kentucky Fried Chicken ten years previously.⁵⁰ Yet some within the restaurant industry were questioning the limitations of his business model: what if a carload of people approached a Wendy's and one of the group did not wish to eat beef? Would they object and encourage the group to go elsewhere? To McDonald's? To Kentucky Fried Chicken? Or even to a full-service diner like Denny's or Cracker Barrel? Thomas rejected this idea for a long time. "I know all the arguments about enlarging menus and the only plausible one just won't hold water," he said. Restaurants like McDonald's that were now considering alternatives to beef were mistaken. "Those guys believe in the minority veto. They believe that if four people are going to eat out together and if one wants chicken, the group won't go to a place that serves hamburgers only. I just don't think that people behave that way. For one thing people eat together because they want to eat together, not because of a particular menu item." Was this argument completely false, then? Thomas did not go that far, but burgers were something special. "Someone might want to veto going to a fish place but not a hamburger restaurant," he proclaimed. As convinced as he seemed to be, he left the door ajar. "That's not to say that Wendy's menu is forever fixed. There may come a time to change it," he conceded. "But," he resolved, "I'll need good reason before Wendy's starts frying fish or chicken."[51]

While the 1970s had been a decade of aggressive expansion for McDonald's and Wendy's, they had been a period of more modest but nonetheless steady growth for southern-style chicken restaurants. The number of franchised chicken restaurants in the United States, dominated by Kentucky Fried Chicken, Popeyes, Church's, and Chick-fil-A, increased from 4,927 in 1973 to 6,708 by 1978, then climbed to 8,147 by 1983. Average sales per store increased too, from around $230,000 every year in 1973 to around $420,000 a decade later.[52]

A 1981 profile of the Washington, D.C., restaurant market by *Washington Post* journalist Courtland Milloy stressed the popularity of chicken outlets among the city's majority African American population. Along Benning Road in the city's northeastern quadrant, Milloy observed "nearly a dozen chicken outlets either on the street or within a few blocks walk. . . . Each one boasts its special drawing cards" with customized menus designed to "break the burger doldrums." Most had opened within the past five to ten years. Holly Farms Fried Chicken had eleven stores in the district. At Chicken George's, named after a character in Alex Haley's *Roots*, Milloy found "bulky armed construction workers with helmets on their heads, wiry brown bodies covered only by jogging clothes, mothers with children at their sides or in their arms and a few young men in open-collared dress shirts who talk of driving all the way from Northwest to get here." The chain's Black owner, Ted Holmes, offered an uncritical interpretation that echoed many reductive historical stereotypes that have been employed to characterize African American culinary cultures.[53] While historian Psyche Williams-Forson has sought to reclaim the preparation of poultry as a space for "self-actualization, self-expression, resistance, even accommodation and power" among Black women, problematic tropes of Black men as thieves with an unrestrained taste for chicken dated back to antebellum America.⁵⁴ "Our research has shown that we should zero in on the minority market because in some areas, like Washington, blacks consume up to 50 percent more chicken than whites," Holmes explained. "Whites like our product, too, don't get me wrong. But they only eat it one time a week when blacks eat it four times a week."⁵⁵

New Menus

While we should not dismiss Ted Holmes's observations as a successful restaurateur out of hand, he understated the scale of change that was affecting restaurants nationwide. Value for money had propelled Wendy's into the first tier of restaurant chains, but circumstances beyond their control would slow down sales, squeeze profits, and force the burger chains to rethink their strategic outlook for the next decade. In order to adjust to this new reality of expensive beef and product fatigue, the burger tradesmen would have to embrace the idea of menu diversity. New items that were not a beef patty in a bread bun had a mixed track record. While the Egg McMuffin at McDonald's had been a success at breakfast time, and its Filet-O-Fish Sandwich was said to have taken off in some Catholic neighborhoods on Fridays, Ray Kroc's untested slice of pineapple with grilled cheese in a bun, the Hula Burger, was a disaster. Attempts to sell a burger-shaped hot dog had been equally unsuccessful, a "floparoo," in the words of company CEO Fred Turner.⁵⁶ Yet in the face of the steady growth of the southern-style chicken franchises, both burger chains and full-service restaurants that did not have poultry options started to add them to their menus. "Chicken seems to have almost universal appeal," Tom Strenk wrote in *Restaurant Business* in 1985. "Today more than ever chicken is perceived as lighter, leaner, and more nutritious than red meat." It was also a pretty straightforward proposition. "For the food operator, chicken has a relatively low food cost, is stable in price, readily available, and incredibly versatile," Strenk said.⁵⁷

Beginning in the late 1970s, McDonald's started test marketing "McChicken" menu items in Dayton, Ohio, and Norfolk, Virginia. Having tried more traditional fried chicken options, McDonald's developed a breaded "deep crispy" offering, produced at the Wilson Dairy and Poultry Company in Cumming, Georgia.⁵⁸ The company gave the McChicken Sandwich a national rollout in 1980, but the company's first serious venture into poultry would prove to be unsuccessful.⁵⁹

The ninety-five-cent sandwich consisted of a breaded chicken steak with tartar sauce and a lettuce leaf inside a sesame seed bun. Was it healthy? It appeared healthier than a Big Mac, though it was still frozen breaded chicken fried in vegetable oil, and it met with a lackluster response from consumers. Two reporters from the *Lancaster New Era* in Pennsylvania conducted their own survey of one hundred chicken eaters. Consumers ranked different fried meals at fast-food restaurants and ultimately concluded that the McChicken was "a loser." How so? "The processed chicken is so bland that you simply can't taste it," said one participant in the survey. "You can taste the bun, lettuce and sauce all right. But there could be *anything* inside that greasy breading," they continued. "Even when we took a hunk of the breaded patty out of the sandwich and tried it, we *still* couldn't taste the chicken," they bemoaned.[60] With disappointing sales, McDonald's had realized by 1983 that the McChicken "wasn't going to fly," to paraphrase the keen wit of the *Wall Street Journal*.[61] Michael R. Quinlan, the company's chief operating officer, said in May, "We've pretty much concluded that our chicken sandwich product is not good enough. It's not generating the results we want."[62] Another director explained, "To date we still have not hit upon the formulation, patty content and distribution method which meets all of our needs."[63] The sandwich would be "sent back to the culinary labs for fine-tuning," wrote W. David Gibson in *Barron's*.[64]

By the time the McChicken Sandwich disappeared from menus, the fast-food market was already in a state of rapid evolution, and the largest burger chains had entered into a fierce contest to attract customers with at least nominally healthier chicken meals. Burger King had launched a chicken sandwich of its own, Jack in the Box presented the Chicken Supreme, and Carl's Jr. had debuted the Hearty Chicken Sandwich. Reviewing the latest in fast-food dining for the *Los Angeles Times* in January 1982, John Pashdag offered Carl's modest praise, describing the restaurant's "entry in the chicken derby" as "the most edible of the lot." In spite of the sandwich being made of further processed poultry, Pashdag added: "The chicken patty actually tastes like chicken—a major accomplishment—and the slightly spicy coating is pretty good. Still, any processed chicken sandwich is to real chicken breast what Instant Breakfast is to ham and eggs. It may not taste bad and it may be as nutritious, but it'll never be the same." In responding to the burger chains' encroachment into its territory, Kentucky Fried Chicken introduced the Chicken Breast Filet Sandwich with an ad campaign proclaiming, "We do chicken right." "His chicken sandwich isn't made of gummy, tasteless, reconstituted shreds of chicken," Pashdag commented. "It's an honest-to-Robert E. Lee chicken breast, cooked in the Colonel's famous original recipe batter, the one with 11 secret herbs and spices," he wrote. He went on to note that "Wendy's deserves a special award of merit." Thomas's popular Breast of Chicken Sandwich was as described, a breast cut with a choice of mayonnaise, ketchup, pickle, onion, lettuce, and mustard.[65]

As McDonald's withdrew the McChicken Sandwich and retreated from the contest, Prudential-Bache Securities analyst Michael Culp explained to the *Boston Globe* that its removal "is not terribly consequential for the chain, but it is symptomatic of the problems involved in rolling out new products. This is also part of McDonald's effort to address the food-quality issue. Burger King and Wendy's have been raking McDonald's over the question of food quality because their food is simply better." Culp forecast, "If McDonald's can improve its food, it will be able to get down in the dirt and fight back in a year or two."[66]

The world's largest restaurant chain wasn't out of ideas, though, nor would it take two years to mount a new assault upon its rivals. The head chef at McDonald's, René Arend, had been working to develop several other menu options. Born in Luxembourg, Arend had been the executive chef at the exclusive Whitehall Club in Chicago, frequented by Ray Kroc. "He asked me to work for him, and at first I said 'I'm a chef, not a hamburger man. What would I do?'" Arend told the *Buffalo News* in 1988.[67] Kroc persisted and asked several times before Arend finally relented. "But when I came I wanted to do for the people out there in the street what I did for those who were rich," he explained.[68] Arend had developed a chicken pot pie and Onion McNuggets, neither of which graduated from the testing phase. Beginning in 1979, he began working on a variation of the McNugget using methods that resembled those of Robert Baker to create a chicken-based snack. The closest Baker had come to a product of this type were Chicken Cubes and Chicken Sticks, both breaded finger foods that utilized deboned Leghorn fowl. Chicken Sticks were designed to have a high meat content as a proportion of the final product. As created by Baker, 90 pounds of poultry meat resulted in 108 pounds of product before the batter coating was added, becoming 135 pounds.[69]

After a little over a year of product development and taste testing, the McNugget progressed to operational testing in 1980, where stores in select markets assessed the kind of equipment that would be needed for its preparation.[70] The *Los Angeles Times*' Jack Smith attended a McNuggets promotional event for the press in the Music Room at the opulent Biltmore Hotel in May 1981. Recalling that his previous visit to the Music Room had been to hear a string trio perform Bach, Brahms, and Vivaldi, he wrote that on this occasion he was greeted by a sign that read "Old McDonald's Farm," a scarecrow, and a string trio that wasn't "Viennese" but that "looked like three bad guys from an old Republic Western." Served in silver tureens, "McNuggets turned out to be chunks of boneless chicken, about the size of a golf ball but elliptical in shape, cooked crisp and brown in a light batter." Noting that famous literary eulogies to chicken were in abundance and stressing the high-brow/low-brow contrasts of the occasion, Smith concluded, "My wife and I had two McNuggets each and would probably have had more, but we were going downstairs to Bernard's for dinner, and I didn't think Bernard would like it if we showed up at his table full of McNuggets."[71]

The product's limited debut, accompanied by televisual promotions on local stations, received little praise from food columnists yet nonetheless returned extremely positive sales figures. McNuggets were described as "McBland" in the *Arizona Republic*, "but isn't that the McDonald's way?"[72] In a slightly later opinion piece, Mike Romkey, whose regular column in the Moline, Illinois, *Daily Dispatch* was titled The Common Connoisseur, echoed this evaluation, opining that McNuggets were moist and tender but lacking in taste and "just didn't measure up after years of munching blissfully on Col. Sanders's chicken, cooked using his secret recipe." The McNuggets "were blandness personified—or should that be chickenonified," and even the condiments were "ho-hum."[73] In spite of mixed reviews, the addition of McNuggets to the menu led to a reported 8 percent increase in sales as a snack that accompanied other meals during the initial trial period. The success of these trials in about sixteen hundred restaurants convinced the company to prepare for a nationwide campaign and the addition of the McNugget to the menu in every restaurant in the United States by June 1983.[74]

It hadn't been a mystery in either the poultry or fast-food industries that McDonald's was readying a product of this type, "pre-formed, battered, deboned meat cubes."[75] Besides early news items like Jack Smith's column, there had been considerable preparation to meet the logistical demands required to roll out a new item on a national scale for a chain that, as of 1983, had 6,094 restaurants.[76] Processing plants required fitting with deboning and meat recovery equipment, supplied by companies such as Utah's Beehive Machinery. "If you're looking for the most *simple, rugged, dependable, easy to operate* deboning equipment on the market with an *infeed capacity of up to 10,000 lbs. per hour* . . . you just found it," the company professed in an advert for the Model S-76 Deboner.[77] Improved deboning technology allowed processors to "reclaim" bits of meat that had previously been hard to reach and had been lost with the carcass. Keystone Foods, a two-plant company with operations in Reidsville, North Carolina, and Nashville, Tennessee, handled the test production of the McNugget, but for the national plan McDonald's needed multiple partners and numerous processing plants.

By late 1981 the corporation was able to reach a handshake agreement with Tyson's, then the seventh largest poultry processor in the nation, a company that claimed to have increased its sales by 3,280 percent between 1958 and 1975.[78] Tyson's already had a strong record of working on further processed chicken as well as breaded products. Moving into the fast-food market also suited Don Tyson's plans to diversify the company's interests beyond its seven present plants. In addition to adding a swine division, the company was seeking to aggressively expand through the acquisition of other businesses while improving export sales around the globe.[79] Becoming the largest producer of Chicken McNuggets, Tyson's agreed to provide McDonald's with around 40 percent of its needs and refit its Nashville, Arkansas, plant, a union facility with around twelve hundred employees, so that it could focus exclusively on the new product.[80] This would amount to around $50 million worth of product, which would help in the "fattening of Tyson Foods margins," wrote Gordon Mitchell.[81] Reaching this agreement with a processor that slaughtered approximately 3.9 million chickens every week represented a significant new partnership for both companies.[82]

In a training video preparing employees for the new offering, puppets representing existing menu items promised that McNuggets were "just about as easy to make as fries." With the company's characteristic precision, McNuggets were delivered to stores in bags weighed to fit the exact capacity of existing fry baskets. They should be cooked for exactly four minutes and fifteen seconds, including being shaken after two minutes and twenty seconds, and drained for five to ten seconds before being transferred to a heated holding cabinet, where trays were similarly sized to fit precisely one bag. The McNuggets could remain there for no longer than thirty minutes before they must be served or discarded; both cooker and holding cabinet featured built-in, preset "duty timers." Besides requiring crew members to keep an eye out to ensure that the McNuggets were not sticking together in the fryer, this strikingly foolproof procedure required very little in the way of initiative on the part of crew members and fit seamlessly within the company's existing operational methodology.[83]

In late 1983 the North American launch began. In a quiet library a man in a suit leans over to the librarian and whispers, "They're here." Unable to control her excitement, she loses her sense of the decorum required by her environment, and turns to him in shock. "They're here!" she exclaims loudly. We move to a dark living room in which a young couple sits on a couch watching television. The girl, dressed in pink, disturbs her boyfriend's amorous intent by sitting up sharply in response to the image on the screen. "Bobby, they're here!" All other thoughts disappear from Bobby's mind as he jumps up and adjusts his blue sweater in anticipation. "They're here?" he responds in disbelief. We then see a McDonald's restaurant at night with fireworks exploding overhead. People are climbing out of their cars and hurrying toward the entrance. Others are departing with large paper bags in their hands.

"McDonald's new Chicken McNuggets," a voice sings as a polystyrene container, guided by an invisible hand, rotates toward the camera to display the cause of such unbridled enthusiasm. "Chunks of chicken, a crispy nugget, dip 'em in a sauce," the advert continues. "Sweet and sour," the librarian says, smiling as she holds a McNugget in the air. "Honey," says the girl in pink. "And barbeque," adds Bobby, sitting beside her. "Hot mustard," the man in the suit says in a deep voice before a youthful McDonald's server places a tray on the counter showing the three portion sizes. "Six, nine, or twenty." "A winner," a father prophetically declares, seated at a table with his children. All of the fifty-odd actors in the commercial, whether in speaking or background roles, are white. This includes the restaurant staff in what appears to be an entirely segregated environment.[84]

It wasn't that McDonald's was uninterested in the African American dollar. Far from it. The company had been deliberately and strategically courting Black franchisees and customers since the 1970s in the promotion of a small-business-driven model of community economic development. For the McNuggets rollout the company released an alternative advertisement specifically designed for Black television audiences, part of a broadly researched and market-tested plan to create commercials that appealed to African American cultural sensibilities.[85] In the "McNugget Mania Chant," a group of five Black teenagers sang, "One McNugget, two McNuggets, three McNuggets, four. Six Chicken McNuggets taste so good you'll ask for more." The chant was based upon "one potato, two potato" and involved similar sequenced hand motions. "Six pieces, nine pieces, twenty pieces too, Chicken McNuggets, McDonald's and you."[86] While the white commercial shows people in professional and domestic settings and stresses family appeal, the Black advertisement employs none of the same tropes. The group of youths aren't even situated within the restaurant itself; instead, they are part of an impromptu social gathering on the sidewalk. A 1985 installment in a series of ads featuring the American Double Dutch League, sponsored by McDonald's, was situated in a similar urban street setting and showed coordinated rope jumpers chanting: "Down at McDonald's where the arches glow, they've got Chicken McNuggets and they're hot to go."[87] While both sets of commercials endeavored to highlight the new product's exciting appeal, the company's African American advertisements stressed themes of community, athleticism, and multigenerational social gatherings, all of which were absent in the comparatively generic scenes designed for white audiences.

In spite of or more likely with the help of these advertisements and a reported $35 million marketing budget for the McNugget Mania campaign, the Chicken McNugget was a staggering success.[88] The television campaign was supported by a prolific print campaign in local newspapers (see Image 9). Per-

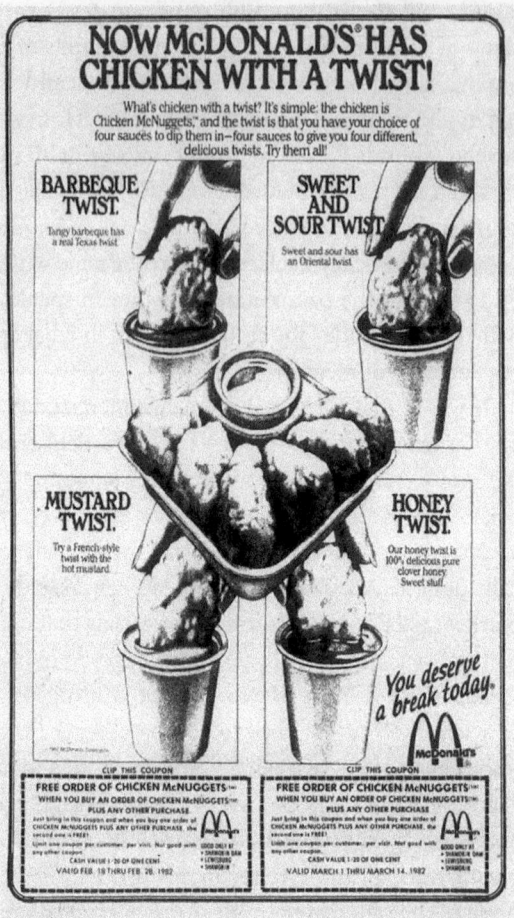

IMAGE 9. The introduction of the Chicken McNugget by McDonald's to North American consumers in 1982 demonstrated a new style of chicken dining and emphasized the taste of the dipping sauces rather than the nugget itself. From *Daily Item* (Sunbury, Pa.), February 18, 1982.

haps we should avoid treating Bobby's awestruck proclamation that "They're here?" with incredulity or irony. The company claimed to have used 5 million pounds of chicken in the opening twelve weeks and projected sales of 3.5 billion McNuggets in 1984.[89] Within months of the national rollout, Michael Roberts, assistant vice president of purchasing at McDonald's, reported, "We sold enough chicken product to position us firmly as the world's second largest chicken restaurant" after KFC.[90] "The frozen boneless chicken business in North America has 'gone crazy—bananas,' since the introduction of the Chicken McNugget last year," reported Ben Fiber of the *Toronto Globe and Mail* in September 1984. He was quoting Steve Poirier, the product manager of McCain Foods, a company based in Florenceville, New Brunswick, that was developing a frozen line of nuggets for Canada as the new snack entered international markets. "McNugget sales are running beyond our most optimistic budget projections right now," said Gary Reinblatt, vice president of marketing for McDonald's Restaurants of Canada. "Our projections in the first place were wild because we had run our own tests based on the U.S. data we had," he continued. "But we've even had to revise all of those figures upward," Reinblatt concluded.[91]

McDonald's had managed to present an item that successfully met the needs of multiple eating trends that were in the ascendance. The company had introduced menu diversity at its restaurants, providing lean white meat over red while at the same time providing a snack that could be fit into increasingly irregular dining patterns. "At the chicken chains, new lunch products generally are finger foods," wrote *Restaurants & Institutions* in April 1982.[92] In capitalizing on the increased popularity of finger foods and stressing that condiments were a central part of the experience, McDonald's had also circumvented the accusations of blandness that had doomed the first incarnation of the McChicken Sandwich. "My own personal evaluation of the product is that it relies on the external sauce to determine its taste," said restaurant industry analyst Keith Mullins in 1985. "It's like the product is changed each month with a different sauce," he praised.[93] As the McNugget Mania campaign eagerly pointed out, boxes were served with a selection of honey, barbeque, hot mustard, and sweet and sour sauces, all designed to enhance or even obscure the relatively limited taste of the nugget itself. The omnipresent red tomato–themed sauce was always another option.

"McDonald's has really started something," wrote *Restaurants & Institutions*. "The success of its McNuggets line has rubbed off on the entire chicken fast-food segment," the magazine reported.[94] The senior vice president of Kentucky Fried Chicken had recognized by the end of 1984 that the "nugget business has great potential for KFC." By 1985 KFC, which already purchased 7 percent of the nation's broilers, was ready to compete with its own Kentucky Nuggets.[95] "Do your chicken nuggets seem to run out of flavor when you run out of sauce?" the company's thirty-second commercials queried in an undisguised jab at McDonald's. All nuggets were not created equal. This being so, you needed to "know your nuggets," a rich voice sang. KFC served "the only chicken nuggets with the Colonel's secret blend of eleven herbs and spices for a taste so good you're going to love them with sauce or even without," the ad proclaimed. The suggestion that McDonald's had infringed upon KFC's turf pervaded the ad campaign: "You wouldn't go to a Chinese restaurant for tacos. Or to an Italian restaurant for egg rolls. So why go to a burger place for chicken nuggets?" In spite of describing them as a "shameless copy," Mike Romkey in Moline wrote that the "Kentucky Nuggets succeed in all the areas where Chicken McNuggets fail," stressing the "mouth-watering effect" of the Colonel's secret herb-and-spice recipe.[96] KFC had correctly recognized the threat presented by McDonald's. The world's largest restaurant chain had unparalleled access to markets in the United States and overseas and an unrivaled logistical capacity and influence upon agribusiness.[97] This meant that McDonald's had enormous potential to eat into the market for quick-service chicken, in which KFC had to date been preeminent.

Other franchised chicken restaurants such as Church's and Chick-fil-A had to confront the same challenge of a potentially shrinking market as burger restaurants encroached upon what had previously been their exclusive domain. "We were already well established in chicken and we thought we could do a better job with nuggets," said Kay Richardson of Church's, explaining that Crispy Nuggets were "shaped and formed" rather than "pressed" as she attempted to capitalize on the sense of mystery surrounding the contents of McNuggets. "Pressing involves grinding up chicken parts. Forming and shaping don't take the parts down to the smallest size. You can't fool anybody with forming and shaping because you can tell what's in the nugget," Richardson said.[98] Chick-fil-A's sales had more than quadrupled between 1977 and 1981, but in the following three years they increased by just 34 percent. By the end of 1982, the company had added a nugget-like offering to its menu and renamed its flagship dish, the One Piece Box, as the more self-explanatory One Sandwich Meal.[99] Nonetheless, Southern Baptist founder S. Truett Cathy's policy of not opening stores on Sundays remained unchanged, "a distinctive principle of my Christian background," he would write.[100]

Burger King and Wendy's, for the past decade the most direct rivals of McDonald's, would be among the nearly twenty chains to add some variation of the McNugget to their menu in the three years following the snack's debut. By the early 1980s, Dave Thomas had assumed a more backseat role and allowed younger men to take the lead in determining the future of Wendy's. Robert Bauer's initial involvement with the company was as a franchisee, but within fifteen years he had risen to vice president of procurement, responsible for the purchasing and distribution of foods for company-owned restaurants. In March 1986 he took time to reflect on how Wendy's had changed course at the end of the 1970s. "As our customers' tastes have changed, Wendy's has adapted," he argued. "And that's what success in today's marketplace is all about—*change and adaptation.*" Bauer tried to pinpoint the locus of the shift in taste: "As more women entered the work force, our customers started to demand lighter fare." He added, "In the late 70's, many consumers became concerned about health considerations associated with beef. They wanted an alternative to our hamburgers." Tyson Foods marketing director Bruce Baird hewed to a similar analysis. "People are more diet and health conscious. They want the convenience of finger foods which gives them an alternative and allows them to make choices about what they're eating," Baird said, explaining the growing preponderance of nuggets in the restaurant and frozen food markets.[101]

Though Bauer would assert that "'me too' products wouldn't do," the addition of breast of chicken sandwiches and nuggets to the Wendy's menu, alongside a range of egg-based breakfast meals, was hardly a unique approach, even if they did include a measure of customization. His promise that "we're expanding our menu by developing new products" represented a modest departure from Thomas's orthodox quick-service restaurant philosophy, which said that limiting the number of items available was the surest way to achieve efficient service.[102] Burger King also briefly resisted the growing trend. While company representative Steve Finn stated in February 1985 that "we're doing pretty well with the menu as it is," by April 1986 Chicken Tenders were ready to hit the market with a $30 million advertising campaign, the soundtrack to which was Marvin Gaye's "Ain't Nothing Like the Real Thing." Tenders were different from McNuggets, Burger King asserted, because they were made exclusively from chicken breasts and were fried in unsaturated vegetable oil, as opposed to the blend of vegetable oil and beef tallow used at McDonald's.[103]

For the poultry processing industry, the surging demand for fast-food products, many of which were made from mechanically reclaimed meat that had previously been of very limited value, was a great boon. Tyson Foods was a supplier of nuggets to both McDonald's and KFC. "Years ago we used to throw them away," remarked Don Tyson, referring to the body parts that contributed to the making of further processed chicken. Further processed products such as nuggets and chicken patties may have been introduced to many consumers through restaurants such as McDonald's, Wendy's, and KFC, but the market for equivalents in the frozen food sections soon followed. "The customer has begun looking for a similar product at the supermarket and food processors are responding to that demand," said George B. Watts, president of the National Broiler Council, in 1982. Companies such as McCarty Foods moved aggressively to capitalize upon these new markets (see Image 10). Reflecting the food processors' view that cookery was increasingly unpopular, Tyson observed, "People say 'I don't want to cook that damn chicken, it takes too long.' They just want to take it out of the package, plunk it in the microwave and serve it."[104]

This emphasis on the ease of preparation in both domestic and commercial kitchens was affirmed by Roberta Jones, writing in *Restaurant Business*: "Further-processed chicken products add flexibility without a lot of skilled labor."[105] For some, the nugget seemed like quite a modern way of consuming

IMAGE 10. The success of the Chicken McNugget spawned a legion of copycat products for both restaurant and domestic markets. This ad from McCarty Foods demonstrates the full potential of further processed chicken while seeking to assuage consumer concerns over the use of unpopular cuts through its emphasis on white breast meat. Courtesy of the Division of Rare and Manuscript Collections, Cornell University Library

chicken. The bone was removed and the product was breaded, adding to the tidiness of the eating experience. And the nugget was popular among children. "Advanced, high-tech kitchens, markets, and food sources will not alter the social and cultural need to share food together—even if 'cooking the family meal' means gathering around a table and pressing coded buttons to activate individual retrieval systems," wrote Joanna Pruess. She went on to add: "Two qualities will prevail in the next decade: convenience and healthfulness."[106]

Proponents of the microwave oven were not modest in their proclamations. Annette Yates's *Out of the Freezer, into the Microwave* promised readers that "if you love good meals . . . you can banish hours of kitchen-slavery yet still produce mouth-watering meals for yourself, family and friends," while Elaine Howard from MRCA Information Services, a trend research firm, declared that "microwave ovens have revolutionized cooking habits—and that's not an overstatement."[107] Recipe books such as Janet Emal and Elizabeth Taylor's *Light and Healthy Microwave Cooking* ambitiously envisioned the device as a replacement for traditional ovens and stoves, a means of preparing entire meals ranging from meat loaf dinners to smoked turkey breasts. They stressed that "microwaving often cuts calories: little or no fat is needed as foods cook in their own moisture," and added, "If you microwave your meals, the calories you *didn't* use for fat can be 'spent' on another food—without exceeding your daily calorie limit." Emal and Taylor even offered a recipe for chicken nuggets "with an Italian accent" among their healthy array of items. They were made with chunks of chicken breast (further processing technology was unavailable to the domestic chef), Parmesan, paprika, Italian seasoning, and lemon wedges, heated on full power for three minutes, rearranged, and then heated for three to four minutes more.[108]

The growth of the number of microwave ovens in American homes was indeed rapid, from 20 percent of homes in 1980 to 60 percent by 1986. In a Campbell Soup Company survey of consumers in 1987, 42 percent of respondents said that they "completely agreed" with the statement that "my microwave is my friend." In this sense of fevered excitement, Phyllis Levy, executive director of Campbell's Microwave Task Force, observed that "people don't talk about their vacuum cleaners that way."[109] The microwave oven, for all of its limitations and for all of the giddy hyperbole about a revolution in household dining, did offer previously unimagined levels of convenience to both busy consumers and those simply disinclined to cook. It also offered a new line of opportunities for poultry companies.

In a short time, Holly Farms, Pilgrim's Pride, and Perdue, the third, fifth, and sixth largest poultry processors in the United States, were joining Tyson Foods in offering lines of frozen chicken nuggets for grocery stores and supermarkets.[110] As ever, the poultry industry was a copycat business. These three firms had all traditionally focused on home sales, although, recognizing the changing market, they were quick to adapt. Only one in ten chickens had been processed beyond dismemberment in 1980. Within a few years of the McNugget's introduction, that number would increase to as many as three in ten.[111] In early 1985 Holly Farms launched the $6 million Time Trimmers campaign to promote its new one-pound bags of chicken nuggets. Breast nuggets cost $3.49, and thigh nuggets were a dollar cheaper. They were accompanied by a series of twenty-minute recipes involving nuggets such as stir-fry, chicken masala, and shish kebab.[112]

Meanwhile, Pilgrim's Pride, based in Pittsburg, in northeastern Texas, invested in what Lonnie Pilgrim described as "state-of-the-art" facilities designed to focus on the market for further processed chicken. A new seventy-five-thousand-square-foot processing plant in Mount Pleasant was just ten miles from Pittsburg and had been built next to a slaughter plant capable of killing eight hundred thousand birds per week.[113] Pilgrim's Pride claimed that the new facility could roll out up to twenty thousand pounds of deboned, cooked, and sliced battered or diced chicken every hour.[114] "There are many other integrators and deboners," said senior vice president Tom Garner, "but they don't have the full arsenal of products we're able to offer." Garner asserted that the range of frozen and nonfrozen chicken products from Pilgrim's was popular with both the fast-food bulk purchasers and the regular supermarket shoppers. The chain restaurants wanted to keep their options open. "We know these people, and I can say that they not only want more suppliers in the field, but are eager to have us enter this arena. They don't like to be dependent on one supplier," he added. And where Perdue had become prominent for selling leaner meat in big cities on the Atlantic coast, Pilgrim's would maneuver to consolidate its presence in the American West. Lonnie Pilgrim had started offering low-fat chickens, he said in 1986, because "we listen better, and respond more quickly, to what customers really want." He explained in more detail: "I think the market is 100% ready for low-fat chicken. We're selling both right now, because that is what our customers have requested. We do label most of our parts as 'lean.' Our chickens are certainly 25% leaner than the conventional chicken we and others sell."[115]

Pilgrim's Pride, Perdue, Tyson, Holly, and ConAgra, the largest processors in the country, expanded the capacity of their vertically integrated chicken empires to fit the new realities of the mid-1980s, when Americans purchased ever-greater quantities of poultry in both restaurants and supermarkets. The idea of marketing chickens as lean would have seemed particularly strange to an earlier generation of poultry men, for whom the idea had been to fatten a chicken to the greatest possible weight. The contracted poultry farmers of the 1980s did continue to raise ever-larger birds per the instructions of processors, yet with an emphasis on voluminous white meat rather than fat. Americans' embrace of a lean and versatile alternative to heavy red meats represented a rational new dietary approach, yet it was one that, for a significant share of the population, would not live up to its promise, encased in breadcrumbs and stripped of some measure of its nutritional value. Even as greater dietary consciousness spread and memberships at health clubs increased, mostly among middle-class and wealthy segments of the population, there were parallel and countervailing trends at play.

Value Dining

As the 1970s made way for the 1980s, fast-food chains of almost every stripe embraced chicken as a new menu option as they adapted to consumers' evolving attitudes. Yet the trend toward menu diversity was not the only major change in emphasis that was taking place within the landscape of American casual dining. An extended period of expansion and success at Wendy's had resided in its ability to tap into long-standing cultural assumptions, offering what for most people constituted very good value for money, a meal that contained a sizable portion of meat and a side with a drink. Thomas had vowed to sell "better hamburgers than McDonald's or Burger King at a cheaper price per ounce."[116] Whether they fit anyone's definitions of better or more popular on the whole than the Big Mac or the Whopper was not the only factor at play. The bottom line was that Thomas offered a competitive price and a product that was larger in size.

By the 1970s, burger-weary consumers increasingly had the option of turning to what were sometimes rather derogatorily described as "ethnic" restaurants such as Pizza Hut and Domino's. Franchise pizza chains experienced in excess of 10 percent annual growth in the number of restaurants through the 1970s and 1980s.[117] However, the restaurant that most aggressively centered its appeal around the concept of "value" was Taco Bell. Like Wendy's, Taco Bell had a very simple original menu, consisting of tacos, burritos, tostadas, and chiliburgers, all of which contained at least one of the same ingredients, beef, a tortilla, beans, cheese, lettuce, and tomato.[118] The company had grown consistently for over a decade when PepsiCo purchased it in 1978 for $130 million, having won a bidding war with the H. J. Heinz Company. PepsiCo had been formed by merging Pepsi-Cola and Frito-Lay in 1965, creating a company that, at the time, exceeded $500 million in annual sales.[119] Its restaurant division had obtained Pizza Hut just months previously in November 1977.

Significantly, this deal represented the fusion of supplier and retailer. Without the name recognition of Coca-Cola, PepsiCo had competed by aggressively negotiating drinks contracts with restaurants and bars. Between 1965 and 1985, PepsiCo's sales volume increased eighteenfold.[120] Taco Bell was already the company's largest purchaser of soft drinks when it was acquired by PepsiCo. In 1983 PepsiCo reached an agreement to supply sodas to Burger King, "a huge shot in the arm" in the midst of the so-called cola wars, according to CEO Roger Enrico, and an alliance the company would maintain until 1990.[121]

In 1978 Taco Bell consisted of nearly nine hundred restaurants, mostly in the Southwest. With Glen Bell having resigned his chairmanship to pursue his interest in restoring historic railways in the Sierra Nevada, PepsiCo appointed John Martin, the former president of La Petite Boulangerie, Hardee's, and Burger Chef, to run the company. "Barreling out of the Southwest," Martin transformed Taco Bell's operational approach through a series of historic innovations, launching the brand into the first tier of American franchise restaurants and over seven thousand units by the mid-1990s and reshaping the framework of competition within the industry.[122]

Martin's first goal was to shake the stigma that "ethnic foods" represented a niche market, eliminating the company's mascot, a barefooted Mexican boy wearing a sombrero, at about the same time Pizza Hut was dispensing with its icon of an Italian chef. Martin also replaced adobe arcades with a more standard European style in the construction of new restaurants.[123] While Taco Bell may still represent "a slice of fantasy Mexican California plopped into suburbia," according to journalist Gustavo Arellano, Martin emphasized the similarities between his fare and that offered by the burger chains.[124] "What's a burger?" he asked. "Ground beef, cheese, tomato, lettuce, and sauce on a bun. Not very different from a taco."[125]

At the center of Martin's vision for the business were two central connected elements: he would introduce technological solutions to drive down labor costs and by doing so create the latitude to reduce in-store prices. The goal was to offer greater value than Taco Bell's rivals: larger meals for less money.

Like Wendy's, the company's operation under Glen Bell had involved preparing fresh ingredients every day. Beef served in tacos was slow cooked and required regular stirring. Vegetables had to be washed and sliced. Beans were stoned and cooked. This was Bell's and Dave Thomas's vision of running a restaurant: bringing in fresh ingredients and cooking them. Less so for John Martin. "Maybe we can simplify this whole thing," he said. "We're really not in the business of making food. We're in the business of feeding people." Cooking food was slow and potentially inconsistent, and Martin worried that the mess involved created a negative impression with the clientele: "Imagine you're coming to work at Taco Bell at 8:00 A.M. From 8:00 until 10:00, all you're doing is slicing and dicing things. By the time the restaurant door opens you look like a bomb has gone off in the walk-in refrigerator because you're covered with lettuce and beans and cheese and garbage. Now you're going to be friendly and attractive to customers? No way. No way."[126]

Martin implemented two new strategies, known as K-Minus (Kitchen-Minus) and TACO (total automation of company operations). K-Minus optimized space by inverting the ratio of seventy to thirty kitchen to seating to thirty to seventy in the opposite direction. More significantly, TACO established a system that would constantly keep track of sales at all branches, transmitting the information to the company headquarters in Irvine, California. Computers, which had previously been largely confined to the office-based side of the business, were installed in every restaurant. The new system allowed up-to-the-minute communication between restaurants, with one manager quickly commuting between multiple sites to troubleshoot problems through the use of pagers or car phones. The company did not conceal its ambition to eliminate as many manual tasks as possible. The vice president for operations support, Ken Harris, envisioned the future of retail sales: "The next step is to automate the POS (point-of-sale) process." Every store would have a network. "Off that network will be a bunch of devices: some will be robotic—taco-making machines; others will be customer communication devices—touch-screen order-entry, drive-through order confirmation boards, handhelds (terminals an employee punches an order into while greeting drive-through customers outside the store); maybe a fax or customer phone order capability.... All of these will come down the line and will be on one network. The TACO network will be the facilitator."[127] In the 1980s many of these ideas remained pipe dreams. Faxing your order to a fast-food restaurant never quite took off. However, by delegating managerial tasks to "team members," the company created "team-managed units" and transferred added responsibilities to its entry-level employees without increasing their compensation. This cost-saving strategy was cleverly packaged as an attempt to "empower" and "encourage ... self-sufficiency" among restaurant staff, wrote Tim Durnford. While Durnford referred to this as an opportunity for team members to "take more ownership of store operations," ownership remained in every sense in the hands of the corporation and franchisees, while staff remained highly replaceable.[128]

In order to hasten production in restaurants' newly remodeled smaller kitchens, Martin implemented a new production regime. "I guess my revelation has been that we were really ripping people off," he said. "The bottom line is, if people come in and spend 100 of their hard-earned pennies in your restaurant and you give them 27 cents worth of food, that is not a good deal."[129] Martin developed a solution to resolve this disequilibrium whereby tacos would be very easy to prepare. Lettuce would arrive pre-shredded, and beans were dehydrated and sealed in sachets that could be readied with boiling water. Condiments such as guacamole and sour cream were delivered in cartridges and loaded into a gun that squeezed them out onto the appropriate morsels.[130] Taco shells were fried off-site, a far cry from the traditional method of preparation, in which cooks pushed pastry around a hot pan with their fingers, sometimes burning themselves in the process.[131]

Rather than ground beef and chicken that were prepared on the premises every day, meat arrived cooked, frozen, and seasoned. The idea of freshness, a priority to consumers if you believed Dave Thomas and many other restaurateurs, was disregarded. How many people would really notice the difference between fresh beef and frozen beef? Martin's gambit was that it did not matter a whole lot. His pitch was one of economics centered almost purely on the basis of value. Cost-effective preprepared ingredients and a simplified kitchen operation allowed Taco Bell to present a menu that could match any of its fast-food sector competitors in terms of both price and quantity, offering tacos at forty-nine cents each. This approach was in line with PepsiCo's broader agenda. "What consumers want most is value," said CEO Wayne Calloway. This did not simply mean cheap. Taco Bell's menu offered items that were distinctly different from a burger and fries in shape, texture, and form yet without using any suspiciously unusual ingredients or flavors. If they seemed a little bland to some, they could, like McNuggets, be doused in spicy sauces, and at least customers were getting quite a lot of food for their money. "Value and volume go hand in hand, just like Harry and Sally," Calloway added.[132]

In the wake of Martin's introduction of TACO and K-Minus and the rollout of Taco Bell's value strategy, would Americans embrace the restaurant as a venue that could be visited over and over again? The explosive expansion of the chain under PepsiCo's ownership indicates that they clearly would. In 1983 there were 1,664 Taco Bell restaurants in the United States. By 1990 there were 3,227, with around 56 percent company owned.[133] Taco Bell was one of the nine largest restaurant chains in the country, and its annual growth rate of 22 percent from the mid-1970s through the late 1980s outstripped that of McDonald's, Burger King, Hardee's, Pizza Hut, Denny's, and Kentucky Fried Chicken. The only chains with higher average annual growth rates than Taco Bell were Domino's at 42 percent and Wendy's at 32 percent.[134]

Though the overall demand for fast food in the United States remained fairly inelastic, steadily growing one decade after the next, franchise restaurants' clientele were often sensitive to price fluctuations at individual chains and ready to transfer their patronage. Even McDonald's, with arguably the second most recognizable brand in the world after Coca-Cola—"billions served"—found that modest price hikes could dissuade customers. Between 1974 and 1988 the company raised prices six times and found that on five of those six occasions store sales declined an average of 3.7 percent.[135] When McDonald's finally started cutting prices in 1989 it was in part a response to Taco Bell's effective approach and in part a reaction to the growth of the double drive-through burger chain Rally's in the West, a company whose strategy was to offer burgers that were about 30 percent cheaper than those offered by the market leaders.[136]

PepsiCo's new approach to value menus and meals represented a defining moment within the fast-food industry, a popular strategy that appealed to the rational economic calculus of many hungry consumers. Just as the Lovettes, Tysons, and Pilgrims considered the management of "pennies and grams" as central to controlling their bottom line, thrifty purchasers who needed convenience and who were operating on tight family budgets counted nickels and dimes saved in a similar fashion.

The 1990s swiftly became a decade of intense value pricing competition and an era of exuberant fast-food excess. In 1989 Wendy's introduced the successful Super Value Menu of items costing ninety-nine cents each. Then in 1991 McDonald's followed suit and debuted its Extra Value Meal menu, bundles that included a burger, sandwich, or McNuggets with fries and a soda for anywhere from $2.49 to $2.99.[137] This was followed in 1993 by its long-standing Supersize It promotion: customers were encouraged in advertising to say the two magic words and upscale their meal for even greater value.[138] Burger King launched its own value campaign in 1994. Pizza Hut, not to be outdone by the other chains, introduced cheese-stuffed crusts in 1995, followed shortly thereafter by the Triple Decker, a pizza that contained six cheeses and four hundred calories per slice and more fat than a stick and a half of butter, an "indulgent choice," said senior vice president Bill Cobb.[139]

When one chain restaurant appeared to have gained an edge, another responded in kind as the value competition got further out of hand. In 1999 Burger King announced a new range of "XL" products. Marketing director Lorraine Thompson explained: "For the past three years, the Burger King marketing focus has been primarily on taste—now we are targeting a specific consumer sector with 'significantly bigger burgers.'" Internal company research indicated that 47 percent of men bought burgers primarily on the basis of size. McDonald's responded with the McXL Sandwich range, and Taco Bell introduced the Border Lights lower-fat range of items, but when they failed to catch on, the company responded with the Bacon Cheeseburger Double Decker Taco.[140]

The provision of sodas constituted an additional element within the competition for consumers. An average soda in the 1950s was around eight ounces. By the 1990s the smallest available soda was normally twelve ounces, but anything up to thirty-two ounces was normally available, albeit loaded with cheap and plentiful ice cubes.[141] The switch from sugar to high-fructose corn syrup, made from genetically modified maize, substantially reduced the cost to produce soft drinks. On the very same day in November 1984, PepsiCo and Coca-Cola announced that they would raise the amount of high-fructose corn syrup in their drinks to 100 percent. Until that point, cans of Pepsi Cola had been a fifty-fifty mixture of fructose and sucrose, while Coke employed a seventy-five/twenty-five split. The biggest producers of fructose—Archer-Daniels-Midland, A. E. Manufacturing, and Cargill—had already raised their output in anticipation of the final switch.[142] The escalating drinks contest reached its culmination in 1992 when the convenience store 7-Eleven replaced its forty-four-ounce Super Big Gulp, successor to the Big Gulp, with the sixty-four-ounce, headline-grabbing Double Gulp, roughly five cans of soda in one very large cup for just $1.09.[143] "We're talking about a wading pool–sized drink here," offered company spokeswoman Karen Raskopf with apparent alacrity.[144]

As the United States hurtled headlong through the 1990s toward a public health crisis, the impending and inevitable consequences of the extravalue transformation in the restaurant business became a cause of increasing concern and attention. While early news reports and reactions to the latest jumbo-sized meal offering may have contained elements of awe and even amusement, some started to question the nation's commitment to the popular ideals of fitness and healthy living. President Clinton's jogging sessions were at times known to conclude at McDonald's. In a highly contested area of debate, clinical explanations for obesity were changing too. Whereas overeating had for years been thought of as a source of comfort sought by individuals with a negative sense of self, by the 1990s it was increasingly believed to be a consequence of discriminatory societal attitudes directed toward people perceived to be overweight. "Daily, when looking at television programs and magazines, they are reminded that 'thin is in' and 'fat is not where it's at,'" observed psychologist Thomas A. Wadden and psychiatrist Albert J. Stunkard in 1993. "Contemptuous attitudes are expressed in jokes heard on the street and on late night talk shows, as well as in the nation's respected news weeklies," they explained. Wadden and Stunkard, pioneering researchers both, contended that body image discrimination could be manifested in a broad range of professional, academic, and social settings ranging from college admissions to job applications to marital opportunities and could even extend to patients' treatment by medical professionals. "In virtually every aspect of life, the overweight are reminded that they live in a society that hates fat," they asserted.[145]

Many academic commentaries on eating in the United States were laced with critical and sweeping condemnations that reflected these broader attitudes. "Think about what it says about our culture when the typical American recognizes 'supersize' as a verb," remarked Dr. Kelly D. Brownell, the director of Yale University's Center for Eating and Weight Disorders in November 1998. Lurking behind concerns for public health was a growing sense of disdain and even revulsion for overweight Americans and their culinary preferences. "The Big Gulp is a sign of American greed and haste," stated psychologist Brian L. Stogner from the University of Michigan–Flint.[146] Meanwhile, biology professor Paul Saltman explained that "the American people are scientifically illiterate. They get all of these conflicting statements from the government, from food manufacturers, from diet companies; and they are unable to sort out what is real, unreal and surreal." Saltman continued: "We are a nation of gluttons. We need to teach ourselves to become epicureans, to appreciate food for what it is," he said. "If we had been exercising as much as we said we were, our weight would have stabilized or gone down. It went up," observed John Foreyt from Baylor University's School of Medicine.[147]

Many measures of health data indicated that obesity rates were rising very quickly. In 1962 around 13 percent of Americans were classified as obese, according to the National Health and Nutrition Examination Survey. This number remained relatively stable through the 1980s before the beginning of a sharp spike toward the decade's end. Around 23 percent of Americans were obese by 1994, and 31 percent by 2000, with the number continuing to climb. Similarly, the number of "extremely obese" Americans stood at around 1 percent from the 1960s through the 1980s before climbing to 3 percent by 1994 and 5 percent by 2000.[148] Even more concerning for many, childhood and adolescent obesity rates were following the same trajectory, from around 5 percent in the 1970s to 10 percent by 1994 and then 14 percent and continuing to climb in 2000.[149]

This statistical reading was not without its critics, though. Molecular geneticist Jeffrey M. Friedman observed in *Science* in 2003 that while the average weight of the U.S. population had increased by an average of seven to ten pounds between 1991 and 2000, this relatively modest gain had pushed many Americans marginally beyond the threshold whereby they were classified as "obese," as measured by their body mass index. Though a one-third increase in rates of obesity in the 1990s appeared to represent a dramatic shift in public health, Friedman observed that "because obesity is defined as a threshold, a relatively small increase in average weight has had a disproportionate effect on the incidence of obesity."[150]

In the public discourse, news stories employing the misnomer of an "obesity epidemic" proliferated, heightening the perceived threat to the body politic presented by overweight Americans to the level of a national emergency. The idea of thinness, argues American studies scholar Charlotte Biltekoff, became inextricably tied to notions of good citizenship, individual discipline, and self-control and was a measure of the greater state of the nation.[151] In spite of healthy eating activists' ostensible goals of encouraging self-actualization through improved physical health, an increasing number of voices came to conclude that the stigmatization of body weight created by the nation's fitness obsession was inflicting more harm than good upon the diverse populations the movement was purporting to serve.[152]

Though the growing fitness and weight-loss industries had greatly benefited from increases in both institutional and individual spending on a great array of health and fitness products since the 1980s, Americans in the late 1990s appeared to be even more dissatisfied with their bodies than ever before. A 1996 study by *Psychology Today* found that 56 percent of women and 43 percent of men were unhappy about their overall physical appearance. When asked which features caused the most displeasure, 71 percent of women and 63 percent of men cited their abdomens, while insufficient muscle tone was also a common cause for concern. "Thinness has become the preeminent yardstick for success or failure, a constant against which every woman can be measured, a gauge that has slowly permeated the male mentality," wrote the report's author, David Garner.[153]

Even as the moral panic concerning obesity deepened and restaurant portion sizes increased, chicken completed its final ascent to the top of the American food chain. In spite of the calorific extravalue meals, which became standard fare in the 1990s, per capita consumption of beef had declined from a high of ninety-four pounds in 1976 to sixty-seven pounds by 1990, a plateau at which it would remain for the next fifteen years. By contrast, chicken consumption, just twenty-eight pounds per person in 1960 and forty-two pounds by 1976, surpassed beef consumption for the first time in 1992 and continued to grow to seventy-seven pounds per person by 2000.[154]

In America's most frequented restaurants, discussions of fresh food had, at least temporarily, been displaced in favor of affordability and scale, what the industry itself defined as "value," a concept many consumers needed or were willing to adopt. With the full array of fast-food options available and within close proximity in many competitive urban and suburban markets, restaurant executives sought to achieve momentum from one quarter to the next with the latest eye-catching, blockbuster meal deal. Menus that had once seemed frozen in time year after year bristled with exclusive seasonal options that were "only available for a limited time." While menu diversity had meant an expansion of options beyond the narrow parameters of beef burgers and fries, the new range of options available often only marginally improved upon the limited nutritional benefits of the older fare, and when restaurants did attempt to introduce low-fat product lines, they were often met with indifference on the part of customers and disappointing sales. The regular clientele of McDonald's, Burger King, Wendy's, or Taco Bell had already, it seemed, committed to a certain type of meal the moment they stepped through the doors or pulled up in the drive-through line.

Others were comfortable living with both the risks and the consequences. Ray Recchi, a popular lifestyle columnist writing for the *South Florida Sun Sentinel*, outlined a defense of fast-food diners in a March 1990 commentary that hinted at a broader populist rejection of overbearing dietary instructions. "Listen up, you health evangelists," Recchi began.

> I don't care what you think is good for me, and I don't care what you think is bad for me. And frankly, I'm starting to feel rather insulted by your assumption that ignorance or stupidity are the only possible reasons I don't agree with you.... Why, oh why, you wonder, do the rest of us keep eating Whoppers, McNuggets and nachos with bean dip when we know for a fact that those things are chock full of bad stuff? ... It is not because we don't believe you.... One would have to be a dolt or an expert at self-delusion to dismiss all the studies about the health benefits of good diet and exercise.... But we also know we can get run over by a fat guy in a car while we're out jogging. In other words, there are no guarantees, save this: Eventually, every last one of us is going to die. So some of us prefer to spend the time we have enjoying the things we like—such as French fries, real butter and cheesecake—and avoiding things we don't like—such as tofu, raw vegetables and unsweetened fruit juices.[155]

Recchi rejected nutritional disclosure agreements that were supported by advocacy organizations such as the Center for Science in the Public Interest: "It may come as a surprise to them that those of us who frequent such places do not want to know that our McNuggets are made out of ground-up chicken skin, or that we would have to jog from Fort Lauderdale to Atlanta to work off the calories contained in a single Whopper."[156] While Ray Recchi, who died of cancer at the age of fifty-one in 1999, was neither a political commentator nor a culture warrior, his March 1990 missive invoked a clear sense that his menu preferences represented personal choices and a form of individual liberty that was being publicly evaluated and condemned.[157] In excoriating what he considered to be unnecessary nutritional guidelines and coercive legislative instruments designed to discourage unhealthful eating, Recchi's commentary suggested the emergence of a growing cultural divide within Americans' culinary attitudes and a rising resistance to scientific instruction in the food space.

The widespread introduction of further processed poultry had met the economic goals that Robert Baker had envisioned, presenting Americans with an alternative form of protein that retrieved unused components of chickens, good edible meat that had been made use of for hundreds of years, transformed into a popular diet and relished by millions. As this was taking place, the United States was simultaneously saturated with images and messages representing the yin and yang of American health: on the one hand, visual and cinematic displays depicting what were often white ideals of physical perfection and beauty, on the other, oversized servings and appeals to people's hunger that were not conducive to these ideals. While academic studies found that a majority of Americans considered obesity to be a failure of both morality and individual discipline, this was complicated by anthropologists who found that prevailing attitudes toward corporeal health were not always shared by people of color and within immigrant communities.[158] In spite of these findings, in their 2009 study of fitness magazine covers, Shari L. Dworkin and Faye Linda Wachs argued that these covers' visual representations created a general sense of "body panic." By displaying the bodies of models that were unattainable to all but a few, the print media encouraged the continued consumption of fitness club memberships, home workout equipment and videos, dietary supplements, and even more fitness magazines in the pursuit of popular aesthetic standards.[159] Americans found themselves in a psychological loop: dining out in record numbers, often working long hours, and then expending more of their earnings on fitness products in order to compensate for the physical impacts of a heavy diet, widespread automobility, and, for a certain segment of the population, sedentary occupations in the expanding service sectors. As the 1990s came to a close there was a burgeoning awareness of this growing paradox within the American diet, a slowly developing critique that would be fully articulated in the new century.

EPILOGUE

The New Century

Entering the 2000s, the poultry industry occupied a central position within the ecology of American businesses, its breakneck efficiency having made chicken dinners a ubiquitous feature within the national diet. It was a celebrated food, a signature provision at barbeques and Superbowl parties, a storied dish in some homes where recipes and the knowledge of secret ingredients were passed on from one generation to the next. Poultry's versatility allowed it to mean different things to different people, lending to many styles of cuisine. Reflecting in 2000 on past trends, Molly O'Neill defined the 1960s as the period when internationalism started to see mainstream appeal: "date-lime chicken; chicken with curry, peanuts, coconut and bananas; chicken with dried mint and fresh lime; and ginger-peach chicken." These recipes made way for "buttermilk pecan-chicken" in the 1970s, "chicken avocado melt" and "chicken nuggets with pineapple sauce" in the 1980s, and "baked spicy pineapple Balinese chicken" and "Caribbean chicken drums" in the 1990s. "I cook with it a few times a week," Mary Rizzio from Traverse City, Michigan, told O'Neill. "It's great for trying out new flavors. You can do anything with it," Rizzio added. Having highlighted the diversity of chicken options available, O'Neill nonetheless observed that the most popular recipe downloaded from a popular website remained "simple roast chicken."[1]

The growth in poultry output in the twentieth century was reflected not simply in larger facilities and faster production speeds but also in the size of birds themselves as more traditional broilers were replaced by increasingly tasteless breeds designed for their high feed conversion ratios and speed of growth. Diners disguised the blandness of modern poultry through invention, the appropriation and adaptation of international styles, and the growing popularity of hot sauces as a standard tabletop accessory, a market that was estimated to have grown by 150 percent between 2000 and 2014.[2] The widespread popularity of spicy and spicy-themed products may well have represented the growing influence of Central American and Asian cuisines upon the evolving face of U.S. dining and a new search for stimulating flavors and experiences, but it could also be a symptom of another wave of fatigue for classical North American staples and the downsides of foods designed for scale and durability.

In many parts of the world and even in some American communities, a measure of corpulence had positive connotations, suggesting financial success, conspicuous consumption, and opulence, even beauty and domesticity in women. Yet large and luxuriant bodies occupied an increasingly controversial role within a public consciousness hard-wired to envision physical healthfulness in a very clearly defined athletic shape and form. While leading anthropologist Cheryl Ritenbaugh went so far as to describe obesity as a "culture-bound syndrome," within the broader public discourse the seemingly incontrovertible crisis in adult and childhood obesity forged a common understanding in the early 2000s that there had to be something fundamentally wrong with the American diet.[3] For young people to be so out of shape at an early age, an essential equilibrium between food and exercise and general well-being must have been lost somewhere along the way. Obesity was no longer considered merely an aesthetic concern that preoccupied some individuals; instead, it had become a long-term threat to the national health worthy of significant public-facing initiatives by successive presidential administrations.[4] A growing number of physicians called for state interventions concerning an array of issues ranging from a ban on the sale of trans-unsaturated fatty acids, or "trans fats," to requirements on restaurants to include nutritional information on menus.[5]

A growing chorus of voices identified popular fast-casual dining habits as central concerns. Within the cultural sphere, journalist Eric Schlosser's international bestseller *Fast Food Nation: The Dark Side of the All-American Meal* leveled a multipronged attack at the chain restaurant industry in 2001, echoing H. L. Mencken's earlier charge that it was creating a widespread homogeneity of dining options at the expense of small businesses and regional variations and highlighting a reliance on slipshod industrial practices that disregarded both food and worker safety, all at the greatest expense of the nation's children, who were subject to the most direct marketing efforts. Following Schlosser, in 2004 filmmaker Morgan Spurlock's "how the other half eats" documentary *Super Size Me* took aim at the bumper-size menu offerings at McDonald's and the consequences of heavy and sustained fast-food dining. Eating only McDonald's meals for thirty consecutive days, Spurlock tracked dramatic and deleterious changes to both his physical and mental health that ensued. *Super Size Me* was critically acclaimed and contributed to the growing levels of opprobrium directed toward fast-food chains by food critics and public health advocates. Just weeks after the release of Spurlock's film, the company described by commentator Greg Critser as "the overlord of Midwestern commodity imperialism" discontinued the Super Size menu as the company's Eat Smart, Be Active campaign sought to remake its image as a purveyor of at least some nutritious items.[6]

The addition of salads and bottled water to fast-food restaurant menus was hardly enough to deter the industry's most committed critics, though. Buoyed by concerns about genetically modified farming practices, the organic food movement had emerged from its countercultural origins and matured into a nearly $8 billion U.S. market by 2000, the first year in which a greater proportion of organic sales were transacted in conventional supermarkets rather than farmers markets and specialized natural food stores.[7] A belief in the inherent superiority of the organic label reached a broad level of mainstream acceptance among middle-class consumers, facilitated by the expansion of premium grocery chains such as Whole Foods Market and the industrial embrace of organic production by companies such as Silk and WhiteWave Foods, both of which were later purchased by Danone.[8] Among the most popular and influential critics of the U.S. food system was science writer Michael Pollan, a journalism professor at the University of California, Berkeley, who, over the course of four books, advanced a sustained and vigorous argument in favor of a locally sourced and largely plant-based diet as a remedy for "America's national eating disorder." He charged that the complexity of the legion of popular processed foods was both unhealthy and excessive, leaving people oblivious to the troubling origins of the meals they were consuming and contributing to a greater overall sense of dysfunction. "Food is about pleasure, about community, about family and spirituality," Pollan wrote, "about our relationship to the natural world, and about expressing our identity." He contended that "most of what we're consuming today is no longer, strictly speaking, food at all, and how we're consuming it—in the car, in front of the television, and, increasingly, alone—is not really eating, at least not in the sense that civilization has long understood the term."[9] Pollan's analysis captured some of the concern and even growing disdain among middle-class consumers for the American fast-food diet and its excesses in the 2000s.

As some turned to what seemed to be lighter alternatives at sandwich shops such as Subway, Panera Bread, Corner Bakery Cafe, and Jimmy John's, where meals were prepared within the clear view of consumers, sales fluctuated at the increasingly out-of-vogue burger chains.[10] Whereas commentators in the early 1980s had charged that beef burger menus had grown tiresome and predictable, critiques of the 2000s were all-encompassing indictments of a widely replicated business model based on low-wage labor and seemingly dubious meat products of both beef and chicken. Critics of this new discourse on food charged that it wasn't new at all: discussions of food in the United States had always been driven more by class anxiety and demonstrations of exclusive forms of consumption than by an objective understanding of working-class dietary habits and preferences. Reflecting a growing rejection of the morality-laden rhetoric of many of the most prominent food writers, historian S. Margot Finn would conclude in 2017 that "many advocates of sustainable food are only interested in eating better to the extent that it is difficult and thus distinguishes them from people unable or unwilling to put in the effort."[11]

In public discourse, fast food had been reimagined not as a respectable convenience but rather as a vice of the ignorant and in some cases those who were economically and geographically deprived. Despite setbacks to their prestige, America's largest restaurants retained a widespread underlying democratic popularity that carried them through the economic doldrums of the early 2000s, providing an open and sanitary environment in which poor people, young and old, continued to feel welcome.[12] McDonald's employees, clad in uniforms bearing the company's new slogan, "i'm lovin' it," continued to serve millions of burgers and Chicken McNuggets on a daily basis. Subsequent to a New York judge describing the McNugget as a "McFrankenstein creation of various elements not utilized by the home cook," the company introduced a new model in 2003 that was slightly smaller and made of more expensive all-white meat, reportedly dropping dark meat from its unknown recipe, a feature of the company's broader effort to redefine its unhealthful image.[13] Nonetheless, further processed chicken products, creatively reshaped as dinosaurs, cars, and even fish in their direct appeals to children, remained ubiquitous on grocery store shelves as they continued to connect to their target markets. The critics said no, but many diners still said yes to mechanically deboned and repurposed chicken parts.

The complicated relationship between Americans and food continued to evolve in the 2000s while entertaining a series of paradoxical trends. As organic food sales climbed, the consumption of carbonated beverages fell precipitously from around fifty-three gallons per capita in 1998 to forty-one gallons by 2014.[14] An estimated one hundred million people attempted to diet an average of four to five times per year, contributing to a $20 billion weight-loss industry.[15] On the airwaves, shows such as NBC's *The Biggest Loser* and VH1's *Celebrity Fit Club* promoted weight loss as both entertainment and competitive sport. Even while NBC maintained its commitment "to helping contestants achieve healthy weight loss and live healthier lifestyles, and to inspiring viewers to do the same," specialists raised concerns about the long-term efficacy and healthfulness of extreme crash dieting.[16] While the U.S. obesity crisis stood strangely juxtaposed with idealized images of lean and muscular bodies, some food writers and chefs presented ideas that somewhat ambivalently rebutted the focus upon seasonal and organically farmed products. In a 2020 study, Emily Contois described an alternative, unpretentious regionalism in the "anti-elitist masculinity" of the 2000s trend for what came to be referred to as "dude food": "Infused with class politics, dude food embodies notions of lowbrow food and eaters, fast-food value menu quantity, and the enthusiastic pursuit of exaggerated eating experiences."[17] Sometimes described as "comfort food," eschewing the pejorative "junk food," dude food represented not so much an explicit retort to healthy food but rather a creative and often localized validation of the American foodways that were most under fire. In embracing novelty burgers, Tater Tots, all-day breakfasts, and lengthy menus of chicken wings doused in sugary and spicy sauces, consumers didn't by necessity abandon personal health; instead, they signaled an intent to maintain late twentieth-century convenience foods as an enduring, albeit modified feature of the American diet.

Even chicken nuggets survived their reputational nadir of the early 2000s both in restaurants and on frozen food aisles and increasingly assumed a role as a legitimate item of home cookery. For many, there appeared to be a place at the table for the original snack-sized ground chicken product, even though it had not yet been recognized as a unique and traditional American meal. When McDonald's debuted Spicy Chicken McNuggets as a new item in 2020, the review by *Washington Post* food writer Emily Heil was reflective of this greater level of acceptance and even a sense of nostalgia. "Fear not, nugg lovers, these are the crunch-coated pellets you know so well, the ones you might have devoured in the back seat of the station wagon on the way to soccer practices or wolfed down on road trips," Heil wrote. "They're McNuggets, my generation's memory-evoking Proustian madeleine, with merely a touch of spice added to a familiar equation." Heil even seemed reconciled to some of the realities of further processed chicken. "Out of the box, I noticed that the new guys are formed just like their classic older siblings, with irregular shapes aimed at making us forget this is actually not a single piece of bird, but rather an amalgam of parts, smooshed together and fried. The tempura-like coating boasts those familiar crags and crannies," she observed.[18] A 2023 essay in the *New York Times* by Adrian J. Rivera echoed Heil's unwillingness to disavow fond childhood memories and associations. Even while acknowledging that his tastes had now shifted away from the realm of processed foods,

Rivera recalled that he visited McDonald's during the pandemic because he "wanted to recapture that magic, the excitement at the prospect of satisfaction and pleasure." Finding these feelings to be elusive, he mourned, "I wish eating a McNugget could still transport me to a time of warmth and love and safety, a time when I didn't know what a madeleine was, when I didn't know any better."[19]

As chicken nuggets entered their third and fourth decades as a feature on restaurant menus, they also took on a new life as an item that could be prepared at home from scratch. However, the recipes of the 2000s represented only a partial endorsement of Robert Baker's earlier vision. The purpose of Baker's designs was to rescue unpopular and often discarded components and refashion them into a versatile new source of protein, benefiting both the poultry industry and economically minded consumers. This surfeit of chicken parts had been generated by shoppers' increasing propensity to purchase plastic-wrapped breasts, legs, and wings rather than carcasses in their entirety. However, modern cookery writers invariably recommended that nuggets should be made from chicken breasts, eschewing the resourceful approach of Robert Baker and for that matter home cooks of decades past like Mrs. E. G. Jenkins from Oskaloosa, Kansas, who scraped the remains away from the bones after she had roasted a bird and prepared chicken croquettes. Despite Baker's best efforts, notions about better and worse cuts of animals, some more valuable and some less, were deep rooted and persistent. In the minds of most, offal remained a form of refuse.

The challenges faced by the most recent generation of poultry workers persisted and remained as intractable as those faced by the last. From time to time, reporters, human rights activists, and federal agencies shone a spotlight on the industry's inner workings and sought interviews with its now majority Latin American labor force. In September 2008 the *Charlotte Observer* concluded a twenty-two-month investigation into workplace safety at House of Raeford Farms, a large North Carolina–based processor with four facilities in the state, three in South Carolina, and another in Louisiana. At the company's Greenville plant, House of Raeford boasted seven million hours without a "lost-time accident," meaning no worker had suffered an injury sufficiently severe to miss time at work. Employees were periodically provided with T-shirts emblazoned with the image of Strut McClucker, the company's safety mascot.

Yet the *Observer* found that House of Raeford's own safety logs revealed that nine workers had suffered broken bones or amputated fingers during this seven-million-hour stretch. When Guatemalan chicken tender packer Cornelia Vicente caught her hand in a conveyor belt in 2003, her right arm was snapped and the tip of her finger severed, but she returned to light duty the following day. Her account was corroborated by Belem Villegas, a former supervisor, who told the *Observer* that as many as twenty workers a day would report hand, wrist, and arm pain but that when she proposed referral to a physician to plant managers, she was told, "If they keep coming to the office, they're going to have to be let go." When James Mabe, the complex manager at House of Raeford's West Columbia plant, was questioned by reporters why there were no records of musculoskeletal injuries reported between July 2003 and April 2007, he explained: "Hispanics are very good with their hands and working with a knife. We've gotten less complaints." He added: "It's more like a natural movement for them."[20]

Human Rights Watch issued a highly credible and thorough report chronicling the challenges poultry workers faced in 2004; the organization returned to the subject fifteen years later in 2019 and issued a second report demonstrating that no real improvements had taken place. The report revealed "alarmingly high rates of serious injury and chronic illness among workers at chicken, hog, and cattle slaughtering and processing plants, as well as business practices that endanger workers and obscure the reality of workplace hazards." This was compounded by the U.S. government's ongoing failure "to implement domestic workplace safety and health standards that would regulate practices in the industry to the benefit of workers' health and safety."[21] Even the respected nonpartisan Government Accountability Office similarly issued dual reports, reviewing the meat and poultry industries in 2005 and then again in 2016.[22] "Since our findings in 2005 on meat and poultry workers facing hazardous work conditions," the agency recorded in 2016, workers "continue to face the types of hazards we cited, including hazards associated with musculoskeletal disorders, chemical hazards, biological hazards from pathogens and animals, and traumatic injury hazards from machines and tools."[23] Many poultry plants are in remote locations, tucked away on the outskirts of rural southern towns, but a substantial body of credible scientific evidence was on display for anyone who cared to lift the rock and look at the collateral damage created along the poultry supply chain. Other studies of note included a 2014 NIOSH survey of workers at a Maryland poultry plant, which found that 81 percent of jobs in receiving, picking, evisceration, deboning, and the "thigh line" required hand activity and force beyond the levels at which controls were recommended, and 34 percent of participants demonstrated carpal tunnel syndrome.[24] This was but one of several such studies into the most common physical ailment associated with poultry line work.[25]

In the absence of strikes at poultry plants in urban environs or the fire and fury of an Imperial Foods disaster, the grinding day-to-day anguishes of poultry workers, the cuts and the slips, the crippled hands, wrists, elbows, and necks, even the average of eight workplace fatalities per year between 2013 and 2017 all failed to prick the American conscience.[26] Even as influential writers such as Carlo Petrini, Marion Nestle, and Michael Pollan shifted culinary conversations among middle-class Americans away from processed foods and generated deep suspicions toward the giants of agribusiness, debates about the treatment of livestock seldom extended beyond their farmyard environs into the hidden realm of the abattoir.

In late September 2017 the National Chicken Council petitioned the USDA to remove the present line speed of 140 birds per minute at most slaughterhouses, arguing that to do so was consistent with President Trump's deregulatory agenda and a necessary step to protect American competitiveness from Brazilian and Chinese rivals.[27] With food and workplace safety advocates rallying in opposition and submitting more than one hundred thousand public comments, the USDA denied the poultrymen's request in January 2018, contending that it remained unconvinced that Food Safety and Inspection Service officers could effectively surveil birds moving in excess of the present speed.[28] In spite of stopping short of issuing an industry-wide green light, the USDA permitted many of the industry's largest operators to increase speeds to 175 birds per minute, easing them into an Obama-era program called the New Poultry Inspection System.[29]

As migration from across the Americas ebbed in the late 2010s, processors increasingly turned to an international workforce of refugees from conflicts in Africa and the Middle East, guided in processors' direction by federal contractors such as Catholic Charities and Lutheran Social Services. In a nation in which 95 percent of the population identified as meat eaters, the work needed to be done, and there was normally someone available who needed the work.[30] There was never an alternative reality in which poultry work was a light and breezy endeavor, free from some measure of risk and physical strain. Work in a slaughterhouse, like jobs in logging, fishing, construction, or mining, carried some inherent dangers associated with the nature of the work involved. Nonetheless, the political protection enjoyed by poultry companies, owing to the imperatives of production and the provision of affordable popular meals, made for an incautious and top-down industrial model that failed to heed the concerns of workers and workplace safety advocates.

Aware that freshness is fleeting, people have always sought to preserve food both as a safeguard against future shortages and in order to afford themselves the discretion to eat different meals at a time of their choosing. In the United States, the innovations that became embedded within processing and preservation in the creation of convenience foods proved to be remarkably resistant to change. In assuming a role as a widely consumed primary source of protein and as a cultural touchstone, further processed chicken products were among the most significant of these postwar inventions. In spite of persistent and often scathing critiques by a wide array of experts, ranging from public health advocates to food writers to celebrity chefs, processed foods, often dried or frozen, remained popular items within the homes of millions of Americans. While freshness may have possessed a certain cachet, food that was robust and durable fit comfortably into the lifestyles of many who were unwilling or unable to spend an extended amount of time cooking on a nightly basis. Outside the home, many processed foods similarly found an enduring popularity in the country's legion of fast-food restaurants, where customers prized snappy industrial efficiency and economically competitive meal deals. Yet for all of the success of the poultry industry and the grand realization of Robert Baker's inventions, affordable American chicken dinners were only able to exist before a backdrop of unquantifiable social costs that the best public relations campaigns that money can buy were unable to fully conceal. As a thousand poultry lines spun on into the future, nearly two hundred birds per minute hurtling along on a fast track from a cage to a cardboard box in a truck, the human damage that was the untold price of these journeys remained unaccounted for.

NOTES

INTRODUCTION

1. Robert Bauer, "Ready-to-Use 'Fresh Like' Products: Wendy's View," *Broiler Industry*, March 1986, 40–42.
2. Wachs and Dworkin, *Body Panic*.
3. Strasser, *Waste and Want*.
4. Jamie Oliver, *Jamie Oliver's Food Revolution*, ABC, March–April 2010; Jamie Oliver, *Jamie's Dream School*, Channel 4, March 2, 2011.
5. DeShazo, Bigler, and Skipworth, "Autopsy of Chicken Nuggets," 1018.
6. Bittman, *Animal, Vegetable, Junk*; Pollan, *Omnivore's Dilemma*; Vileisis, *Kitchen Literacy*.
7. Vileisis, *Kitchen Literacy*, 5–8.
8. Specht, *Red Meat Republic*, 239. See also Bobrow-Strain, *White Bread*; Levenstein, *Revolution at the Table*; Veit, *Modern Food*.
9. Conkin, *Revolution*; Daniel, *Breaking the Land*; Fitzgerald, *Every Farm*.
10. Deener, *Problem with Feeding Cities*.
11. Watson, *Golden Arches East*.
12. Langdon, *Orange Roofs*, 144–145.
13. Sylvia Allegretto, Marc Doussard, Dave Graham-Squire, Ken Jacobs, Dan Thompson, and Jeremy Thompson, "Fast Food, Poverty Wages: The Public Cost of Low-Wage Jobs in the Fast-Food Industry," University of Illinois Department of Urban & Regional Planning, UC Berkeley Labor Center, October 15, 2013, https://laborcenter.berkeley.edu/pdf/2013/fast_food_poverty_wages.pdf; National Employment Law Project, "New York Department of Labor Wage Board for Fast-Food Workers," May 2015, https://www.nelp.org/wp-content/uploads/Fact-Sheet-New-York-Labor-Department-Fast-Food-Wage-Board.pdf.
14. Cobb, *Selling of the South*; Schulman, *From Cotton Belt to Sunbelt*.
15. There is an extensive literature addressing the history of beef in the United States. On the era of the Beef Trust (the five largest meatpacking companies), see Specht, *Red Meat Republic*; Yeager, *Competition and Regulation*; Young, *Pure Food*. On the culture of meatpacking workers, see Cohen, *Making a New Deal*; Register, *Packinghouse Daughter*. On meatpacking in Chicago, see Barrett, *Work and Community*; Pacyga, *Slaughterhouse*; Slayton, *Back of the Yards*; Wade, *Chicago's Pride*. On meatpacking workers and labor conflict, see Halpern and Horowitz, *Meatpackers*; Horowitz, *Negro and White*; Kopple, *American Dream*; Rachleff, *Hard Pressed*. On industrial restructuring and meatpacking plants within communities, see Andreas, *Meat Packers and Beef Barons*; Broadway and Stull, *Slaughterhouse Blues*; Hamilton, *Trucking Country*; Pachirat, *Every Twelve Seconds*.
16. Brooks, *D. W. Brooks*; Pilgrim, *One Pilgrim's Progress*.
17. Baldwin, *Taco Titan*; Kroc and Anderson, *Grinding It Out*; Love, *McDonald's*; Monaghan, Anderson, and Rayburn, *Pizza Tiger*; Thomas, *Dave's Way*.
18. Schlosser, *Fast Food Nation*; Striffler, *Chicken*.

19. L. Fink, *Maya of Morganton*.
20. Schwartzman, *Chicken Trail*.
21. Gray, *We Just Keep Running the Line*.
22. Stuesse, *Scratching Out a Living*. See also Ribas, *On the Line*, for a similar account of racial tensions within the southern pork-processing sector.
23. Simon, *Hamlet Fire*.
24. Josephson, *Chicken*.
25. Omo-Osagie, *Commercial Poultry Production*; Broadway and Stull, *Slaughterhouse Blues*.
26. Waltz, *Hog Wild*.
27. "McDonald's to Be Sponsor of '94 Soccer World Cup," *Wall Street Journal*, April 7, 1992, B8.
28. Fleischman, *Communist Pigs*, 4.

CHAPTER 1. Dr. Baker and Mr. Nugget

1. *The Wire*, "The Detail," HBO, June 9, 2002.
2. McKenna, "Father of the Chicken Nugget."
3. Bayles made clear that the "sleazoid" types she was referring to included political strategist Lee Atwater.
4. Martha Bayles, "TV: Where's the Chicken?," *Wall Street Journal*, January 13, 1986, 1.
5. *Red Dwarf II*, "Kryten," BBC Two, September 6, 1988.
6. Carol Ritter, "He Brought You the Chicken Hot Dog," *Sunday Democrat and Chronicle* (Rochester, N.Y.), March 21, 1982, 1B, box 8, #21/26/4030, Robert C. Baker Papers, Cornell University, Ithaca, N.Y. Hereafter cited as Baker Papers.
7. "Biographical Sketch: Robert C. Baker," box 3, Baker Papers.
8. Ritter, "He Brought You," 1B.
9. Robert C. Baker, "Nutritional Aspects of Food Science," box 6, Baker Papers.
10. Langdon, *Orange Roofs*, 59–77.
11. Robert C. Baker, "Food Science—the Future," talk presented at the 75th Anniversary Birthday, New York State College of Agriculture and Life Sciences, May 12, 1979, 2, box 6, Baker Papers.
12. Robert C. Baker, "The Problem of Food Waste," 22, box 8, Baker Papers.
13. Baker, "Food Waste—Can We Prevent?," 3, box 8, Baker Papers; Baker, "Problem of Food Waste," 23.
14. Baker, "Problem of Food Waste," 23.
15. Robert C. Baker, "Underutilized Species of Fish: A New Food Source," *League for International Food Education Newsletter*, April 1978, box 8, Baker Papers.
16. Baker, "Problem of Food Waste," 23.
17. Ibid., 23.
18. Hayse and Marion, "Eviscerated Yield," 4.
19. Baker, "Problem of Food Waste," 24.
20. John E. Grajek to B. M. Palmer, March 15, 1943, Poultry, 1943, Petition of John W. Grajek, Milwaukee, Wisconsin, box 765, Records of the Office of Price Administration, RG 188, National Archives at College Park, Md. Hereafter cited as Records of the Office of Price Administration.
21. Robert C. Baker, "The Utilization of Problematic Animal Raw Material for Production of Human Foods from Poultry and Fish," talk given at the Third Advanced Seminar on Food Technology in Bogotá, Colombia, June 15–20, 1978, 1, box 6, Baker Papers.

22. United States Department of Agriculture, *Agricultural Statistics 1979*, 394.
23. Baker, "Food Science," 2–3.
24. Devereux, "Famine," 6.
25. Olsson, *Agrarian Crossings*.
26. Cullather, *Hungry World*.
27. Devereux, "Famine," 6; Jay Ross, "Ethiopia Reports Millions Threatened by New Famine," *Washington Post*, June 4, 1974, A1.
28. "Starvation in West Africa and Bangladesh," *Washington Post*, July 3, 1973, A16.
29. Looper, "Food, Famine," 2.
30. Thomas O'Toole, "Major U.S. Role Urged to End World Hunger: U.S. Urged to Lead Fight to Abolish World Hunger," *New York Times*, December 11, 1979, A1. For more on Borlaug and his role in the Green Revolution, the development of high-yield crops, and his standing in debates over global food supply, see Mann, *Wizard*.
31. Presidential Commission on World Hunger, "Overcoming World Hunger," 5, 8.
32. Ehrlich, *Population Bomb*, xi, 4, 5, 18.
33. Cook, *Fight for Food*, 197.
34. Ehrlich, *Population Bomb*, 21.
35. Nickerson, *Homage to Malthus*, 9, 16. It may be of some interest that Russell Kirk provides an introduction to this volume. One would be correct to deduce from this that Soames Nickerson was conservative in her political views. For further information on neo-Malthusianism, see Linnér, *Return of Malthus*.
36. Bates, *Projection for Survival*, 15, 89–91.
37. Paarlberg, "Enough Food," 290.
38. Robert Hanley, "Mowers Replace Feed Grain in New Suburb," *New York Times*, March 15, 1988, https://timesmachine.nytimes.com/timesmachine/1988/03/15/826188.html?pageNumber=29.
39. AP, "Farmland Fading under City Sprawl," *New York Times*, late edition, July 15, 1987, B28; Robert Hanley, "Mowers Replace Feed Grain in New Suburb," *New York Times*, late edition, March 15, 1988, B1.
40. Sabin, *Bet*.
41. Baker, "Problem of Food Waste," 22.
42. McCollum and Simmonds, *American Home Diet*, 62–63.
43. Ladies of Perry, Kansas, and Vicinity, *Perry Home Cook Book*, 17–18.
44. Eisenhower and Chew, *United States Department of Agriculture: Yearbook of Agriculture 1932*, 848. This figure includes specialty egg-laying hens.
45. United States Department of Agriculture, *Agricultural Statistics 1979*, 403.
46. Robert C. Baker, "URGENT! New Poultry Products Needed!," *Broiler Industry*, October 1975, 18.
47. "Are Consumers Ready? Researchers Develop Egg-Based Pizza Using Whites," box 8, Baker Papers.
48. Robert C. Baker, "Further-Processing of Broilermeat," 1986, 3, box 6, Baker Papers.
49. Robert C. Baker, "New Products for the Future," 47, box 6, Baker Papers.
50. Robert C. Baker, "What Goes into Chicken Hot Dogs?," *Dutchess Life*, June 1989, 12, box 8, Baker Papers.
51. "No End of Products We Can Make from Poultry!," *Broiler Industry*, September 1985, 14.
52. Baker, Darfler, and Bourne, "Effect of Level of Skin," 1989, 1990–1992, 1994–1995, 1995.
53. Baker, "What Goes?"

54. Baker, "URGENT!," 20.

55. E. R. Maesso, R. C. Baker, M. C. Bourne, and D. V. Vadehra, "Effect of Some Physical and Chemical Treatments in the Binding Quality of Poultry Loaves," *Journal of Food Science* 35 (1970): 440–443, 441, box 1, Baker Papers.

56. Ibid., 442.

57. E. R. Maesso, R. C. Baker, and D. V. Vadehra, "The Effect of Vacuum, Pressure, pH and Different Meat Types on the Binding Ability of Poultry Meat," *Poultry Science* 49, no. 3 (May 1970): 699.

58. Baker, "URGENT!," 20.

59. Ibid.

60. Carol L. Cleaveland, "Cornell's Col. Sanders: Poultry Expert Developing New Products from Chicken," *Post-Standard* (Syracuse, N.Y.), November 2, 1982, D1; Paul B. Brown, "Food Processors," *Forbes*, January 4, 1982, 205.

61. Yong. H. Kim, "Tasty, Dark-Meat Chicken Burgers Developed at Cornell," New York State College of Agriculture and Life Sciences, Cornell University. September 14, 1983, box 8, Baker Papers; Cleaveland, "Cornell's Col. Sanders."

62. Mark D. Frank, "Will Chicken Burgers Make Diners Squawk?," *Detroit Free Press*, n.d., folder 15, box 6, Baker Papers.

63. American Meat Institute, *U.S. Meat and Poultry Consumption*, 2.

64. Schnepf, "Consumers," 16.

65. McDepk, http://www.mcdepk.com/50/downloads/history_listing.pdf, accessed November 27, 2013.

66. Ibid.

CHAPTER 2. "The Poor Hen, She Has Become a Machine!"

The epigraph is drawn from Hinman and Harris, *Story of Meat*, 249.

1. United States Department of Agriculture, *USDA Yearbook of Agriculture 1919*, 308.

2. Hinman and Harris, *Story of Meat*, 146.

3. Perry, Banker, and Green, *Broiler Farms' Organization*, 3.

4. Pilgrim, *One Pilgrim's Progress*, 153.

5. Jeff Blyskal, "Sleepless Nights in Iowa," *Forbes*, October 25, 1982, 172.

6. N. R. Kleinfeld, "Americans Go Chicken Crazy," *New York Times*, December 9, 1984, sec. 3, 1.

7. Fitzgerald, *Every Farm*, 21–28.

8. Gisolfi, *Takeover*.

9. Williams, *Delmarva's Chicken Industry*, 11–13.

10. Ibid., 15.

11. Gisolfi, "Roots."

12. Thompson, "'Safety First,'" 1.

13. Hover and Pittman, *Profitable Farming*, 259, 254.

14. T. D. Manford Jr. to Lyndon B. Johnson, June 3, 1944, Congressional, 1944, January–December, box 18, Records of the Office of Price Administration.

15. Charles and Stuart, *Commercial Poultry Farming*, 357.

16. Lewis, *Poultry Keeping*, 267–269.

17. *Los Angeles Herald*, August 27, 1906, 4.

18. James A. Rodgers, "Poultry Raiser Must Determine the 'Best Ration' for Himself," *Los Angeles Times*, June 27, 1920, VIII22.

19. Lewis, *Poultry Keeping*, 321.

20. Valentine, *How to Keep Hens*, 242.
21. Lewis, *Poultry Keeping*, 322.
22. R. P. Hart, "The Poultry Yard: Citified Fontana Man Keeps His Hens in an 'Apartment-House,'" *Los Angeles Times*, July 2, 1933, H11.
23. "Chicago's Factory for Producing Eggs," *Baltimore Sun*, July 21, 1938, 6.
24. Avery McBee, "Mechanized Hens: Poultry Farm near Cockeysville Employs Factory Methods," *Baltimore Sun*, July 14, 1935, SM6.
25. "1,586,787 Autos Produced in 1919, 580,000 Persons Employed in Industry by 170 Concerns," *Washington Post*, March 21, 1920, 55.
26. H. R. Tolley and L. M. Church, "Corn-Belt Farmers' Experience with Motor Trucks," United States Department of Agriculture Bulletin No. 931, Washington, D.C., February 25, 1921, 2.
27. Frank Ridgway, "Trucks Growing in Popularity among Farmers: Rush Produce and Milk to Chicago Terminal," *Chicago Daily Tribune*, November 17, 1935, C4.
28. Hinman and Harris, *Story of Meat*, 186–187.
29. Ibid., 191, 193, 194, 195.
30. Lewis, *Main Street*, 118.
31. Deutsch, *Building a Housewife's Paradise*, chap. 1.
32. Riis, *How the Other Half Lives*, 115.
33. May, *Canning Clan*, 322. See also Zeide, *Canned*.
34. Van Syckle, "Changes in Food Consumption," 232.
35. Ibid., 247.
36. McCollum and Simmonds, *American Home Diet*, preface, 39.
37. H. L. Mencken, "Bad Food Fanciers," *Chicago Tribune*, June 13, 1926, quoted in Dubasky, *Gist of Mencken*, 772. For some examples of the influences of ethnic cuisines upon American food, see Avakian and Haber, *From Betty Crocker*, esp. chaps. 10, 13; Brown and Mussell, *Ethnic Regional Foodways*; Chen, *Chop Suey USA*; Coe, *Chop Suey*; Diner, *Hungering for America*; Shortridge and Shortridge, *Taste of American Place*.
38. Rodgers, *Impossible H. L. Mencken*, 443.
39. H. L. Mencken, "Victualry as a Fine Art," in Mencken, *Prejudices: Sixth Series*, 184–185. See also Harper, "Anti–Chain Store Movement," 29.
40. Levenstein, *Revolution at the Table*, 162.
41. Levinson, *Great A&P*, 8.
42. Hasia Diner argues that the abundance offered by the United States led to the creation of new Italian American and Jewish American cuisines based upon the habits of elites within the immigrants' countries of origin and religious traditions. For Diner, it is abundance as much as availability that is responsible for reforming new immigrant ethnicities centered around food. However, the anecdotal nature of the study's sources make it difficult to determine the full extent of the penury experienced in Europe by those immigrants who were not Irish. See Diner, *Hungering for America*.
43. Federal Trade Commission, Chain Store Enquiry, *Growth and Development of Chain Stores*, 66–67, quoted in Harper, "Anti–Chain Store Movement," 449.
44. Department of Commerce, *Survey of Current Business*, quoted in Harper, "Anti–Chain Store Movement," 454.
45. 1939 Census of Business, *Retail Trade, Vol. 1, Part 1*, table 20, 179–182, quoted in Harper, "Anti–Chain Store Movement," 455.
46. Levinson, *Great A&P*, 8.
47. Strasser, "Woolworth to Wal-Mart," 51.

48. John E. Grajek, "Petition for Amendment, Part 1429, Poultry and Eggs, Revised Maximum Price Regulation No. 269, 'Poultry,'" December 18, 1942, 3, Poultry, 1943, Petition of John W. Grajek, Milwaukee, Wisconsin, box 765, Records of the Office of Price Administration.

49. Chester B. Franz to St. Louis Chamber of Commerce, March 15, 1943, Poultry and Eggs Miscellaneous—General, box 11, Records of the Office of Price Administration.

50. Theodore W. Henrichs, "Voice of the People: Poultryman's Troubles," *Chicago Tribune*, December 26, 1942, 8.

51. Williams, *Delmarva's Chicken Industry*, 36.

52. "All Chickens in Storage to Go to Military," *Chicago Daily Tribune*, December 30, 1943, 1.

53. Minutes of the Poultry and Egg Procurement Board, May 20, 1944, Poultry and Egg Procurement Board Meetings, box 11, Records of the Office of Price Administration.

54. Minutes of the Poultry and Egg Procurement Board, July 1, 1944, Poultry and Egg Procurement Board Meetings, box 11, Records of the Office of Price Administration.

55. Ibid.

56. Walter H. Waggoner, "Price of Poultry Increased by OPA: Rise, to Cost $15,000,000 to Be in Effect May, June and First Half of 1945," *New York Times*, April 21, 1944.

57. Joseph F. McGowan to Raymond Einhorn, November 29, 1943, Poultry: Telegrams, Activity Reports, Misc. Material, box 17, Records of the Office of Price Administration.

58. Joseph Montgomery to Raymond Einhorn, September 26, 1944, Poultry: Telegrams, Activity Reports, Misc. Material, box 17, Records of the Office of Price Administration.

59. Prentiss H. Brown to David J. Ward, September 14, 1943, Congressional, 1943, January–September, box 18, Records of the Office of Price Administration.

60. "Harlem Dealer Sent to Jail by OPA for Price Cheating," *New York Amsterdam News*, August 21, 1943, 1.

61. Williams, *Delmarva's Chicken Industry*, 39.

62. United States Department of Agriculture, *Agricultural Statistics 1945*, 371, 384.

63. Ibid., 387.

64. United States Department of Agriculture, *Agricultural Statistics 1943*, 342; *Agricultural Statistics 1945*, 382. The USDA defines the South Atlantic region as Delaware, Maryland, Virginia, West Virginia, North Carolina, South Carolina, Georgia, and Florida.

65. "Wickard Urges Further Increases in Poultry Meat Production," 1943, Poultry and Eggs Miscellaneous—General, Records of the Office of Price Administration.

66. Williams, *Delmarva's Chicken Industry*, 40.

67. Charles E. Kellogg, "What Is Farm Research?" 17–32, quoted in Stefferud, *Yearbook*, 22, 17.

68. Chester Bowles to Robert A. Taft, August 12, 1943, Congressional, 1943, January–September, box 18, Records of the Office of Price Administration.

69. "Feeding Chickens in Spring," *Baltimore Sun*, April 14, 1940, M14.

70. Bowles to Taft, August 12, 1943.

71. "Holly's System Unique: Here's How It Works," *Broiler Industry*, April 1968, 38.

72. "Holly's Quiet Miracle: Brands ½ Billion Lbs.," *Broiler Industry*, October 1975, 33; "Holly's Deep Chill Profitable in '74!," *Broiler Industry*, September 1975, 14.

73. "Hidden Nite—Holly Farms," 1969, folder 98, box 701, Local 525 Collection, Southern Labor Archives, Georgia State University, Atlanta. Hereafter cited as Local 525 Collection.

74. United States Department of Agriculture, *Agricultural Statistics 1971*, 422.

75. "Poultry Science Hall of Fame," https://cals.ncsu.edu/prestage-department-of-poultry-science/about/hall-of-fame/, accessed October 25, 2019.

76. *The Fifty: Sincerely Bill France*, video, Indianapolis: Ligner Group Productions for ESPN Video, 1998, quoted in Pierce, *Real NASCAR*, 16.

77. Vance Packard, "Millions in Moonshine," *American Magazine*, September 1950, 46–47.

78. "Charlie A. Felts, interview with Aaron Lancaster, Appalachian State University, Spring 2011," in Lancaster, "Chasing," 78.

79. R10958747, Wilkes County, North Carolina, U.S. Census, 1790, Race and Slave Status; R10958739, Wilkes County, North Carolina, U.S. Census, 1860, Race; R10958744, Wilkes County, North Carolina, U.S. Census, 1910, Race; R10958745, Wilkes County, North Carolina, U.S. Census, 1930, Race; R10958735, Wilkes County, North Carolina, U.S. Census, 1970, Comprehensive, all in Social Explorer, https://www.socialexplorer.com/us-census-data, accessed May 19, 2015.

80. R10958735, Wilkes County, North Carolina, U.S. Census, 1970, Comprehensive; United States Department of Commerce, Bureau of the Census, "Characteristics," 3.

81. Pierce, *Real NASCAR*, 225, 286.

82. Company-owned farm production accounted for the remaining 20 percent of total broiler production. Roy, *Contract Farming*, 28.

83. Gisolfi, "Roots," 48.

84. Lloyd et al., *Cost of Broiler Production*.

85. C. Howard Smith, "How Holly Farms Grows a Million Broilers a Week," *Broiler Industry*, August 1965, 38.

86. Ibid., 38.

87. Ibid., 44.

88. Omo-Osagie, *Commercial Poultry Production*, 99, 104–105.

89. The plight of poultry contractors achieved widespread notoriety in the 2000s through the popular documentary film *Food, Inc.* (2008). The subject was revisited in greater detail in *Under Contract: Farmers and the Fine Print* (2017). For more on the Tyson Foods tournament, see Leonard, *Meat Racket*.

90. Ahmed and Sieling, "Two Decades," 36.

91. "Federal Compress Sale of Certain Property Is Approved by Holders," *Wall Street Journal*, September 30, 1968, 4; "Federal Compress Unit Buys Eckhart Milling for Cash," *Wall Street Journal*, July 14, 1964, 10.

92. "Federal Co. to Acquire Halberts Inc., 6 Units," *Wall Street Journal*, May 6, 1969, 7.

93. MBPXL represented the merger of Missouri Beef Packers and Kansas Beef Packers, formerly known as the Excel Packing Company, in 1974. In 1979 MBPXL was purchased by Cargill and was renamed Excel in 1982.

94. William A. Haffert, "How Companies Rate in Hourly Capacity," *Broiler Industry*, March 1976, 17. Incidentally, Armour and Company revived its fortunes in the 1950s through the popularity of Dial, its popular brand of soap developed from meat by-products. In 1970 Greyhound Corporation, the bus operator, purchased Armour-Dial, and its headquarters departed from Chicago, the city with which it was most closely associated. See "Armour Holders Vote Plan for Greyhound to Own All of Common," *Wall Street Journal*, December 21, 1970, 8; "Greyhound to Control 90% of Armour Stock," *Chicago Tribune*, July 4, 1969, C9; Hamilton, *Trucking Country*, 135–138, 154. See also D. Fink, *Cutting*.

95. "USDA Asked to Speed O.K. of Overseas Automation," *Broiler Industry*, July 1973, 22, 23.

96. Ibid., 23, 24.
97. "Fried Chicken in a Can: The 'Philadelphia Story,'" *Broiler Industry*, May 1967, 34; "Holly's Quiet Miracle," 34.
98. Blank, *Chicken Real*.
99. "Now It Is Retailer Who Demands Dry Chilled," *Broiler Industry*, April 1968, 28.
100. "Holly's System Unique," 40.
101. "Now It Is Retailer," 30.
102. Ibid., 36.
103. "Holly's System Unique," 42.
104. "Holly's Quiet Miracle," 30.
105. "Now It Is Retailer," 30.
106. Hyman, "Rethinking the Postwar Corporation," 197–198.
107. "34 Firms Do 70% of U.S. Volume," *Broiler Industry*, October 1970, 12.
108. Townsend, *Up the Organization*.
109. Hyman, "Rethinking the Postwar Corporation," 205–207.
110. "Tyson's Goal: $1 Billion Sales in 1985," *Broiler Industry*, April 1982, 34.
111. "Nation's Top Broiler Firms," *Broiler Industry*, December 1983, 22; "Valmac Takeover Completed," *Wall Street Journal*, January 17, 1985, 46.
112. "Tyson Foods Buys Another Plant; May Add Burger King as Client," *Broiler Industry*, January 1985, 12.
113. Ray A. Goldberg, "Broiler Dynamics—Past and Future," *Broiler Industry*, July 1976, 15–16; Betsy Morris and Roy Harris Jr., "ConAgra to Buy Greyhound Unit for $166 Million," *Wall Street Journal*, June 30, 1983, 8; Marj Charlier, "ConAgra Agrees to Acquire 50% of a Meatpacker," *Wall Street Journal*, June 1, 1987, 1.
114. Michael Fritz, "Contented Pigs?," *Forbes*, August 7, 1989, 118.
115. "Tyson Foods Bids for Holly Farms," *New York Times*, October 12, 1988, D1.
116. Striffler, *Chicken*, 65.
117. Ted Bailey, "ConAgra and Holly Farms Enter into Definitive Agreement for Holly Farms to Merge with ConAgra," *Business Wire*, November 17, 1988, 1.
118. "Holly Farms Move Blocked," *New York Times*, November 26, 1988, A32.
119. "Holly Farms, ConAgra Say Court Won't Keep Them Apart," *Orlando Sentinel*, January 4, 1989, C6; "Holly Seeks Restraining Order," *Oklahoma City Journal Record*, May 16, 1989.
120. "Tyson Closes Holly Farms Offer," *Oklahoma City Journal Accord*, July 19, 1989.
121. Scott Charton, "Chicken King's Quest for Rival Took Patience: Tyson Foods Chairman Bided His Time in the Protracted Tussle for Holly Farms," *Orlando Sentinel*, July 9, 1989, D1; "Nation's Top Broiler Companies, 1988," *Broiler Industry*, December 1988, 48.
122. Kim Clark, "Tyson Foresees No Layoffs at Holly Farms; Top Chicken Man Claims 'Fun' Image," *Baltimore Sun*, August 18, 1989, 2B.
123. Burrough and Helyar, *Barbarians at the Gate*.
124. Clark, "Tyson Foresees," 2B.
125. Mollie Rorrer, "Union Accepted at Holly Farms," *Richmond-Times Dispatch*, March 17, 1989, A18; Frank Swoboda, "Labor's Love Lost at Holly Farms: N.C. Chicken Producer Embroiled in Dispute with Teamsters," *Washington Post*, May 3, 1990, E1.
126. "Tyson Foods Ordered by Court to Negotiate with Teamsters Union," *Wall Street Journal*, March 15, 1995, B4.
127. Holly Farms Corporation; Tyson Foods, Incorporated v. National Labor Relations

Board, nos. 93-1710, 93-1882, United States Court of Appeals, Fourth Circuit, decided, March 10, 1995.

128. Paul M. Barrett, "Top Court to Hear Tyson Appeal of Labor-Law Status of Truckers," *Wall Street Journal*, November 7, 1995, B8.

129. Holly Farms Corp. v. National Labor Relations Board, 517 U.S. 392 (1996). Whereas the Court unanimously agreed that truck drivers were nonagricultural employees, forklift truck drivers were voted in the same category by a 5–4 decision with support from Justices Breyer, Ginsburg, Kennedy, Souter, and Stevens.

130. David Amey, "Nation's Top Broiler Companies," *Broiler Industry*, December 1989, 50.

131. Arthur Buckler, "Tyson Foods Isn't Chicken-Hearted about Expansion," *Wall Street Journal*, January 18, 1994, B4.

132. "We Went to the Public for Money!," *Broiler Industry*, October 1960, 61.

133. R. Charles Brooks, "Structure and Performance of the U.S. Broiler Industry," *Farm Structure*, Committee on Agriculture, Nutrition and Forestry, United States Senate (April 1980), 196–215, 205.

134. Ibid.

135. Jeff Blyskal, "Food Processors," *Forbes*, January 2, 1984, 207.

136. Laura Jereski, "Food Distributors: In the Supermarket Business, the Bigger You Are the More Money You Make—up to a Point," *Forbes*, January 13, 1986, 152.

137. Lichtenstein, *Retail Revolution*, 43.

138. Mark Clifford, "The Supermarket Seesaw," *Forbes*, August 26, 1985, 76.

139. Ibid.

140. Robert Reno, "Regulators Ratify Wall Street Excess as National Policy," *Newsday*, March 11, 1987, 47.

141. Terry Bivens, "Feeding on Food Firms the Merger Menu Offers a New Dish," *Philadelphia Inquirer*, October 27, 1985, F1.

142. Executive Order 12,291, February 17, 1981, 3 C.F.R. 127 (1982); Linder, "I Gave My Employer," 113–114.

143. Merrill Brown, "Senate Panel Criticizes Reagan Merger Policy," *Washington Post*, October 28, 1981, D9; Martin Sikora, "Reagan: The Merger Catalyst," *Mergers and Acquisitions* 39, no. 7 (July 2004): 3.

144. Reno, "Regulators Ratify," 47.

145. Companies that sold popular branded foods offered strong returns to investors through most of the 1980s. Leading brands such as Kellogg, ConAgra, H. J. Heinz, Hershey, and General Mills offered average returns on equity of 27.7 percent, 26 percent, 19.5 percent, 19.9 percent, and 19.1 percent, respectively, between 1980 and 1985. *Forbes*'s top thirty-five branded food companies offered a median average of 16.8 percent, while the top twelve commodity companies and top ten meatpacking companies averaged 15.2 percent and 14.5 percent, respectively, over the same five-year span. Even when commodity prices started to rise again in the late 1980s many packaged food brands were able to maintain profitability by passing prices on to consumers. "The media provided exceptional free advertising for price hikes by putting every dry cornfield in Iowa on the evening news," observed market analyst George Dahlman in 1989; see "Food Processors," *Forbes*, January 14, 1985, 148–150; Janet Novack, "Food Processors," *Forbes*, January 9, 1989, 144–149.

146. National Chicken Council, "Per Capita Consumption of Poultry and Livestock, 1965 to Forecast 2022, in Pounds," https://www.nationalchickencouncil.org/about-the

-industry/statistics/per-capita-consumption-of-poultry-and-livestock-1965-to-estimated-2012-in-pounds/, accessed November 15, 2023.

147. McKenna, *Big Chicken*.
148. Zuidhof et al., "Growth, Efficiency, and Yield."
149. Havenstein et al., "Carcass Composition."

CHAPTER 3. Broken Bones, Broken Laws, and the Rise of AMC Local 525

1. Statement: Alma Gryder, 1957, folder 111, box 702, Local 525 Collection. All statements are located in this folder and box.
2. Statement: Jennie Joines, 1957.
3. Statement: Alma Gryder, 1957.
4. Statement: Margaret Elledge, 1957.
5. Statement: Alma Gryder, 1957.
6. Ibid.
7. Statement: Carrie Johnson, 1957.
8. Statement: Jennie Joines, 1957.
9. Emanuel Coutlakis to Louis Perloff, September 4, 1957, folder 111, box 702, Local 525 Collection.
10. Statement: Jennie Joines, 1957.
11. Statement: Carrie Johnson, 1957.
12. Statement: Alma Gryder, 1957.
13. Statement: Carrie Johnson, 1957.
14. Statement: Margaret Shoemaker, 1957.
15. Statement: Alma Gryder, 1957.
16. Ibid.
17. Hearing before the Subcommittee on Legislation Affecting the Food and Drug Administration of the Committee on Labor and Public Welfare, United States Senate, 84th Cong., 2nd sess., on S. 3176, May 9, 1956, n. 17, p. 20, quoted in Charles Coble, "The Department of Agriculture's Regulation of Poultry under the Poultry Products Inspection Act of 1957," Harvard University, January 25, 1997, https://dash.harvard.edu/bitstream handle/1/10018981/ccoble.pdf?sequence=1&isAllowed=y.
18. See Christensen, *Paradox*.
19. Linder, "I Gave My Employer," 68–90.
20. "Winston Holly Farms' Workers on Strike: A Fact Sheet," folder 95, box 701, Local 525 Collection.
21. Ibid.
22. "Notes, Holly Farms Poultry Co. 7/3/57," folder 95, box 701, Local 525 Collection.
23. John Russell to Sheriff of Wilkes County, July 5, 1957, via Western Union, folder 95, box 701, Local 525 Collection.
24. Warren Olney III to John Russell, July 10, 1957, folder 95, box 701, Local 525 Collection.
25. Emanuel Coutlakis to Patrick E. Gorman, May 1, 1971, folder 103, box 701, Local 525 Collection.
26. "Holly Farms Poultry Industries, Inc., and Local 525, Meat, Food and Allied Workers Union, Amalgamated Meat Cutters & Butcher Workmen of North America, AFL-CIO. Cases Nos. 11-CA-4725, 11-CA-4295, 11-CA-4421. Memorandum Brief," 1–3, folder 105, box 701, Local 525 Collection.
27. Statement of Daisy Allen, folder 105, box 701, Local 525 Collection.

28. Note by Cornelius A. Simmons, folder 102, box 701, Local 525 Collection. While folder 102, in which Cornelius Simmons's letter can be found, is titled "1970, Correspondence, Monroe," the letter is undated, and it is hard to be certain that 1970 was indeed the year in which it was written. Though the famous Greensboro sit-in protests occurred in 1960, other areas within the state evolved at different speeds. In 1956 North Carolina passed into law the Pearsall Plan, legislation that transferred responsibility for desegregation over to local authorities, the aim being to thwart *Brown v. Board of Education*. Desegregation remained a contentious issue into the late 1960s. See Richardson, "'Not Gradually,'" 353. See also Chafe, *Civilities and Civil Rights*; Hanchett, *Sorting Out*.

29. Patrick E. Gorman to C. F. Lovette, February 25, 1972, folder 103, box 701, Local 525 Collection.

30. "National Labor Relations Board, Holly Farms Poultry Industries, Inc., Employer, and Local 525, Meat, Food and Allied Workers Union, Amalgamated Meat Cutters and Butcher Workmen of North America, AFL-CIO, petitioner. Case No. 11-RC-3221. November 16, 1973. Tally of Ballots," folder 107, box 701, Local 525 Collection.

31. *Local 525 Stewardgram*, May 1966, 3, folder 39, box 696, Local 525 Collection. All issues of the *Stewardgram* are in this folder and box.

32. *Local 525 Stewardgram*, April 1969, 3.

33. *Local 525 Stewardgram*, May 1966, 2.

34. *Local 525 Stewardgram*, August 1969, 1.

35. *Local 525 Stewardgram*, June–July 1967, 4.

36. Paul Hoffman, "Tobacco: Leaf to Cigarette: From Leaf to Pack Taking a Tobacco Tour," *New York Times*, September 26, 1976, 11.

37. Redburn, "Protest and Policy," 51.

38. Agger, Goldrich, and Swanson, *Rulers*, 352–353, quoted in ibid., 53.

39. Ibid., 52.

40. Frazier, "Durham," quoted in Leslie Brown, *Upbuilding Black Durham*, 14.

41. Ibid., 18.

42. See Greene, *Our Separate Ways*.

43. Ibid., 11.

44. "Gold Kist Workers Strike," *Raleigh News & Observer*, July 26, 1978, folder 20, box 13, Local 525 Collection; Laura Green Langley, interview with Lane Windham, November 15, 1989, transcript in author's possession.

45. Laura Green to John Russell, August 1, 1965, 1, folder 8, box 31, Local 525 Collection.

46. Laura Green to John Russell, November 24, 1965, folder 8, box 31, Local 525 Collection.

47. Ibid., 1. Timothy Pachirat considers some of the potential psychological consequences of being a "killer" and how the position is regarded by slaughterhouse workers in *Every Twelve Seconds*, 149–152.

48. Malizia, "Earnings Gap," 19–20.

49. "Union Proposals to Gold Kist Company," 1, folder 22, box 2, Local 525 Collection.

50. "Agreement between Gold Kist Poultry, Durham, North Carolina and Amalgamated Meat Cutters and Butcher Workmen of North America and Local Union 525, Effective July 13, 1975 to July 15, 1978," 9–11, 26, folder 1, Gold Kist Legal Challenge, Local 525 Collection.

51. Ibid., Exhibit B, 1.

52. Progressive Labor Party, "Road to Revolution III," *PL Magazine* 8, no. 3 (November 1971): 8–24.

53. See Georgakis and Surkin, *Detroit*; Ranney, *Living and Dying*; Antaya, "The New Left."
54. *WAM Newsletter*, no. 5, June 18, 1974, 2, 3, 1, folder 21, box 20, Local 525 Collection.
55. Ibid., 2.
56. *WAM Newsletter*, no. 2, June 27, 1974, 3, folder 21, box 20, Local 525 Collection.
57. *WAM Newsletter*, no. 1, June 10, 1974, 4, folder 20, box 20, Local 525 Collection.
58. Karen Walker, interview by author, November 15, 2013.
59. Ibid.
60. *WAM Newsletter*, no. 9, December 2, 1974, 2, folder 21, box 20, Local 525 Collection.
61. Laura Green, urgent message, folder 21, box 20, Local 525 Collection.
62. Walker interview. Incidentally, throwing gall bladders at one another was a popular activity at Gold Kist in Durham. "We had great, great gall bladder fights," Walker recalled.
63. Ibid.
64. Ortiz and Jacobs, *Safety and Health Assessment*, 6.
65. Karen Walker, Larry Brandon, Anne Smith, Lloyd Brewer, and Johnny Elliott, Plaintiffs, v. Local 525, Meat, Food and Allied Workers Union, etc., et al., Defendants, "Plaintiff Karen Walker's Answer to Union Defendants' First Interrogations," no. A-C-76-534, United States District Court for the Western District of North Carolina, Asheville Division, folder 1, Gold Kist Legal Challenge, Local 525 Collection.
66. "Gold Kist North Carolina Poultry Division, Durham, N.C., Personnel Transaction: Karen Elizabeth Walker," March 31, 1977, folder 22, box 20, Local 525 Collection.
67. D. Wilson Still to John Russell, September 6, 1978, folder 22, box 20, Local 525 Collection.
68. Walker interview.
69. Barbara Green to Harry R. Poole, April 24, 1978, folder 22, box 20, Local 525 Collection.
70. Ibid.
71. "Gold Kist Workers Reject Offer," August 1, 1978; and John Russell to Leon B. Schachter, August 25, 1978, both in folder 20, box 13, Local 525 Collection.
72. "Gold Kist Workers on Strike," July 28, 1978, folder 20, box 13, Local 525 Collection.
73. Russell to Schachter, August 25, 1978, 2.
74. Ibid.
75. Betty W. Mushak, "Pickets Man Lines at Gold Kist Firm," *Durham Morning Herald*, July 26, 1978, folder 20, box 13, Local 525 Collection.
76. *On the (Picket) Line*, July 1978, folder 7, box 25, Local 525 Collection.
77. "Gold Kist and United Food and Commercial Workers International Union, AFL-CIO, Local 525," National Labor Relations Board, case no. 11-CA-7901, 4.
78. Russell to Schachter, August 25, 1978, 2.
79. "Gold Kist and United Food and Commercial Workers," 7–10.
80. Ibid., 12.
81. Gold Kist Inc. and Amalgamated Meat Cutters and Butcher Workmen of North America, AFL-CIO, CLC, Local 525, "Respondent's Answering Brief to General Counsel's Exceptions," United States of America before the National Labor Relations Board, case no. 11-CA-7901, 2.
82. Ibid., 4, 29.
83. Ibid., 15.

84. Alison Howard, "Testimony Begins on Violence during Gold Kist Strike," *Durham Morning Herald*, September 8, 1978, B18, folder 7, box 25, Local 525 Collection.
85. "Gold Kist and United Food and Commercial Workers," 17.
86. Ibid., 18–19.
87. Ibid., 20–24.
88. Russell to Schachter, August 25, 1978, 3.
89. Ibid., 2–4.
90. "Gold Kist Poultry, Durham, North Carolina, Offers a Reward," *Durham Morning Herald*, August 26, 1978, folder 20, box 13, Local 525 Collection.
91. Ted Mellnik, "N.C. Urban-Rural Income Gap Widens," *Charlotte Observer*, May 17, 1992, 1D.
92. *Hamlet: Out of the Ashes*, North Carolina Occupational Safety and Health Project, Chapel Hill, videocassette, 02 Productions, 1994; for a more extensive exploration of the fire, the workers involved, and the Roe family's involvement in the poultry business, see Simon, *Hamlet Fire*.
93. William A. Haffert Jr., "Broiler Industry's Third Great Revolution!," *Broiler Industry*, January 1985, 100–112.
94. "At Shoney's the Focus Is on Details," *New York Times*, June 8, 1984, D1–5.
95. C. E. Yandle and Jim Barnett, "The Road to Ruin," *Raleigh News & Observer*, December 10, 1991, 8A.
96. "Haverpride Farms: The 'New Kid on the Block,'" *Broiler Industry*, November 1984, 30.
97. Yandle and Barnett, "The Road to Ruin," 10A–11A.
98. Ibid., 9A; "Civil Docket for Case #: 1:89-CV-01215-MHS, Cagle's Inc. v. Imperial Foods, Inc., et al.," U.S. District Court, Northern District of Georgia (Atlanta); James Greiff and Ken Garfield, "Debt Dogged Imperial's Owner—Then the Fire," *Charlotte Observer*, September 15, 1991, 12A.
99. Greiff and Garfield, "Debt Dogged," 10A.
100. Steve Riley, "Hamlet Twice Had Threatened to Close Plant," *Raleigh News & Observer*, September 19, 1991, 1B, 8B.
101. Statement by Phillip J. Kirk Jr., President, North Carolina Citizens for Business and Industry, Legislative Research Commission Committee on Fire and Occupational Safety, State Legislative Building, Raleigh, January 6, 1992, 1, box 36, North Carolina Occupational Safety and Health Project Records, Southern Historical Collection, Wilson Library, University of North Carolina at Chapel Hill.
102. George Watts, "Hamlet's Tragedy Was an Exception," *Charlotte Observer*, November 18, 1992, 15A; Clayton Loflin, "Not a Poultry Processor," *Raleigh News & Observer*, November 9, 1991, 13A.
103. Jane Ruffin, "Dreams of Better Days," *Raleigh News & Observer*, December 9, 1991, 7A–8A.
104. "Nuclear Site Choices Delayed Sites in Richmond, Chatham and Wake Counties to Be Studied," *Richmond County News Record*, March 24, 1990; Alison Davis, "Nuclear Waste Site Finalists Approved," *Greensboro News Record*, May 1, 1990, 1; "N.C. Court Rules against Counties in Radioactive Waste Site Suits," *Rock Hill Herald*, February 3, 1993, 10A; Jim Molis, "North Carolina Nuclear Waste Dump Woes Imperil Bond Deal," *Bond Buyer*, July 28, 1997, 30.
105. *Hamlet: Out of the Ashes*.
106. Transcript of an interview conducted by Frank Trogdon, Joe Bolton, Doug Jones,

and David Poole of the North Carolina Department of Labor with unidentified former Imperial Food Products employee, November 7, 1991, commencing 1:08 p.m., 7, North Carolina Department of Labor, Raleigh, N.C.

107. Ibid., 13.

108. Imperial Food Products, Inc., Fire Investigation interview statement, September 9, 1991, commencing 3:13 p.m., 6, North Carolina Department of Labor, Raleigh, N.C.; interview transcript, November 7, 1991, commencing 1:08 p.m., 6.

109. Transcript of interview conducted by Frank Trogdon, Joe Bolton, and Charles W. Johnson of the North Carolina Department of Labor with unidentified former Imperial Food Products employee, November 8, 1991, commencing 9:00 a.m., 11, North Carolina Department of Labor, Raleigh, N.C.; transcript of interview conducted by Frank Trogdon, Joe Bolton, Doug Jones, and David Poole of the North Carolina Department of Labor with unidentified former Imperial Food Products employee, November 7, 1991, commencing 8:54 a.m., 31, North Carolina Department of Labor, Raleigh, N.C.

110. Interview transcript, November 7, 1991, commencing 1:08 p.m., 6, 16.

111. Interview transcript, November 7, 1991, commencing 8:54 a.m., 51–52.

112. Interview transcript, November 8, 1991, commencing 9:00 a.m., 42.

113. Chicken Processing Plant Fires Hamlet, North Carolina (September 3, 1991) and North Little Rock, Arkansas (June 7, 1991), report 057, 1992, 10–11, USFA Fire Investigation Technical Report Series, TriData Corp., Arlington, Va., Federal Emergency Management Agency, Washington, D.C.

114. Paige Williams, "Jackson Rallies Hamlet: 'Save Our Workers!,'" *Charlotte Observer*, September 11, 1991, 6A.

115. Rachel Buchanan, "Hamlet Fire Rally Held," *Raleigh News & Observer*, October 19, 1991, 1B–2B.

116. Jesse Jackson, address before the Democratic National Committee, New York, July 14, 1992, https://www.c-span.org/video/?c4693350/user-clip-hamlet-nc-jesse-jackson-dnc.

117. Bob Hall, "Chicken Empires," *Southern Exposure* 17, no. 2 (Summer 1989): 19.

118. Bruce Ingersoll, "Faster Slaughter Lines Are Contaminating Much U.S. Poultry," *Wall Street Journal*, November 16, 1990, A1.

119. "Repetitive Motion Injuries in North Carolina," North Carolina Occupational Safety and Health Project, 1987, box 32, NCOSH Collection, University of North Carolina, Chapel Hill.

120. Christopher Drew, "Repetitive-Motion Injuries Cut Wider Swath," *Chicago Tribune*, November 3, 1988, 6.

121. Linder, "I Gave My Employer," 54n118; "Confronting Repetitive Motion Illnesses in the Workplace," Employment and Housing Subcommittee, Committee on Government Operations, House of Representatives, 102nd Cong., 1st sess., March 28, 1991, 121, https://babel.hathitrust.org/cgi/pt?id=pur1.32754075295976&seq=1.

122. "Dramatic Rise in Repetitive Motion Injuries and OSHA's Response," Employment and Housing Subcommittee, Committee on Government Operations, House of Representatives, 101st Cong., 1st sess., June 6, 1989, 64.

123. Albert R. Karr, "U.S. Proposes $2.6 Million Fine against IBP," *Wall Street Journal*, July 22, 1987, 1.

124. Albert R. Karr, "IBP Inc. to Pay $975,000 in Fines on OSHA Charges," *Wall Street Journal*, November 25, 1988, 1.

125. Albert R. Karr, "OSHA Urges Record Penalty for Meatpacker," *Wall Street Journal*, October 31, 1988, 1.

126. Al Zack, Eleanor Kennelly, and Jim Lyons, "Morrell Co. Hit with Largest OSHA Fine Ever," *Business Wire*, October 28, 1988, 1.

127. Albert R. Karr, "United Brands' Morrell Unit Settles Charges by OSHA," *Wall Street Journal*, March 22, 1990, A16.

128. Hall, "I Feel What Women Feel."

129. S. Kiken, W. Stringer, L. Fine, T. Sinks, and S. Tanaka, *Health Hazard Evaluation Report: HETA-89-307-2009, Perdue Farms, Inc., Lewiston, North Carolina, Robersonville, North Carolina* (Cincinnati, Ohio: U.S. Department of Health and Human Services, Public Health Service, Centers for Disease Control, National Institute for Occupational Safety and Health, February 1990), 1–4.

130. Ibid., 14, 16.

131. Linder, "I Gave My Employer," 118.

132. Barnaby J. Feder, "A Spreading Pain, and Cries for Justice," *New York Times*, June 5, 1994, 92.

133. Michael Weisskopf and David Maraniss, "Forging an Alliance for Deregulation," *Washington Post*, March 12, 1995, A01.

134. "Labor Dept. Relents on Repetitive Strain," *New York Times*, March 21, 1995, D19; Steve Lohr, "Administration Balks at New Job Standards on Repetitive Strain," *New York Times*, June 12, 1995, D1.

135. Sara Fritz, "Critics Question Clintons' Ties to Tyson Scion," *Los Angeles Times*, June 12, 1994, OCA1; Lichtenstein, *A Fabulous Failure*, chap. 1.

136. Ayers, *Southern Journey*, 94–107.

137. See Striffler, *Chicken*; L. Fink, *Maya of Morganton*; Schwartzman, *Chicken Trail*.

138. Pachirat, *Every Twelve Seconds*.

139. See L. Fink, *Maya of Morganton*; Schwartzmann, *Chicken Trail*; Stuesse, *Scratching Out a Living*.

CHAPTER 4. The Business of Feeding People

1. Thomas, *Dave's Way*, 70, 72.
2. Alberts, *Good Provider*.
3. Thomas, *Dave's Way*, 72.
4. Baldwin, *Taco Titan*, 60.
5. McDepk, "McDonald's Stores," http://www.mcdepk.com/50/downloads/history_listing.pdf, accessed November 27, 2013. Website no longer exists.
6. "Sales and Market Share by Company," *Restaurant Business*, September 1974.
7. Wyckoff and Sasser, *Chain-Restaurant Industry*, 100.
8. Ibid., 111.
9. Davis and Robinson, "R. David Thomas."
10. Ibid.
11. Thomas, *Dave's Way*, 107.
12. Rhyne, "An Evaluation," 195.
13. "International Franchise Association's Interest in Size Standards," in U.S. Congress, Senate, Committee on Small Business, *Small Business Administration's Size Standards*, 97th Cong., 1st sess., 1981, Committee Print, 248–249.
14. See also Schlosser, *Fast Food Nation*, 102.
15. Rhyne, "An Evaluation," 195.
16. Critser, *Fat Land*, 112.
17. Edward L. Hudgins, "Helping Small Business by Eliminating the Small Business Administration," *Backgrounder*, May 13, 1985, 4.

18. Emerson, *New Economics*, 14–15; Bernstein, *Sambo's*.
19. Schnepf, *Consumers*, 16.
20. United States Department of Agriculture, Economic Research Service, "Table 10, Food Expenditures Data Set," http://www.ers.usda.gov/data-products/food-expenditures.aspx#, accessed December 31, 2013.
21. Thomas, *Dave's Way*, 116.
22. Wyckoff and Sasser, *Chain-Restaurant Industry*, 95.
23. Emerson, *New Economics*, 116–118.
24. Wyckoff and Sasser, *Chain-Restaurant Industry*, 101.
25. *U.S. Meat and Poultry Consumption: An Overview* (Washington, D.C.: American Meat Institute, 2009), 2.
26. Edward Clifford, "Stable Beef Prices Forecast as High Feed Cost Spurs Sales," *Globe and Mail* (Toronto), October 11, 1980, B16.
27. United States Department of Agriculture, *Agricultural Statistics 1989*, 260.
28. United States Department of Agriculture, *Agricultural Statistics 1976*, 396, 403; United States Department of Agriculture, *Agricultural Statistics 1981*, 394, 401; United States Department of Agriculture, *Agricultural Statistics 1989*, 350.
29. Judy Herders, "Despite High Beef Prices: The Best Meat Bargains This Week Are . . . ," *Chicago Tribune*, April 26, 1979, D3.
30. Seth S. King, "Cattle Drop Seen Lifting Beef Prices: Beef Prices Up 37% in Year Drop Cited in Cattle," *New York Times*, April 20, 1979, D11.
31. Ibid., D1.
32. Jeff Byssal, "The Burger Boom Slows Down," *Forbes*, October 11, 1982, 45.
33. Jane Y. Wallace, "Menus Have Changed, Often Dramatically," *Restaurants & Institutions*, March 15, 1981, 38.
34. Mehlman Petrzela, *Fit Nation*, 153–158.
35. Alan Maltun, "Stomachs Flat, Profits Fat in Health Boom," *Los Angeles Times*, September 2, 1979, 5.
36. William Overend, "Flocking to the Body Temples with the Gym Generation," *Los Angeles Times*, May 6, 1981, G1, G6.
37. For a more expansive exploration of *Rocky* and white popular culture, see Cowie, *Stayin' Alive*.
38. Glassner, *Bodies*, 93, 247.
39. Charles Gaines, "Hulk Triumphant," *Esquire*, June 1986, 117–118.
40. Michele Donley, "Health Clubs Bulk Up to Wrestle for Hot Market," *Crain's Chicago Business*, November 21, 1988, 3; Kathleen Doheny, "An Exercise in Caution: Finding Your Way through the Health Club Jungle in Five Easy Steps," *Los Angeles Times*, February 16, 1988, OC D1; Ronald Sullivan, "Health Clubs Shut for Violations," *New York Times*, August 25, 1982, B22.
41. Glassner, *Bodies*, 208.
42. Jordan Sollitto, "Women Gyms Put Weight on Muscle Tone," *Los Angeles Times*, September 10, 1985, E1; Dirk Johnson, "Health Conscious Collegians Jamming Gyms," *New York Times*, May 9, 1985, B1; Johnson, "The New Campus Craze: Fitness," *Sun Sentinel*, July 16, 1985, 3D; Bill Richards, "Misshapen Identities: Despite the Hype Surrounding the Fitness Craze, Most People Are More Interested in Style Than Sweat," *Wall Street Journal*, April 21, 1986, 75; Lynne Helm, "Home Gyms Get a Workout: More Homes Are Reflecting the Fitness Craze with Gyms That Offer Private Workouts," *Sun Sentinel*, July 31, 1987, 1E.

43. James C. G. Conniff, "The Great Home Fitness Craze," *New York Times Magazine*, October 8, 1989, 47–50.

44. Ritenbaugh, "Body Size and Shape," 179; Garner, "Body Image."

45. Mayer, *Health*, 135, 150. The "basic seven" food groups were introduced by the USDA in 1943 and consisted of "1. Leafy, green, and yellow vegetables. 2. Citrus fruits, tomatoes, raw cabbage, and Salad Greens. 3. Potatoes and other vegetables and fruits. 4. Milk and milk products. 5. Meat, poultry, fish, dried beans and peas, and nuts. 6. Bread, flour, and cereals. 7. Butter and fortified margarine." The "basic four," by contrast, consisted of "1. Vegetables and fruits. 2. Milk. 3. Meat. 4. Cereals and breads." "The basic four system is not satisfactory," Mayer wrote. "There is no reason, for example, to classify potatoes and spinach together" (135–137).

46. Jeanne Goldberg and Jean Mayer, "Food and Common Sense: 3 Essentials for Safe Weight Reduction," *Los Angeles Times*, January 22, 1981, 130, 131.

47. "Chickens Stampeding Beef Customers," *Broiler Industry*, July 1981, 12.

48. N. R. Kleinfield, "America Goes Chicken Crazy," *New York Times*, December 9, 1984, Business sec., 1.

49. Wyckoff and Sasser, *Chain-Restaurant Industry*, 96.

50. Pete Berlinski, "Why Wendy's Way Works," *Restaurant Business*, February 1978, 93.

51. Wyckoff and Sasser, *Chain-Restaurant Industry*, 96.

52. Emerson, *New Economics*, 67.

53. Courtland Milloy, "Washington's Fried Chicken Wars," *Washington Post*, September 7, 1981, B1.

54. Williams-Forson, *Building Houses*, 2.

55. Milloy, "Washington's Fried Chicken Wars," B1.

56. Lisa Bertagnoli, "McDonald's: Company of the Quarter Century," *Restaurants & Institutions*, July 10, 1989, 48.

57. Tom Strenk, "Broader Menus Spice Up Chicken Sales," *Restaurant Business*, January 20, 1985, 97.

58. "Wilson May Brand Frozen Chicken," *Broiler Industry*, July 1975, 14; "McDonald's Ready to Expand 'McChicken,'" *Broiler Industry*, July 1975, 14.

59. Paul Ingrassia and David P. Garino, "Burger Battle: After Their Slow Year, Fast-Food Chains Use Ploys to Speed Up Sales," *Wall Street Journal*, April 4, 1980, 1.

60. "'McChicken' Doesn't Turn On This Duo," *Broiler Industry*, April 1980, 14.

61. Ingrassia and Garino, "Burger Battle," 1.

62. "McDonald's Executives Meet the Press," *Restaurants & Institutions*, June 1, 1983, 100.

63. "Chef Arend and His Magic Wand Produce the McNugget," *Broiler Industry*, December 1983, 82.

64. W. David Gibson, "Did McDonald's Deserve a Break?," *Barron's National Business and Financial Weekly*, September 5, 1983, 7.

65. John Pashdag, "Fast-Food Frolics: Checking Out the Major Quick-as-a-Wink Dining Chains," *Los Angeles Times*, January 26, 1982, 8, 11.

66. Scott Hume, "Chains Move Quality to the Front of the Burner," *Boston Globe*, May 11, 1983, 1.

67. Janice Okun, "Rene Arend, McDonald's Chef: Meet the Inventor of Chicken McNuggets," *Buffalo News*, October 7, 1988.

68. Leonard Sloane, "McDonald's Chef Looks for Quality," *New York Times*, April 20, 1981, D2.

69. Marshall, *New Marketable Poultry*, 1.
70. Sloane, "McDonald's Chef."
71. Jack Smith, "Combining Chicken/Catch-a-Story," *Los Angeles Times*, May 24, 1981, pt. VI, p. 1.
72. "McNuggets: Bits of Bland," *Arizona Republic*, July 18, 1982, D9.
73. Mike Romkey, "McDonald's: Yes; Chicken McNuggets: No," *Daily Dispatch* (Moline, Ill.), November 3, 1984, 21.
74. "Tyson Gets 40% of McNuggets," *Broiler Industry*, January 1982, 18; "McDonald's Executives Meet the Press," *Restaurants & Institutions*, June 1, 1983, 100.
75. "Tyson Gets 40%," 18.
76. Emerson, *New Economics*, 111.
77. Beehive Model s-76 Deboner advertisement, *Broiler Industry*, January 1982, 18.
78. "Tyson Gets 40%," 18; "Nation's Top Broiler Firms," *Broiler Industry*, December 1991, 22; "Tyson Expects to Have $1 Billion Sales by 1986," *Broiler Industry*, April 1981, 26.
79. "Tyson Expects," 26.
80. "Tyson Gets 40%," 18; Associated Press, "McNugget Controversy Causes Role Reversal; Businessmen Picket Union Food at Nashville," *Baxter Bulletin*, May 18, 1983, 14A.
81. Gordon Mitchell, "Chicken McNuggets and Other Processed Poultry Are Fattening Tyson Foods Margins," *Barron's National Business and Financial Weekly*, September 13, 1982, 37, 50, 62.
82. "Nation's Top Broiler Firms" (1991), 22.
83. McDonald's, "Chicken McNuggets," video, 1983.
84. McDonald's, "They're Here!," advertisement, 1983.
85. Chatelain, *Franchise*, 74–75.
86. McDonald's, "McNugget Mania Chant," advertisement, 1983.
87. Chatelain, *Franchise*, 164.
88. "Tyson's Resumes Making Nuggets for McDonald's," *Broiler Industry*, August 1983, 14.
89. Mary Haley, "With a Little Bit of Pluck: Fast-Food Chains Cash In on New-Found Delight with Chicken Chunks," *St. Petersburg Times*, February 25, 1985, 3E.
90. "Chef Arend and His Magic Wand Produce the McNugget," *Broiler Industry*, December 1983, 82.
91. Ben Fiber, "Chicken Nuggets Hit Gold for Fast Food Producers," *Globe and Mail*, September 12, 1984, B11.
92. "Chains," *Restaurants & Institutions*, April 1982, 91.
93. Haley, "With a Little Bit of Pluck," 3E.
94. "Chicken: Breakfast and Sandwich Program Worth Crowing About," *Restaurants & Institutions*, July 24, 1985, 125.
95. "As KFC Enters Nugget Business, Supplier's Role to Change, Too," *Broiler Industry*, December 1984, 10.
96. Mike Romkey, "CC Tries the Colonel's Nuggets," *The Dispatch*, January 5, 1985, 18.
97. As of 1988, McDonald's had the second highest number of foreign restaurants for any American restaurant chain, around 2,600 to KFC's 2,800. However, the volume of sales in the company's international restaurants, an average of around $1.6 million per site, was more than double the turnover at the average international KFC. Emerson, *New Economics*, 164–165.
98. Haley, "With a Little Bit of Pluck," 3E.
99. Barbara Rudolph, "The Up-and-Comers," *Forbes*, June 4, 1984, 176.
100. Cathy, *It's Easier*, 69.

101. Robert E. Bauer, "Ready-to-Use 'Fresh Like' Products: Wendy's View," *Broiler Industry*, March 1986, 40–42; Haley, "With a Little Bit of Pluck," 3E.

102. Bauer, "Ready-to-Use," 40–42.

103. Haley, "With a Little Bit of Pluck," 3E; Jeremy Iggers, "New Ammunition in the Chicken Wars," *Detroit Free Press*, April 2, 1986, 22.

104. Brown, "Food Processors," 205.

105. Roberta Jones, "Chicken, Dressed, and Undressed," *Restaurant Business*, May 20, 1988, 236.

106. Joanna Pruess, "The Future of Foodservice: Food Buying," *Restaurant Business*, May 20, 1987, 164.

107. Yates, *Out of the Freezer*, cover copy; Patricia Tennison, "Convenience Cooking Has Found Its Niche," *Orlando Sentinel*, August 20, 1987, G20.

108. Emal and Taylor, *Light and Healthy Microwave Cooking*, 6, 34.

109. Carole Sugarman, "Americans in the Age of the Microwave: If It Can Be Microwaved 'the Sky's the Limit,'" *Washington Post*, January 14, 1987, E1.

110. "Nation's Top Broiler Companies," *Broiler Industry*, December 1985, 20–22.

111. Hall, "Chicken Empires," 16.

112. "Holly Pumps $6 Million into Deep-Chilled Nugget Campaign," *Broiler Industry*, March 1985, 63.

113. "'Bo' Pilgrim Tells Why He Made the Plunge," *Broiler Industry*, April 1986, 12.

114. "Poultry Processing & Marketing," *Broiler Industry*, April 1986, 34.

115. "New State-of-Art Plant Aims for Foodservice," *Broiler Industry*, April 1986, 18, 22.

116. Wyckoff and Sasser, *Chain-Restaurant Industry*, 101.

117. Emerson, *New Economics*, 71.

118. Baldwin, *Taco Titan*, 138.

119. *Wall Street Journal*, June 9, 1965, 8. "We have had no communications from the Justice Department," said Herbert L. Barnet, the chairman of the Pepsi-Cola Company. "Pepsi-Cola is embarking on a new, great era both for Pepsi-Cola and the stockholders," he indelicately but nevertheless accurately observed. "We're still a growing baby and we expect to go many places in the U.S. as well as abroad. While the merger represented a diversification into snack foods for Pepsi-Cola, it significantly provided access to foreign markets for Frito-Lay's. At the time Pepsi-Cola owned and franchised over 900 bottling plants in 108 countries," the *Wall Street Journal* reported.

120. Enrico and Kornbluth, *Other Guy Blinked*, 22.

121. Ibid., 80; "Burger King Picks Pepsi," *New York Times*, August 12, 1987, D5.

122. *Restaurant Business*, March 20, 1985, 190; Jakle and Sculle, *Fast Food*, 262.

123. Jakle and Sculle, *Fast Food*, 259.

124. Arellano, *Taco USA*, 63.

125. Jakle and Sculle, *Fast Food*, 260.

126. Leonard A. Schlesinger, "Taco Bell Corp," Harvard Business School case study 9-692-058, 2, 10.

127. Ibid., 6, 12.

128. Durnford, "Redefining Value," 78.

129. Ibid., 76.

130. Schlesinger, "Taco Bell Corp," 10.

131. Arellano, *Taco USA*, 58.

132. Emerson, *New Economics*, 40.

133. Schlesinger, "Taco Bell Corp," 22.

134. Emerson, *New Economics*, 37.
135. Ibid., 32.
136. Ibid., 57, 92, 95. McDonald's reduced the price of hamburgers from seventy-five cents to fifty-nine cents and of cheeseburgers from eighty-five cents to sixty-nine cents.
137. Glenn Collins, "Egg McMuffins, Priced to Move: McDonald's Reinvents a Promotion in Fast-Food Frenzy," *New York Times*, April 4, 1997, D1.
138. Theresa Howard, "McDonald's Revamps Value Meal with Eye on Size," *Nation's Restaurant News*, February 14, 1994, 3.
139. Bruce Horovitz, "Portion Sizes and Fat Content 'Out of Control,'" *USA Today*, February 20, 1996, 1A.
140. Ian Darby, "Burger King Opts to Battle on Size," *Marketing*, August 19, 1992, 2; Horovitz, "Portion Sizes," 1A.
141. Smith, *Encyclopedia*, 259.
142. Thomas E. Ricks and Delia Flores, "Pepsi, Coke Raise to 100% the Corn Syrup Bottlers Can Use to Sweeten Cola Drinks," *Wall Street Journal*, November 7, 1984, 6.
143. Carole Sugarman, "Exploding Portions: America Sizes Up," *Washington Post*, October 11, 1995, E1.
144. Horovitz, "Portion Sizes," 1A.
145. Wadden and Stunkard, "Psychosocial Consequences," 163–164.
146. Sean McCarthy, "It's Big but Is It Better? 'Supersizing' Means Bigger Servings and Even Bigger People," *The Province* (Vancouver, B.C.), November 25, 1998, B16.
147. Scott LaFee, "The Skinny on Fat: Large Portions Help Make Americans Large People," *San Diego Tribune*, February 2, 1995, Food-1.
148. National Center for Health Statistics, https://www.cdc.gov/nchs/data/hestat/overweight/overweight_adult.pdf; *Prevalence of Overweight, Obesity, and Extreme Obesity among Adults: United States, Trends 1976–1980 through 2005–2006*, December 2008, 3.
149. Fryar, Carroll, and Ogden, *Prevalence of Overweight*, 4.
150. Friedman, "War on Obesity," 856.
151. Biltekoff, *Eating Right*, 124–125.
152. See Campos, *Obesity Myth*; Glassner, *Gospel of Food*; Williams-Forson, *Eating While Black*.
153. Garner, "Body Image."
154. National Chicken Council, "Per Capita Consumption of Poultry and Livestock, 1965 to Estimated 2021, in Pounds," https://www.nationalchickencouncil.org/about-the-industry/statistics/per-capita-consumption-of-poultry-and-livestock-1965-to-estimated-2012-in-pounds/, accessed March 30, 2021.
155. Ray Recchi, "Health-Nut Attitude Is a Whopping Pain," *South Florida Sun Sentinel* (Fort Lauderdale), March 11, 1990, 1E.
156. Ibid.
157. Jonathon King, "Ray Recchi Dies of Cancer," *South Florida Sun Sentinel*, September 10, 1999, https://www.sun-sentinel.com/news/fl-xpm-1999-09-10-9909100366-story.html, accessed June 7, 2022.
158. Peter Brown, "Cultural Perspectives," 188–191; Massara, *¡Qué gordita!*.
159. Wachs and Dworkin, *Body Panic*.

EPILOGUE

1. Molly O'Neill, "Big Bird: When Americans Want Dinner, Chicken Rules the Roost," *New York Times*, May 7, 2000, SM103.
2. Randall, "Quartz: America's Taste for Hot Sauce Fueled by Immigrants," *AsAmNews*, January 29, 2014.
3. C. Ritenbaugh, "Obesity as a Culture-Bound Syndrome," *Culture, Medicine and Psychiatry* 6347 (1982): 61, quoted in Gremillion, "The Cultural Politics."
4. Biltekoff, *Eating Right*, 127–128.
5. Grotz, "Look at Food Industry Responses"; Margaret Webb Pressler, "A Super-Size Backlash: Restaurant Menus Feature More with Less," *Washington Post*, August 6, 2003, E1.
6. Greg Critser, "Survival of the Fittest: McDonald's Must Revisit Menu to Keep Its Super-Size Empire," *Calgary Herald*, November 24, 2002, B11; Dave Minauti, "Morris Joins McDonald's Move to Attack Fat: End of the Super Size Menu Hailed as Good News for Waistlines," *Daily Record* (Morristown, N.J.), March 4, 2004, A1.
7. Belasco, *Appetite for Change*; Dimitri and Greene, *Recent Growth Patterns*.
8. Fromartz, *Organic, Inc.*
9. Pollan, *The Omnivore's Dilemma*, 4, 7–8.
10. Ameet Sachdev, "As Choices Fatten, Fast-Food Sales Thin; Burger, Chicken Chains Feel Pinch," *Chicago Tribune*, September 13, 2002, 3:1.
11. Finn, *Discriminating Taste*, 207. See also Naccarato and Lebesco, *Culinary Capital*.
12. Sherri Day, "McDonald's to Slim Down Operations: The Fast-Food Giant Announced That It Is Closing 175 Outlets and Cutting Hundreds of Jobs," *Orlando Sentinel*, November 9, 2002, C1; Glassner, *Gospel of Food*, 150.
13. Delroy Alexander, "The McNugget Makeover," *Chicago Tribune*, October 5, 2003, sec. 5, pp. 1, 7.
14. Elena Holodny, "The Epic Collapse of American Soda Consumption in One Chart," *Business Insider*, March 10, 2016, https://www.businessinsider.com/americans-are-drinking-less-soda-2016-3.
15. ABC News Staff, "100 Million Dieters, $20 Billion: The Weight-Loss Industry by the Numbers," May 7, 2012, https://abcnews.go.com/Health/100-million-dieters-20-billion-weight-loss-industry/story?id=16297197.
16. Jennifer Konlin, "A Big Reveal Touches a Nerve," *New York Times*, February 7, 2014, https://www.nytimes.com/2014/02/09/fashion/Biggest-Loser-Rachel-Frederickson.html; Gina Kolata, "After 'The Biggest Loser,' Their Bodies Fought to Regain Weight," *New York Times*, May 2, 2016, https://www.nytimes.com/2016/05/02/health/biggest-loser-weight-loss.html.
17. Contois, *Diners, Dudes, and Diets*, 20.
18. Emily Heil, "McDonald's New Spicy Nuggets Aren't Really All That New—and Thank Goodness for That," *Washington Post*, Weblog post, September 25, 2020.
19. Adrian J. Rivera, "I Am Mourning the Loss of Something I Loved: McNuggets," *New York Times*, February 28, 2023.
20. Kerry Hall, Ames Alexander, and Franco Ordoñez, "The Cruelest Cuts," *Charlotte Observer*, September 30, 2008, https://www.charlotteobserver.com/news/special-reports/cruelest-cuts/article9012839.html.
21. Human Rights Watch, "Blood, Sweat, and Fear"; Human Rights Watch, "'When We're Dead,'" 2.
22. Government Accountability Office, *Workplace Safety and Health: Safety*.

23. Government Accountability Office, *Workplace Safety and Health: Additional Data*, 21.
24. Ramsey et al., *Evaluation*, i.
25. Cartwright et al., "Prevalence"; Harmse et al., "Impact," 197; Kirchberg et al., "Carpel Tunnel Syndrome"; Musolin et al., *Evaluation*.
26. Human Rights Watch, "'When We're Dead,'" 2.
27. National Chicken Council to Carmen Rottenberg, Acting Under Deputy Secretary for Food Safety, September 1, 2017, 7–8, https://www.fsis.usda.gov/wps/wcm/connect/7734f5cf-05d9-4f89-a7eb-6d85037ad2a7/17-05-Petition-National-Chicken-Council-09012017.pdf?MOD=AJPERES.
28. Nicole Erwin, "USDA Denies Poultry Industry's Request to Speed Up the Slaughter Line," NPR, January 31, 2018, https://www.npr.org/sections/thesalt/2018/01/31/581956147/usda-denies-poultry-industrys-request-to-speed-up-the-slaughter-line; Carmen Rottenberg to Michael Brown, January 29, 2018, https://www.fsis.usda.gov/wps/wcm/connect/235092cf-e3c0-4285-9560-e60cf6956df8/17-05-FSIS-Response-Letter-01292018.pdf?MOD=AJPERES.
29. Austin Alonzo, "How to Get a Processing Line Speed Waiver," *Watt Poultry USA*, August 2019, 14–19.
30. Maura Judkis, "You Might Think There Are More Vegetarians Than Ever. You'd Be Wrong," *Washington Post*, August 3, 2018, https://www.washingtonpost.com/news/food/wp/2018/08/03/you-might-think-there-are-more-vegetarians-than-ever-youd-be-wrong/.

BIBLIOGRAPHY

Agger, Robert E., Daniel Goldrich, and Bert E. Swanson. *The Rulers and the Ruled: Political Power and Impotence in American Communities*. New York: Wiley, 1964.

Ahmed, Ziaul Z., and Mark Sieling. "Two Decades of Productivity Growth in Poultry Dressing and Processing." *Monthly Labor Review*, April 1987. Washington, D.C.: Bureau of Labor Statistics.

Alberts, Robert C. *The Good Provider: Henry J. Heinz and His 57 Varieties*. Boston: Houghton-Mifflin, 1973.

American Meat Institute. *U.S. Meat and Poultry Consumption: An Overview*. Washington, D.C.: American Meat Institute, 2009.

Andreas, Carol. *Meat Packers and Beef Barons: A Company Town in a Global Economy*. Boulder: University of Colorado Press, 1994.

Antaya, Sean. "The New Left at Work: Workers' Unity, the New Tendency, and Rank-and-File Organizing in Windsor, Ontario, in the 1970s." *Labour / Le Travail* 85 (Spring 2020): 53–89.

Arellano, Gustavo. *Taco USA: How Mexican Food Conquered America*. New York: Scribner, 2012.

Avakian, Arlene Voski, and Barbara Haber, eds. *From Betty Crocker to Feminist Food Studies: Critical Perspectives on Women and Food*. Amherst: University of Massachusetts Press, 2005.

Ayers, Edward L. *Southern Journey: The Migrations of the American South, 1790–2020*. Baton Rouge: Louisiana State University Press, 2020.

Baker, Robert C. "The Problem of Food Waste." *New York's Food & Life Sciences Quarterly* 11, no. 2 (1978): 22–23. New York State College of Agriculture and Life Sciences, a Statutory College of the State University at Cornell University, Ithaca, N.Y.

Baker, Robert C., J. M. Darfler, and M. C. Bourne. "The Effect of Level of Skin on the Quality of Chicken Frankfurters." *Poultry Science* 47, no. 6 (November 1968): 1989–1996. Box 1, #21/26/4030, Robert C. Baker Papers, Cornell University, Ithaca, N.Y.

Baldwin, Debra Lee. *Taco Titan: The Glen Bell Story*. Arlington, Tex.: Summit, 1999.

Barrett, James R. *Work and Community in the Jungle: Chicago's Packinghouse Workers, 1894–1922*. Urbana: University of Illinois Press, 2002.

Bates, Leon. *Projection for Survival*. Sherman, Tex.: Bible Believers Evangelical Association, 1977.

Belasco, Warren J. *Appetite for Change: How the Counterculture Took on the Food Industry*. 2nd ed. Ithaca, N.Y.: Cornell University Press, 2007.

Bernstein, Charles. *Sambo's: Only a Fraction of the Action; The Inside Story of a Restaurant Empire's Rise and Fall*. Burbank, Calif.: National Literary Guild, 1984.

Biltekoff, Charlotte. *Eating Right in America: The Cultural Politics of Food and Health*. Durham, N.C.: Duke University Press, 2013.

Bittman, Mark. *Animal, Vegetable, Junk: A History of Food from Sustainable to Suicidal.* Boston: Houghton, Mifflin, Harcourt, 2021.

Blank, Les, dir. *Chicken Real: The Story of Holly Farms Poultry Industries.* Flower Films, 1970.

Bobrow-Strain, Aaron. *White Bread: A Social History of the Store-Bought Loaf.* Boston: Beacon Press, 2012.

Broadway, Michael J., and Donald Stull. *Slaughterhouse Blues: The Meat and Poultry Industry in North America.* Belmont, Calif.: Wadworth Cengage Learning, 2013.

Brooks, D. W. *D. W. Brooks, Gold Kist and Seven Presidents: An Autobiography.* Atlanta: D. W. Brooks Family, 1993.

Brown, Leslie. *Upbuilding Black Durham: Gender, Class, and Black Community Development in the Jim Crow South.* Chapel Hill: University of North Carolina Press, 2008.

Brown, Linda Keller, and Kay Mussell. *Ethnic Regional Foodways United States: Performance of Group Identity.* Knoxville: University of Tennessee Press, 1984.

Brown, Peter J. "Cultural Perspectives on the Etiology and Treatment of Obesity." In *Obesity: Theory and Therapy,* 2nd ed., edited by Thomas A. Wadden and Albert J. Stunkard, 179–193. New York: Raven Press, 1993.

Burrough, Bryan, and John Helyar. *Barbarians at the Gate: The Fall of RJR Nabisco.* New York: Harper & Row, 1989.

Campos, Paul. *The Obesity Myth: Why America's Obsession with Weight Is Hazardous to Your Health.* New York: Gotham Books, 2004.

Cappellazzi, Marcello, and Sally Lee, dirs. *Under Contract: Farmers and the Fine Print.* Rural Advancement Foundation International, 2017.

Cartwright, Michael S., et al. "The Prevalence of Carpal Tunnel Syndrome in Latino Poultry-Processing Workers and Other Latino Manual Workers." *Journal of Occupational and Environmental Medicine* 54, no. 2 (February 2012): 198–201.

Cathy, S. Truett. *It's Easier to Succeed Than to Fail.* Petaling Jaya, Malaysia: Thomas Nelson, 1990.

Chafe, William H. *Civilities and Civil Rights: Greensboro, North Carolina, and the Black Struggle for Freedom.* New York: Oxford University Press, 1980.

Charles, T. Burr, and Homer O. Stuart. *Commercial Poultry Farming.* Danville, Ill.: Interstate, 1950.

Chatelain, Marcia. *Franchise: The Golden Arches in Black America.* New York: Liveright, 2020.

Chen, Yong. *Chop Suey USA: The Story of Chinese Food in America.* New York: Columbia University Press, 2014.

Christensen, Rob. *The Paradox of Tar Heel Politics: The Personalities, Elections, and Events That Shaped Modern North Carolina.* Chapel Hill: University of North Carolina Press, 2010.

Cobb, James C. *The Selling of the South: The Southern Crusade for Industrial Development, 1936–1990.* Urbana: University of Illinois Press, 1993.

Coe, Andrew. *Chop Suey: A Cultural History of Chinese Food in the United States.* New York: Oxford University Press, 2009.

Cohen, Lizabeth. *Making a New Deal: Industrial Workers in Chicago, 1919–1939.* New York: Cambridge University Press, 1989.

Conkin, Paul K. *A Revolution down on the Farm: American Agriculture Since 1929.* Lexington: University Press of Kentucky, 2008.

Contois, Emily J. H. *Diners, Dudes, and Diets: How Gender and Power Collide in Food Media and Culture.* Chapel Hill: University of North Carolina Press, 2020.

Cook, J. Gordon. *The Fight for Food*. New York: Dial Press, 1957.
Cowie, Jefferson. *Stayin' Alive: The 1970s and the Last Days of the Working Class*. New York: New Press, 2010.
Critser, Greg. *Fat Land: How Americans Became the Fattest People in the World*. New York: Mariner Books, 2004.
Cullather, Nick. *The Hungry World: America's Cold War Battle against Poverty in Asia*. Cambridge, Mass.: Harvard University Press, 2010.
Daniel, Pete. *Breaking the Land: The Transformation of Cotton, Tobacco, and Rice Cultures Since 1880*. Urbana: University of Illinois Press, 1985.
Davis, Peter, and Richard Robinson. "R. David Thomas and Wendy's: Classic Entrepreneurship." *Journal of the International Academy for Case Studies* 6, no. 1 (April 2000): 112–131.
Deener, Andrew. *The Problem with Feeding Cities: The Social Transformation of Infrastructure, Abundance, and Inequality in America*. Chicago: University of Chicago Press, 2020.
deShazo, Richard, Steven Bigler, and Leigh Baldwin Skipworth. "The Autopsy of Chicken Nuggets Reads 'Chicken Little.'" *American Journal of Medicine* 126, no. 11 (November 2013): 1018–1019.
Deutsch, Tracey. *Building a Housewife's Paradise: Gender, Politics, and American Grocery Stores in the Twentieth Century*. Chapel Hill: University of North Carolina Press, 2010.
Devereux, Stephen. "Famine in the Twentieth Century." IDS Working Paper 105. Brighton: Institute of Development Studies, 2000.
Dimitri, Carolyn, and Catherine Greene. *Recent Growth Patterns in the U.S. Organic Foods Market*. USDA Economic Research Service, AIB-777, September 2002.
Diner, Hasia R. *Hungering for America: Italian, Irish, and Jewish Foodways in the Age of Migration*. Cambridge, Mass.: Harvard University Press, 2001.
DuBasky, Mayo, ed. *The Gist of Mencken: Quotations from America's Critic*. Metuchen, N.J.: Scarecrow Press, 1990.
Durnford, Tim. "Redefining Value: For Whom the Taco Bell Tolls." *Cornell Hotel and Restaurant Administration Quarterly* 38, no. 3 (June 1997): 74–80.
Ehrlich, Paul R. *The Population Bomb*. New York: Ballantine Books, 1968 [1971 ed.].
Eisenhower, Milton S., and Arthur P. Chew. *United States Department of Agriculture: Yearbook of Agriculture 1932*. Washington, D.C.: United States Government Printing Office, 1932.
Emal, Janet, and Elizabeth Taylor. *Light and Healthy Microwave Cooking*. Los Angeles: HP Books, 1986.
Emerson, Robert L. *The New Economics of Fast Food*. New York: Van Nostrand Reinhold, 1990.
Enrico, Roger, and Jesse Kornbluth. *The Other Guy Blinked: How Pepsi Won the Cola Wars*. New York: Bantam, 1986.
Fink, Deborah. *Cutting into the Meatpacking Line: Workers and Change in the Rural Midwest*. Chapel Hill: University of North Carolina Press, 1998.
Fink, Leon. *The Maya of Morganton: Work and Community in the Nuevo New South*. Chapel Hill: University of North Carolina Press, 2003.
Finn, S. Margot. *Discriminating Taste: How Class Anxiety Created the American Food Revolution*. New Brunswick, N.J.: Rutgers University Press, 2017.
Fitzgerald, Deborah. *Every Farm a Factory: The Industrial Ideal in American Agriculture*. New Haven, Conn.: Yale University Press, 2003.
Fleischman, Thomas. *Communist Pigs: An Animal History of East Germany's Rise and Fall*. Seattle: University of Washington Press, 2020.

Frazier, E. Franklin. "Durham: The Capital of the Black Middle Class." In *The New Negro: An Interpretation*, edited by Alain Locke, 331–341. New York: Albert and Charles Boni, 1925. Reprint, New York: Atheneum/Macmillan, 1992.

Friedman, Jeffrey M. "A War on Obesity, Not the Obese." *Science* 299, no. 5608 (February 2003): 856–858.

Fromartz, Samuel. *Organic, Inc.: Natural Foods and How They Grew*. Orlando, Fla.: Harcourt Books, 2006.

Fryar, Cheryl D., Margaret D. Carroll, and Cynthia L. Ogden. *Prevalence of Overweight, Obesity, and Severe Obesity among Children and Adolescents Aged 2–19 Years: United States, 1963–1965 through 2015–2016*. September 2018. National Center for Health Statistics.

Garner, David. "Body Image in America: Survey Results." *Psychology Today*, February 1, 1997. https://www.psychologytoday.com/us/articles/199702/body-image-in-america-survey-results.

Georgakis, Dan, and Marvin Surkin. *Detroit I Do Mind Dying: A Study in Urban Revolution*. New York: St. Martin's Press, 1975.

Gisolfi, Monica R. "The Roots of Agribusiness in the American South." In *The Best American History Essays 2008*, edited by David Roediger, 35–54. New York: Palgrave Macmillan, 2008.

———. *The Takeover: Chicken Farming and the Roots of American Agribusiness*. Athens: University of Georgia Press, 2017.

Glassner, Barry. *Bodies: Why We Look the Way We Do (and How We Feel about It)*. New York: G. P. Putnam's Sons, 1988.

———. *The Gospel of Food: Why We Should Stop Worrying and Enjoy What We Eat*. New York: Harper Collins, 2007.

Government Accountability Office. *Workplace Safety and Health: Additional Data Needed to Address Continued Hazards in the Meat and Poultry Industry*. GAO-16-337. April 25, 2016. https://www.gao.gov/products/gao-16-337.

———. *Workplace Safety and Health: Safety in the Meat and Poultry Industry, While Improving, Could be Further Strengthened*. GAO-05-96. January 12, 2005. https://www.gao.gov/products/gao-05-96.

Gray, LaGuana. *We Just Keep Running the Line: Black Southern Women and the Poultry Processing Industry*. Baton Rouge: Louisiana State University Press, 2014.

Greene, Christina. *Our Separate Ways: Women and the Black Freedom Movement in Durham, North Carolina*. Chapel Hill: University of North Carolina Press, 2005.

Gremillion, Helen. "The Cultural Politics of Body Size." *Annual Review of Anthropology* 34 (2005): 13–32.

Grotz, V. Lee. "A Look at Food Industry Responses to the Rising Prevalence of Overweight." *Nutrition Reviews* 64, no. 1 (February 2006): s48–s52.

Hall, Bob. "Chicken Empires." *Southern Exposure* 17, no. 2 (Summer 1989): 12–17.

———. "I Feel What Women Feel." *Southern Exposure*, Summer 1989. Reissued June 1, 2021. https://www.facingsouth.org/2021/06/archives-i-feel-what-women-feel.

Halpern, Rick, and Roger Horowitz. *Meatpackers: An Oral History of Black Packinghouse Workers and Their Struggle for Racial and Economic Equality*. London: Prentice Hall International, 1996.

Hamilton, Shane. *Trucking Country: The Road to America's Wal-Mart Economy*. Princeton, N.J.: Princeton University Press, 2008.

Hanchett, Thomas W. *Sorting Out the New South City: Race, Class, and Urban Development in Charlotte, 1875–1975*. Chapel Hill: University of North Carolina Press, 1998.

Harmse, Johannes L., et al. "The Impact of Physical and Ergonomic Hazards on Poultry Abattoir Processing Workers: A Review." *International Journal of Environmental Research and Public Health* 13, no. 2 (February 2016): 197–220.

Harper, Frederick John. "The Anti-Chain Store Movement in the United States, 1927–1940." PhD dissertation, University of Warwick, 1981.

Havenstein, G. B., et al. "Carcass Composition and Yield of 1991 vs 1957 Broilers When Fed 'Typical' 1957 and 1991 Broiler Diets." *Poultry Science* 73, no. 12 (December 1994): 1795–1804.

Hayes, Jack, ed. *Will There Be Enough Food? The 1981 Yearbook of the United States Department of Agriculture*. Washington, D.C.: United States Government Printing Office, 1981.

Hayse, P. L., and W. W. Marion. "Eviscerated Yield, Component Parts, and Meat, Skin, and Bone Rations in the Chicken Broiler." *Poultry Science* 52 (1973): 718–722. Cited in C. W. Carlson, W. W. Marion, B. F. Miller, and T. L. Goodwin. "Factors Affecting Poultry Meat Yields." North Central Regional Research Publication No. 226, Bulletin 630, Agricultural Experiment Station, South Dakota State University, Brookings, May 1975. Box 1, #21/26/4030, Robert C. Baker Papers, Cornell University, Ithaca, N.Y.

Hinman, Robert B., and Robert B. Harris. *The Story of Meat*. Chicago: Swift & Company, 1939.

Horowitz, Roger. *Negro and White, Unite and Fight! A Social History of Industrial Unionism in Meatpacking, 1930–1990*. Urbana: University of Illinois Press, 1997.

Hover, J. Milton, and Marvin S. Pittman. *Profitable Farming*. Evanston, Ill.: Row, Peterson, and Co., 1932.

Human Rights Watch. "Blood, Sweat, and Fear: Workers' Rights in U.S. Meat and Poultry Plants." January 24, 2005. https://www.hrw.org/report/2005/01/25/blood-sweat-and-fear/workers-rights-us-meat-and-poultry-plants.

———. "'When We're Dead and Buried Our Bones Will Keep Hurting': Workers' Rights under Threat in U.S. Meat and Poultry Plants." September 4, 2019. https://www.hrw.org/report/2019/09/04/when-were-dead-and-buried-our-bones-will-keep-hurting/workers-rights-under-threat.

Hyman, Louis. "Rethinking the Postwar Corporation: Management, Monopolies, and Markets." In *What's Good for Business: Business and American Politics Since World War II*, edited by Kim Phillips-Fein and Julian E. Zelizer, 195–211. New York: Oxford University Press, 2012.

Jakle, John A., and Keith A. Sculle. *Fast Food: Roadside Restaurants in the Automobile Age*. Baltimore, Md.: Johns Hopkins University Press, 2002.

Johnston, Josée, and Shyon Baumann. *Foodies: Democracy and Distinction in the Gourmet Foodscape*. 2nd ed. New York: Routledge, 2015.

Josephson, Paul R. *Chicken: A History from Farmyard to Factory*. Medford, Mass.: Polity, 2020.

Kenner, Robert, dir. *Food, Inc*. Magnolia Pictures, 2008.

Kirchberg, Gordon J., et al. "Carpel Tunnel Syndrome: Classical Clinical Symptoms and Electrodiagnostic Studies in Poultry Workers with Hand, Wrist, and Forearm Pain." *Southern Medical Journal* 87, no. 3 (March 1994): 328–331.

Kopple, Barbara, dir. *American Dream*. Prestige Films, 1990.

Kroc, Ray, and Robert Anderson. *Grinding It Out: The Making of McDonald's*. New York: St. Martin's Griffin, 1977.

Ladies of Perry, Kansas, and Vicinity. *The Perry Home Cook Book*. Oskaloosa, Kans.: Independent Publishing Company, 1920.

Lancaster, Aaron Ennis. "Chasing the Good Ol' Boys and Girls of Wilkes County, North Carolina." MA thesis, Appalachian State University, August 2013.

Langdon, Philip. *Orange Roofs, Golden Arches: The Architecture of American Chain Restaurants*. New York: Knopf, 1986.

Leonard, Christopher. *The Meat Racket: The Secret Takeover of America's Food Business*. New York: Simon and Schuster, 2014.

Levenstein, Harvey. *Paradox of Plenty: A Social History of Eating in Modern America*. Berkeley: University of California Press, 1993.

——. *Revolution at the Table: The Transformation of the American Diet*. Berkeley: University of California Press, 2003.

Levinson, Marc. *The Great A&P and the Struggle for Small Business in America*. New York: Hill and Wang, 2011.

Lewis, Harry R. *Poultry Keeping: An Elementary Treatise Dealing with the Successful Management of Poultry*. 2nd ed. Philadelphia: J. B. Lippincott Co., 1919.

Lewis, Sinclair. *Main Street: The Story of Carol Kennicott*. New York: Harcourt, Brace and Howe, 1920.

Lichtenstein, Nelson. *A Fabulous Failure: The Clinton Presidency and the Transformation of American Capitalism*. Princeton, N.J.: Princeton University Press, 2023.

——. *The Retail Revolution: How Wal-Mart Created a Brave New World of Business*. New York: Metropolitan Books, 2009.

——, ed. *Wal-Mart: The Face of Twenty-First Century Capitalism*. New York: New Press, 2006.

Linder, Marc. "I Gave My Employer a Chicken That Had No Bone: Joint Firm-State Responsibility for Line-Speed-Related Occupational Injuries." *Case Western Law Review* 46, no. 1 (Fall 1995): 33–143.

Linnér, Björn-Ola. *The Return of Malthus: Environmentalism and Post-war Population-Resource Crises*. Isle of Harris, UK: White Horse Press, 2003.

Lloyd, Ray, et al. *Cost of Broiler Production*. Delaware Agricultural Extension Service, Newark, 1961.

Locke, Alain, ed. *The New Negro: An Interpretation*. New York: Albert and Charles Boni, 1925. Reprint, New York: Atheneum/Macmillan, 1992.

Looper, J. Don. "Food, Famine, and a Realistic View." In *Will There Be Enough Food? The 1981 Yearbook of the United States Department of Agriculture*, edited by Jack Hayes, 2–8. Washington, D.C.: United States Government Printing Office, 1981.

Love, John F. *McDonald's: Behind the Arches*. New York: Bantam, 1988.

Maesso, E. R., R. C. Baker, M. C. Bourne, and D. V. Vadehra. "Effect of Some Physical and Chemical Treatments in the Binding Quality of Poultry Loaves." *Journal of Food Science* 35 (1970): 440–443. Box 1, #21/26/4030, Robert C. Baker Papers, Cornell University, Ithaca, N.Y.

Maesso, E. R., R. C. Baker, and D. V. Vadehra. "The Effect of Vacuum, Pressure, pH and Different Meat Types on the Binding Ability of Poultry Meat." *Poultry Science* 49, no. 3 (May 1970): 697–700. Box 1, #21/26/4030, Robert C. Baker Papers, Cornell University, Ithaca, N.Y.

Malizia, Emil. "Earnings Gap in North Carolina: A Study. The Earnings of North Carolinians." June 1975. Department of State and Regional Planning, University of North Carolina.

Mann, Charles. *The Wizard and the Prophet: Two Remarkable Scientists and Their Dueling Visions to Shape Tomorrow's World*. New York: Penguin Books, 2018.

Marshall, Joseph H. *New Marketable Poultry and Egg Products, 12: Chicken Sticks*. April

1963. Departments of Agricultural Economics and Poultry Husbandry, Cornell University.

Massara, Emily Bradley. *¡Qué gordita! A Study of Weight among Women in a Puerto Rican Community*. New York: AMS Press, 1989.

May, Earl Chapin. *The Canning Clan: A Pageant of Pioneering Americans*. New York: Macmillan, 1937.

Mayer, Jean. *Health*. New York: D. Van Nostrand Company, 1974.

McCollum, Elmer V., and Nina Simmonds. *The American Home Diet: An Answer to the Ever Present Question What Shall We Have for Dinner*. Detroit: Frederick C. Mathews Company, 1920.

McKenna, Maryn. *Big Chicken: The Incredible Story of How Antibiotics Created Modern Agriculture and Changed the Way the World Eats*. Washington, D.C.: National Geographic Partners, 2017.

———. "The Father of the Chicken Nugget." *Slate*, December 28, 2012. https://slate.com/human-interest/2012/12/robert-c-baker-the-man-who-invented-chicken-nuggets.html.

Mehlman Petrzela, Natalia. *Fit Nation: The Gains and Pains of America's Exercise Obsession*. Chicago: University of Chicago Press, 2022.

Mencken, H. L. *Prejudices: Sixth Series*. New York: Knopf, 1927.

Monaghan, Tom, Robert Anderson, and John Rayburn. *Pizza Tiger*. Englewood, Colo.: Newstrack, 1987.

Musolin, Kristin, et al. *Evaluation of Musculoskeletal Disorders and Traumatic Injuries among Employees at a Poultry Processing Plant*. NIOSH, CDC. March 2014. https://www.cdc.gov/niosh/hhe/reports/pdfs/2012-0125-3204.pdf.

Naccarato, Peter, and Kathleen Lebesco. *Culinary Capital*. London: Berg, 2012.

Nestle, Marion. *Food Politics: How the Food Industry Influences Nutrition and Health*. Berkeley: University of California Press, 2002.

Nickerson, Jane Soames. *Homage to Malthus*. Port Washington, N.Y.: Kennikat Press, 1975.

Olsson, Tore C. *Agrarian Crossings: Reformers and the Remaking of the U.S. and Mexican Countryside*. Princeton, N.J.: Princeton University Press, 2017.

Omo-Osagie, Solomon Iyobosa, II. *Commercial Poultry Production on Maryland's Eastern Shore: The Involvement of African Americans, 1930s to 1990s*. Lanham, Md.: University Press of America, 2012.

Ortiz, Daniel J., and David E. Jacobs. *A Safety and Health Assessment of Two Chicken Processing Plants*. Atlanta: Georgia Institute of Technology, May 1990.

Paarlberg, Don. "Enough Food? Sure, If We Don't Play It Dumb." In *Will There Be Enough Food? The 1981 Yearbook of the United States Department of Agriculture*, edited by Jack Hayes, 282–293. Washington, D.C.: United States Government Printing Office, 1981.

Pachirat, Timothy. *Every Twelve Seconds: Industrialized Slaughter and the Politics of Sight*. New Haven, Conn.: Yale University Press, 2011.

Pacyga, Dominic A. *Slaughterhouse: Chicago's Union Stockyard and the World It Made*. Chicago: University of Chicago Press, 2015.

Perry, Janet E., David E. Banker, and Robert C. Green. *Broiler Farms' Organization, Management, and Performance*. Agriculture Information Bulletin no. 748. Economic Research Service Report. Washington, D.C.: U.S. Department of Agriculture, Economic Research Service, 1999.

Petrini, Carlo. *Slow Food: The Case for Taste*. New York: Columbia University Press, 2003.

Phillips-Fein, Kim, and Julian E. Zelizer, eds. *What's Good for Business: Business and American Politics Since World War II*. New York: Oxford University Press, 2012.

Pierce, Daniel S. *Real NASCAR: White Lightning, Red Clay, and Big Bill France*. Chapel Hill: University of North Carolina Press, 2010.

Pilgrim, Lonnie. *One Pilgrim's Progress: How to Build a World-Class Company, and Who to Credit*. Nashville, Tenn.: Thomas Nelson, 2005.

Pollan, Michael. *The Omnivore's Dilemma: A Natural History of Four Meals*. New York: Penguin Books, 2008.

Presidential Commission on World Hunger. "Overcoming World Hunger: The Challenge Ahead. Report of the Presidential Commission on World Hunger. An Abridged Version." Washington, D.C.: U.S. Department of Education, June 1980.

Progressive Labor Party. *Road to Revolution III: The Continuing Struggle against Revisionism*. New York: Progressive Labor Party, 1970.

Rachleff, Peter J. *Hard Pressed in the Heartland: The Hormel Strike and the Future of the Labor Movement*. Boston: South End Press, 1993.

Ramsey, Jessica G., et al. *Evaluation of Carpal Tunnel Syndrome and Other Musculoskeletal Disorders among Employees at a Poultry Processing Plant*. NIOSH, CDC. March 2015. https://www.cdc.gov/niosh/hhe/reports/pdfs/2014-0040-3232.pdf.

Ranney, David. *Living and Dying on the Factory Floor: From the Outside In and the Inside Out*. Oakland, Calif.: PM Press, 2019.

Redburn, Francis Stevens. "Protest and Policy in Durham, North Carolina." PhD dissertation, University of North Carolina, Chapel Hill, 1970.

Register, Cheri. *Packinghouse Daughter: A Memoir*. St. Paul: Minnesota Historical Society Press, 2000.

Rhyne, Elizabeth Holmes. "An Evaluation of the Small Business Administration's Business Loan Guarantee Program." PhD dissertation, Harvard University, 1985.

Ribas, Vanesa. *On the Line: Slaughterhouse Lives and the Making of the New South*. Berkeley: University of California Press, 2015.

Richardson, Michael B. "'Not Gradually . . . but Now': Reginald Hawkins, Black Leadership, and Desegregation in Charlotte, North Carolina." *North Carolina Historical Review* 82, no. 3 (July 2005): 347–379.

Riis, Jacob A. *How the Other Half Lives: Studies among the Tenements of New York*. New York: Charles Scribner's Sons, 1890.

Ritenbaugh, Cheryl K. "Body Size and Shape: A Dialogue of Culture and Biology." *Medical Anthropology* 13, no. 3 (1991): 173–180.

Rodgers, Marion Elizabeth, ed. *The Impossible H. L. Mencken: A Selection of His Best Newspaper Stories*. New York: Doubleday, 1991.

Roy, Ewell Paul. *Contract Farming, U.S.A*. Danville, Ill.: Interstate Printers & Publishers, 1963.

Sabin, Paul. *The Bet: Paul Ehrlich, Julian Simon, and Our Gamble over Earth's Future*. New Haven, Conn.: Yale University Press, 2013.

Schlosser, Eric. *Fast Food Nation: The Dark Side of the All-American Meal*. Boston: Houghton Mifflin, 2001.

Schnepf, Randy. *Consumers and Food Price Inflation*. Washington, D.C.: Congressional Research Service, September 13, 2013.

Schulman, Bruce J. *From Cotton Belt to Sunbelt: Federal Policy, Economic Development, and the Transformation of the South, 1938–1980*. Durham, N.C.: Duke University Press, 1994.

Schwartzman, Kathleen C. *The Chicken Trail: Following Workers, Migrants, and Corporations across the Americas*. Ithaca, N.Y.: ILR Press, 2013.
Shortridge, Barbara Gimla, and James R. Shortridge. *The Taste of American Place: A Reader on Regional and Ethnic Foods*. Lanham, Md.: Rowman and Littlefield, 1998.
Simon, Bryant. *The Hamlet Fire: A Tragic Story of Cheap Food, Cheap Government, and Cheap Lives*. New York: New Press, 2017.
Slayton, Robert A. *Back of the Yards: The Making of a Local Democracy*. Chicago: University of Chicago Press, 1986.
Smith, Andrew F. *Encyclopedia of Junk Food and Fast Food*. Westport, Conn.: Greenwood Press, 2006.
Specht, Joshua. *Red Meat Republic: A Hoof-to-Table History of How Beef Changed America*. Princeton, N.J.: Princeton University Press, 2019.
Spurlock, Morgan, dir. *Super Size Me*. Samuel Goldwyn Films, 2004.
———. *Super Size Me 2: Holy Chicken!* Samuel Goldwyn Films, 2017.
Stefferud, Aldred, ed. *The Yearbook of Agriculture, 1943–1947: Science in Farming*. Washington, D.C.: U.S. Government Printing Office, 1947.
Strasser, Susan. *Waste and Want: A Social History of Trash*. New York: Henry Holt and Company, 1999.
———. "Woolworth to Wal-Mart: Mass Merchandising and the Changing Culture of Consumption." In *Wal-Mart: The Face of Twenty-First Century Capitalism*, edited by Nelson Lichtenstein, 31–56. New York: New Press, 2006.
Striffler, Steve. *Chicken: The Dangerous Transformation of America's Favorite Food*. New Haven, Conn.: Yale University Press, 2005.
Stuesse, Angela. *Scratching Out a Living: Latinos, Race, and Work in the Deep South*. Berkeley: University of California Press, 2016.
Thomas, Dave. *Dave's Way: A New Approach to Old-Fashioned Success*. New York: Berkley, 1992.
Thompson, Willard C. "'Safety First' in the Poultry Yard." *Hints to Poultrymen* 8, no. 6 (March 1920). New Brunswick: New Jersey Agricultural Experiment Station, Department of Animal Husbandry.
Townsend, Robert. *Up the Organization: How to Stop the Corporation from Stifling People and Strangling Profits*. New York: Fawcett Press, 1970.
United States Department of Agriculture. *Agricultural Statistics 1945*. Washington, D.C.: United States Government Printing Office, 1945.
———. *Agricultural Statistics 1971*. Washington, D.C.: United States Government Printing Office, 1971.
———. *Agricultural Statistics 1976*. Washington, D.C.: United States Government Printing Office, 1976.
———. *Agricultural Statistics 1979*. Washington, D.C.: United States Government Printing Office, 1979.
———. *Agricultural Statistics 1981*. Washington, D.C.: United States Government Printing Office, 1981.
———. *Agricultural Statistics 1989*. Washington, D.C.: United States Government Printing Office, 1989.
———. *USDA Yearbook of Agriculture 1919*. Washington, D.C.: United States Government Printing Office, 1920.
United States Department of Commerce, Bureau of the Census. "Characteristics of the Low Income Population, 1970." In *Current Population Reports: Consumer Income*,

series P-60, no. 81. Washington, D.C.: United States Government Printing Office, November 1971.

Valentine, C. S. *How to Keep Hens for Profit*. New York: Macmillan, 1910.

Van Syckle, Calla. "Changes in Food Consumption in the United States and Certain Factors Affecting It." PhD dissertation, Iowa State College, 1941.

van Tulleken, Chris. *Ultra-Processed People: Why Do We All Eat Stuff That Isn't Food . . . and Why Can't We Stop?* London: Penguin Random House, 2023.

Veit, Helen Zoe. *Modern Food, Moral Food: Self-Control, Science, and the Rise of Modern American Eating in the Early Twentieth Century*. Chapel Hill: University of North Carolina Press, 2015.

Vileisis, Ann. *Kitchen Literacy: How We Lost Knowledge of Where Food Comes From and Why We Need to Get It Back*. Washington, D.C.: Island Press, 2008.

Wachs, Faye Linda, and Shari L. Dworkin. *Body Panic: Gender, Health, and the Selling of Fitness*. New York: NYU Press, 2009.

Wadden, Thomas A., and Albert J. Stunkard, eds. *Obesity: Theory and Therapy*. 2nd ed. New York: Raven Press, 1993.

———. "Psychosocial Consequences of Obesity and Dieting: Research and Clinical Findings." In *Obesity: Theory and Therapy*, 2nd ed., edited by Thomas A. Wadden and Albert J. Stunkard, 163–177. New York: Raven Press, 1993.

Wade, Louise Carroll. *Chicago's Pride: The Stockyards, Packingtown, and Environs in the Nineteenth Century*. Urbana: University of Illinois Press, 2002.

Waltz, Lynn. *Hog Wild: The Battle for Workers' Rights at the World's Largest Slaughterhouse*. Iowa City: University of Iowa Press, 2018.

Warner, Melanie. *Pandora's Lunchbox: How Processed Food Took Over the American Meal*. New York: Scribner, 2013.

Watson, James L. *Golden Arches East: McDonald's in East Asia*. Stanford, Calif.: Stanford University Press, 1997.

Williams, William H. *Delmarva's Chicken Industry: 75 Years of Progress*. Georgetown, Del.: Delmarva Poultry Industry, 1998.

Williams-Forson, Psyche A. *Building Houses Out of Chicken Legs: Black Women, Food, and Power*. Chapel Hill: University of North Carolina Press, 2006.

———. *Eating While Black: Food Shaming and Race in America*. Chapel Hill: University of North Carolina Press, 2022.

Wyckoff, D. Daryl, and Earl W. Sasser. *The Chain-Restaurant Industry*. Lexington, Mass.: Lexington Books, 1978.

Yates, Annette. *Out of the Freezer, into the Microwave*. Kingswood, UK: Eliot Right Way Books, 1984.

Yeager, Mary A. *Competition and Regulation: The Dynamics of Oligopoly in the Meat Packing Industry, 1870–1920*. Greenwich, Conn.: JAI Press, 1981.

Young, James Harvey. *Pure Food: Securing the Federal Food and Drugs Act of 1906*. Princeton, N.J.: Princeton University Press, 1989.

Zeide, Anna. *Canned: The Rise and Fall of Consumer Confidence in the Canned Food Industry*. Oakland: University of California Press, 2018.

Zuidhof, M. J., et al. "Growth, Efficiency, and Yield of Commercial Broilers from 1957, 1978, and 2005." *Poultry Science* 93, no. 12 (December 2014): 2970–2982.

INDEX

A&P (Great Atlantic & Pacific Tea Company), 43, 71
Allen, Daisy, 70
Amalgamated Meat Cutters (AMC) Local 272, 9–10
Amalgamated Meat Cutters (AMC) Local 525, 9–10; disaffection toward union leadership, 74–78; Gold Kist Durham union campaign, 67, 71–73; Holly Farms Monroe union campaign, 68–71; Holly Farms Wilkesboro union campaign, 63–65; 1978 strike at Gold Kist, 78–82
American Double Dutch League, 109
American Federation of State, County and Municipal Employees, 79
American Journal of Medicine, 3
American Magazine, 50
Animal husbandry, 34, 37, 50, 62
Archer-Daniels-Midland, 27, 57, 122
Arellano, Gustavo, 118
Arend, René, 106
Arizona Republic, 107
Armour & Company, 54, 57, 71
Asheville, N.C., 69, 71, 74
Atkins, Robert, 102

Bailey, A. Eugene, 47
Baker, Robert C.: development of new chicken products, 23, 27–32, 93, 106, 126, 132, 135; food waste, 20–23, 27; life and career, 16–20
Baltimore Sun, 40
Bangladesh, 24
Banks, Margaret, 83
Bare, Bonnie, 63–65
Barron's, 105
Bates, Leon, 26
Battery farming, 38–40, 48
Bauer, Robert, 1, 112–113
Bayles, Martha, 17–18
Bazemore, Donna, 8, 88
Beef consumption, 1, 6, 28, 31–33, 42, 44, 93; as dietary component, 101–102; in fast-food restaurants, 97–99, 102–103, 117–118
Bell, Glen, 8, 94, 118
Biggest Loser, The, 130–131
Billings, Pearl, 63
Biltekoff, Charlotte, 124
Bivens, Terry, 60–61
Blanchard, Ada, 82–84
Borlaug, Norman, 25
Bowles, Chester, 48
Broadway, Michael J., 9
Brockington, Thelma, 80
Broiler Industry, 1, 10, 29, 48, 51–53, 55, 59, 83
Brooks, D. W., 8, 25
Brown, Leslie, 72
Brown, Prentiss, 46
Brownell, Kelly D., 123
Buffalo News, 106
Bullis, Jean, 64
Bureau of Agricultural Economics, 46
Bureau of Labor Statistics, 87
Burger Chef, 118
Burger King, 57, 95, 98, 120, 125; addition of chicken products, 93, 105–106, 112–113, 117–118; Chicken Tenders, 113; value dining, 117–118, 121; Whopper, 117, 125
Burroughs, Anza, 81
Burroughs, Walter, 81

Calloway, Wayne, 120
Campbell, Gail, 83
Campbell Soup Company, 56, 115
Cargill, 122
Carl's Jr. Restaurants, 105
Carter, Jimmy, 25, 59, 99
Case Farms, 8
Catholic Charities, 134
Cathy, S. Truett, 8, 112
Celebrity Fit Club, 130
Center for Science in the Public Interest, 125
Chapin, Harry, 25
Charlotte Observer, 132–133

Chicago, Ill., 7–8, 40, 45, 54, 56, 58, 77, 106
Chicago Daily Tribune, 40, 44
Chicken George's, 103
Chicken hot dogs, 29–32
Chicken McNugget: criticisms of, 2–3, 17–18; development at McDonald's, 106–107; enduring popularity, 130–132; industrial production, 107–108, 115–117; launch and marketing, 106–111; rivals introduce competing products, 111–116
Chick-fil-A, 8, 103, 112
Chubby Chickfried Chicken, 52
Church's Fried Chicken, 103, 112
Clinton, Bill, 89, 122
Cobb, Bill, 121
Coca-Cola, 32, 60, 118, 121–122
C. O. Lovette Produce Company, 49
Columbus, Ohio, 94–95
Commission Against Racism, 78–79
Communist Party USA, 74
ConAgra Foods, 57–59, 116,
Contois, Emily, 131
Cook, J. Gordon, 25–26
Cornell University, 2, 10, 16–19, 21, 30–31, 34, 99, 114
Corner Bakery Cafe, 129
Corporate mergers, 56–61, 117–118
Coutlakis, Emanuel, 63, 69
COVID-19 pandemic, 14
Cracker Barrel, 102
Critser, Greg, 97, 129
CSX Transportation, 84
Cullather, Nick, 24
Culp, Michael, 106
Cumming, Ga., 83–84, 104

Dairy Queen, 95
Danone, 129
DeLay, Tom, 89
Delmarva Peninsula, 36, 46–47, 66
Democratic National Convention, 86
Denny's, 102, 120
Denver, John, 25
Derg (Provisional Military Administrative Council), 24
Deutsch, Tracey, 41
Devereux, Stephen, 24
Domino's Pizza, 5, 20, 92, 97, 117, 120
Drucker, I., 46
Durham, N.C., 11–12, 71–82, 90

Durnford, Tim, 119
Dworkin, Shari L., 126

Eggs: as dietary component, 102; as ingredient, 28–30, 104, 111, 113; Leghorn fowl and, 23; source of farm income, 35–39, 49; wartime procurement, 45
Ehrlich, Paul R., 25, 27
Eisenhower, Dwight, 96
Elledge, Margaret, 64
Emal, Janet, 115
Enrico, Roger, 118
Environmental Protection Agency, 89
Esquire, 100

Famine, 24–27
Farm Bloc, U.S. Senate, 47
Federal Bureau of Investigation, 69
Federal Compress & Warehouse, 52
Federal Emergency Management Agency, 85
Federal Meat Inspection Act, 66
Feldstein, Morris, 46
Felts, Charlie, 49
Fiber, Ben, 110
Fink, Leon, 8, 11, 89
Finn, S. Margot, 130
Finn, Steve, 113
Fitness industry, 99–101, 122–126, 128
Fleischman, Thomas, 13–14
Food and Drug Administration (FDA), 65–66
Food Safety and Inspection Service, 134
Forbes, 35
Ford Motor Company, 5, 43, 50, 92
Foreyt, John, 123
Frank, Mark, 32
Franz, Chester B., 44
Frazier, E. Franklin, 71
Friedman, Jeffrey M., 123–124
Frito-Lay, 117
Fulton, Lawrence, 81

Gaines, Charles, 100
Gainesville, Ga., 45–46
Garner, David, 124
Garner, Tom, 116
Garvin, Francis, 56, 65
Gaye, Marvin, 113
General Foods, 61
General Motors, 60
German Democratic Republic, 13–14

Gibson, W. David, 105
Gisolfi, Monica, 36–37
Glassner, Barry, 100–101
Glen Allen, Va., 9–10
Glover, Dreama, 80
Glover, Jere, 97
Gold Kist, 11–12, 56, 67, 71–82
Gorman, Patrick, 69–70
Grajek, John, 23
Gravani, Robert, 17
Gray, LaGuana, 8–9
Great Atlantic & Pacific Tea Company (A&P), 43, 71
Great Depression, 20, 34–36, 47
Green, Barbara, 77–78
Green, Laura, 72–75, 90
Green Revolution, 24
Greensboro, N.C., 71, 86
Greyhound Lines, 57
Grocery stores: further processed chicken products, 116–117; growing control of market, 60; introduction of dry-chilled chicken, 55–56; relationship with poultry processors, 49, 58, 66; salesmanship, 41–43
Gryder, Alma, 63–65
Gryder, Grace, 64–65, 91

Haffert, William A., 83
Haggart Manufacturing Company, 39
Haley, Alex, 103
Hamlet, N.C., 8–9, 11, 67, 82–86, 90
Hardee's Restaurants, 98, 118, 120
Harris, Ken, 119
Harris, Robert B., 40–41
Hart, R. P., 38–39
Harvey, John, 60
Havenstein, Gerald, 62
Haverpride Farms, 83
Hayse, P. L., 22
Heil, Emily, 131–132
Heinz, Henry J., 94
Helms, Jesse, 69
Henrichs, Theodore W., 44
Herring, Annie, 80–81
Hester, Percy, 80
High-fructose corn syrup, 122
Hinman, Robert B., 34, 40–41
H. J. Heinz Company, 117
Hobby House, 94
Hoffman, Paul, 71

Holiday Spas Health Clubs of California, 100
Holly Farms, 11, 14, 35, 103; acquisition by Tyson Foods, 57–59; anti-union practices, 63–71, 90–91; innovations in production, 48–56, 115–116
Holmes, Ted, 103–104
House of Raeford Farms, 133–134
Hover, J. Milton, 37
Howard, Elaine, 115
Human Rights Watch, 133

Imperial Food Products, 9, 67–68, 82–85, 90, 133
India, 24
Industry consolidation, 56–61
International Association of Machinists and Aerospace Workers (IAM), 79
International Brotherhood of Teamsters, 69
International Brotherhood of Teamsters Local 592, 59
International Franchise Association, 96
Iowa Beef Packers (IBP), 54, 87

Jack in the Box, 99, 105
Jackson, Jesse, 86, 90
Jarrell, Bertha, 83
Jenkins, E. G., 28, 132
Jennings, Spencer, 70
Jesse Jones Sausage Company, 71
Jim Crow segregation, 70–72
Jimmy John's, 129
John Morrell Company, 87–88
Johnson, Carrie, 64–65, 68, 90–91
Johnson, Junior, 50
Joines, Jennie, 63–65, 68, 81, 91
Jones, Roberta, 113–114
Josephson, Paul, 9
Joyner, Larry, 80

Kahn, Alfred E., 99
Kellogg, Charles E., 47
Kena FP-28, 30–31
Kentucky Fried Chicken (KFC), 5, 120; competition with McDonald's, 105, 110–113; Gold Kist and, 74; Holly Farms and, 49, 81; as market leader, 95, 102–103
Keystone Foods, 107
Kirk, Phillip, 84
Kissing Case, 69
K-Mart, 71

Kroc, Ray, 8, 95, 104, 106
Ku Klux Klan, 69

Labron, Betty, 80
Lancaster New Era, 105
Lantos, Tom, 87
La Petite Boulangerie, 118
League for International Food Education, 22
League for Peace and Democracy, 79
Leake, Pete, 75–76, 78
Leghorns, 23, 31, 37, 40, 106
Leiner, Robert W., 80–81
Levenstein, Harvey, 43
Levinson, Marc, 43
Levy, Phyllis, 115
Lewis, Harry, 38
Lewis, Sinclair, 41
Liggett & Myers Tobacco Company (L&M), 71, 75
Linowitz, Sol, 25–26
Loflin, Clayton, 84
Looper, J. Don, 25
Los Angeles Herald, 38
Los Angeles Times, 38–39, 99, 105–106
Lovette, Charles, 49–50, 61, 121
Lovette, Fred, 35, 121; anti-unionism, 63–65, 70; development of Holly Farms, 49, 54–57
Lowery, Carl, 80
Lutheran Social Services, 134
Lyle Farms, 83

Mabe, James, 133
MacLeod, Annie Mae, 80–81
Malthus, Thomas, 26
Maltun, Alan, 99–100
Marel, 54
Marion, W. W., 22
Martin, Joann, 80
Martin, John, 118–120
Matthews, Guy, 81
Mayer, Jean, 25, 101–102
McBee, Avery, 40
McCarty Foods, 113–114
McCollum, Elmer V., 28, 42
McDonald's, 1, 5–6, 12–14, 16, 121; Big Mac, 117; Dollar Menu, 6; Eat Smart, Be Active menu, 129; Egg McMuffin, 104; expansion, 32–33, 96–98; Extra Value Meal Menu, 121; Filet-O-Fish Sandwich, 104; Hula Burger, 104; introduction of further processed chicken products, 104–113; McChicken Sandwich, 104–106, 111; McXL Sandwich, 121; Onion McNuggets, 106; production model, 92–93, 102, 107–108; Richard and Maurice McDonald, 92; Ronald McDonald, 95. *See also* Chicken McNugget; Kroc, Ray
McGowan, Joseph, 45
Meat Cutters Workers Action Movement Newsletter (WAM), 74–75
Memphis, Tenn., 52, 57
Mencken, H. L., 42–43, 128
Microwave cookery, 115
Milloy, Courtland, 103
Missouri Beef Packers-Excel (MBPXL), 54
Mitchell, Gordon, 108
Moline Daily Dispatch, 107
Monfort, 54
Monroe, N.C., 11, 50, 69–71, 84
Monsanto Company, 27
Montgomery, Joseph, 45–46
Morganton, N.C., 8, 11
Mullins, Keith, 111
Murnaghan, Francis, 59

National Association for Stock Car Auto Racing (NASCAR), 49–50
National Association of Manufacturers, 89
National Broiler Council, 84, 113
National Cattlemen's Beef Association, 99
National Chicken Council, 134
National Grocers' Bulletin, 39
National Health and Nutrition Examination Survey, 123
National Institute for Occupational Safety and Health (NIOSH), 87–88, 133
National Labor Relations Act (Wagner Act), 59
National Labor Relations Board (NLRB), 59, 65, 70, 80–81
National Live Stock and Meat Board, 102
Nesmith, Anthony, 81
Nestle, Marion, 134
New Deal, 7, 47
New Poultry Inspection System, 134
New York Amsterdam News, 46
New York City, 36, 46, 90, 94
New York Times, 27, 35, 71, 131
Nichols, Mack, 64
North, Oliver, 100
North American Free Trade Agreement (NAFTA), 8

North Carolina Citizens for Business and Industry, 84
North Carolina Radioactive Waste Management, 84
Northeast Battery Broiler Producers Association, 48

Obama, Barack, 134
Obesity, 101–102, 121–126, 128–131
Occupational Safety and Health Administration (OSHA), 35; cases against meat packers, 87–88; Imperial Food Products, 85; proposed reforms, 89; work of draw hands, 76–77
Office of Price Administration (OPA), 44–48
Oliver, Jamie, 3
Omaha, Nebr., 54
Omo-Osagie, Solomon Iyobosa, II, 9
O'Neill, Molly, 127
Overend, William, 100

Packard, Vance, 49
Panera Bread, 129
Pashdag, John, 105
People's Republic of China, 24, 74
PepsiCo, 14, 60, 93, 117–122
Perdue, Frank, 35
Perdue, James, 80
Perdue Farms, 8, 54, 61, 88, 115–116
Petrini, Carlo, 134
Philadelphia, Pa., 36, 46
Philadelphia Inquirer, 60–61
Pierce, Daniel S., 49
Piggly Wiggly, 43
Pilgrim, Lonnie, 8, 35, 116
Pilgrim's Pride, 35, 61, 86, 115–116
Pillsbury–J. M. Smucker, 56–57, 61
Pittman, Marvin S., 37
Pizza Hut, 5, 20, 92, 117–118, 120–121
Poirier, Steve, 110
Pollan, Michael, 129, 134
Poole, Geneva, 80
Poole, Harry, 77–78
Popeyes Louisiana Kitchen, 103
Porter, Nellie, 63, 65
Poultry Products Inspection Act, 65
Presidential Commission on World Hunger, 25
Production line work, 54–55
Progressive Labor Party (PLP), 74, 78–79

Pruess, Joanna, 115
Psychology Today, 124
Pure Food and Drug Act, 41–42

Quaker Oats Company, 57, 61
Quinlan, Michael R., 105

Raleigh News & Observer, 84
Rally's, 121
Ralston Purina Company, 56–57
Raskopf, Karen, 122
Ratliff, Elaine, 82–83
Reagan, Ronald, 60–61
Recchi, Ray, 125–126
Redburn, Francis Stevens, 71–72
Red Dwarf, 18
Reinblatt, Gary, 110–111
Reno, Robert, 60–61
Repetitive motion injuries (RMIs), 66; growth in incidence rates in 1980s and 1990s, 86–90; persistence in twenty-first century, 133–135; work of draw hands, 76–77
Restaurant Business Magazine, 10, 102, 104, 106, 113
Restaurants & Institutions, 111
Revolutionary Socialist Youth, 78–79
Revolutionary Workers Party, 79
Rhode Island Red, 19
Richmond, Va., 50, 90, 101
Richmond County, N.C., 84
Ridgway, Frank, 40
Riis, Jacob, 41
Rimmer, Arnold, 18
Ritenbaugh, Cheryl, 128
Ritter, Carol, 19
Rivera, Adrian J., 131–132
Rizzio, Mary, 127
R. J. Reynolds–Nabisco, 58, 61
Roberts, Michael, 110
Robinson, Louisiana, 69–70
Rochester Democrat and Chronicle, 19
Rockefeller Foundation, 24
Rocky, 100
Rodgers, James A., 38
Roe, Brad, 84
Roe, Emmett, 83–84
Romkey, Mike, 107, 111–112
Ross 308, 62
Rusch, Bill, 35
Russell, John, 12, 68–82

Safeway, 49, 58
Saltman, Paul, 123
Sara Lee Corporation, 57, 61
Schauer, John J., 69
Schlosser, Eric, 13, 128
Schwartzman, Kathleen, 8, 89
Science, 123–124
Selassie, Haile, 24
7-Eleven, 122–123
Sevette, Dennis, 64
Shoemaker, Margaret, 65
Shoney's, 83
Sikora, Martin, 61
Simmonds, Nina, 28, 42
Simmons, Cornelius, 70, 81
Simon, Bryant, 9, 11
Simon, Julian, 27
Slocum, Rob R., 34
Small Business Act, 96
Small Business Administration (SBA), 96–97
Smith, C. Howard, 50
Smith, Jack, 106–107
Smith, Rudy, 100
Smithfield Foods, 9
Snyder, Harold, 60
Soames Nickerson, Jane, 26
Southern Exposure, 88
South Florida Sun Sentinel, 125
Soviet Union (USSR), 24–25
Spam, 31
Specht, Joshua, 4
Spurlock, Morgan, 128–129
Stallone, Sylvester, 100
Steele, Cecile, 36
St. Louis Chamber of Commerce, 44, 54
Stogner, Brian L., 123
Strenk, Tom, 104
Striffler, Steve, 8, 89
Stull, Donald, 9
Stunkard, Albert J., 122–123
Subway, 129
Successful Farming, 102
Swift & Company, 47, 54, 56–57, 71

Taco Bell, 5–6, 8, 94, 125; expansion, 32, 97; restructuring of business model, 117–122
Taft, Robert A., 48
Taylor, Elizabeth, 115
Taylor, R. Lee, 58
Temperanceville, Va., 50, 54, 59
Thomas, Dave, 1, 92, 112, 118, 120; growth of Wendy's, 94–98; reluctance to sell chicken items, 102–103. *See also* Wendy's
Thompson, Lorraine, 121
Thompson, Willard C., 37
Tobacco Workers International Union, 72
Toronto Globe and Mail, 110
Townsend, Robert, 56–57
Triangle Shirtwaist Factory fire, 90
Trump, Donald, 134
Turner, Fred, 104
Tyson, Don, 35, 57–59, 89, 108, 113
Tyson, John, 57
Tyson Foods, 9, 11, 52, 86; expansion and industry consolidation, 56–62; fire at North Little Rock facility, 85; relationship to McDonald's, 14, 107–108

Union Stock Yards, Chicago, 40
United Food and Commercial Workers (UFCW), 9, 67, 87–88
United States Department of Agriculture (USDA), 46, 99; dietary guidelines, 101–102; food scarcity, 25, 27; promotion of scientific farming methods, 34, 37, 47; regulation of poultry industry, 7, 35, 65–66, 86–87, 134
United States Department of Commerce, 43
United States Department of Justice Antitrust Division, 59–61
United States Department of Labor, 7, 85, 87, 89
United States Fire Administration, 85
United States Government Accountability Office, 133
United States House of Representatives, 89

Valentine, C. S., 38
Valmac Industries, 57
Value meals, 12, 93, 98, 117–125, 131
Vicente, Cornelia, 132–133
Vietnam War, 95, 100
Vileisis, Ann, 4
Villegas, Belem, 133

Wachs, Faye Linda, 126
Wadden, Thomas A., 122–123
Walker, Karen, 74–80
Wallace, Jane, 99
Wall Street (New York), 60–61
Wall Street Journal, 17–18, 105
Ward, David J., 46

War Food Administration (WFA), 44–45
Washington, D.C., 36, 103–104
Washington Post, 24, 40, 84, 103, 131
Watts, George B., 113
Webb, Graydon, 96
Wendy's: addition of chicken products, 1, 12, 14, 92–94, 102–103, 105; expansion, 5, 32–33, 95–98, 112–113, 117; Super Value Menu, 121. *See also* Thomas, Dave
Whole Foods Market, 129
Wilkesboro, N.C., 11, 48, 50, 53–55, 58, 63–69
Wilkes County, N.C., 49–50
Wilkins, Rose, 83
Williams, William H., 47
Williams-Forson, Psyche, 103
Wink, Peter, 39
Winston-Salem, N.C., 58, 68–69
Winton, Gene, 64
Wire, The, 16
World War I, 36, 48
World War II, 35–36, 43–48
Wynn, William H., 87–88

Yates, Annette, 115

POLITICS AND CULTURE IN THE TWENTIETH-CENTURY SOUTH

A Common Thread: Labor, Politics, and Capital Mobility in the Textile Industry
BY BETH ENGLISH

"Everybody Was Black Down There": Race and Industrial Change in the Alabama Coalfields
BY ROBERT H. WOODRUM

Race, Reason, and Massive Resistance: The Diary of David J. Mays, 1954–1959
EDITED BY JAMES R. SWEENEY

The Unemployed People's Movement: Leftists, Liberals, and Labor in Georgia, 1929–1941
BY JAMES J. LORENCE

Liberalism, Black Power, and the Making of American Politics, 1965–1980
BY DEVIN FERGUS

Guten Tag, Y'all: Globalization and the South Carolina Piedmont, 1950–2000
BY MARKO MAUNULA

The Culture of Property: Race, Class, and Housing Landscapes in Atlanta, 1880–1950
BY LEEANN LANDS

Marching in Step: Masculinity, Citizenship, and The Citadel in Post–World War II America
BY ALEXANDER MACAULAY

Rabble Rousers: The American Far Right in the Civil Rights Era
BY CLIVE WEBB

Who Gets a Childhood?: Race and Juvenile Justice in Twentieth-Century Texas
BY WILLIAM S. BUSH

Alabama Getaway: The Political Imaginary and the Heart of Dixie
BY ALLEN TULLOS

The Problem South: Region, Empire, and the New Liberal State, 1880–1930
BY NATALIE J. RING

The Nashville Way: Racial Etiquette and the Struggle for Social Justice in a Southern City
BY BENJAMIN HOUSTON

Cold War Dixie: Militarization and Modernization in the American South
BY KARI FREDERICKSON

Faith in Bikinis: Politics and Leisure in the Coastal South since the Civil War
BY ANTHONY J. STANONIS

Womanpower Unlimited and the Black Freedom Struggle in Mississippi
BY TIYI M. MORRIS

New Negro Politics in the Jim Crow South
BY CLAUDRENA N. HAROLD

Jim Crow Terminals: The Desegregation of American Airports
BY ANKE ORTLEPP

Remaking the Rural South: Interracialism, Christian Socialism, and Cooperative Farming in Jim Crow Mississippi
BY ROBERT HUNT FERGUSON

The South of the Mind: American Imaginings of White Southernness, 1960–1980
BY ZACHARY J. LECHNER

The Politics of White Rights: Race, Justice, and Integrating Alabama's Schools
BY JOSEPH BAGLEY

The Struggle and the Urban South: Confronting Jim Crow in Baltimore before the Movement
BY DAVID TAFT TERRY

Massive Resistance and Southern Womanhood: White Women, Class, and Segregationist Resistance
BY REBECCA BRUCKMANN

I Lay This Body Down: The Transatlantic Life of Rosey E. Pool
BY LONNEKE GEERLINGS

Partners in Gatekeeping: How Italy Shaped U.S. Immigration Policy Over Ten Pivotal Years, 1891–1901
LAUREN BRAUN-STRUMFELS

Radical Volunteers: Dissent, Desegregation, and Student Power in Tennessee
KATHERINE J. BALLANTYNE

Nuggets of Gold: Further Processed Chicken and the Making of the American Diet
BY PATRICK DIXON

Southern by the Grace of God: Religion, Race, and Civil Rights in Hollywood's American South
BY MEGAN HUNT

www.ingramcontent.com/pod-product-compliance
Lightning Source LLC
Chambersburg PA
CBHW031439160426
43195CB00010BB/788